GETTING REAL... about growing up!

To dear Yiana,
Wishing you a wondrous Journey ♡ Amrita

Amrita Hobbs

GETTING REAL BOOKS
AND WORKSHOPS

Editing: Jonathan and Brian Priest.

Graphic Design: Marcel Priest, Robin Ellis, Amrita Hobbs.

Front cover Photography: Christabelle Barany
www.byronbay-photography.com

Front cover concept: Jacob Baldwin, Amrita Hobbs

Inside Photography: Christabelle Barany,
Kanan Alexander, Amrita Hobbs.

National Library of Australia

Hobbs, Amrita.

GETTING REAL... about growing up!

ISBN 1 876494 58 1

1. Youth – Life skills guide.
2. Self actualisation, (Psychology).
I. Title.

158.0835

GETTING REAL BOOKS

Mullumbimby Australia

info@amritahobbs.com

www.amritahobbs.com

Printed by Penfold Buscombe, Queensland. Australia

The production of this book has not cost the Earth. We used paper made from sugar cane fibre and non-toxic inks.

What adults say…

"I have known Amrita Hobbs for several years and am aware of the innovative Rites of Passage work she does. I am sure that this book will prove to be an invaluable resource for young people, parents, teachers, youth workers and others who mentor young people. The information is clear and accessible and there are lots of comments and real life stories to highlight the issues. I highly recommend this book and Amrita's work."
Christie Anthony MD, a Holistic Family Physician

"This is an amazing book! It speaks hauntingly to the teenager inside every adult. It helped me to the bridge gaps between me and my own parents. It also alerted me to the ones that had begun to grow between me, as a parent and my own teenagers. This book can help everyone make sense of the Journey."
David, a father

"As a parent and a survivor of child abuse, I'd like to thank you. You've hit the nail on the head. GETTING REAL… about growing up! is written in a language that teenagers can relate to and understand. It's the most positive piece of work for young people that I've read. This book has helped my daughter to believe what has happened to her and to come to terms with her experience of sexual abuse... and a lot more."
Sharon, a mother

"GETTING REAL… about growing up! communicates compellingly to young people who may be struggling to make sense of their rapidly changing worlds – both inside and outside. After reading the book I realised it had helped me greatly in counselling troubled teenagers. I gained a clearer understanding of many of the challenges that they face – personally, in the family and also the global crisis."
Jonathan, a Metaphysical Counsellor

"This is real information to guide youth through the most important time in anyone's life. It's good to see such positive input in a society that often brings youth down… after all they are the future of the world."
Jacob Baldwin, President, Community Awareness Task Force

"The journey from childhood innocence to mature and responsible adult can be a very scary and treacherous one. Having made the journey one often looks back and wonders how it was endured. Many of us form beliefs about ourselves based on how we were perceived. Some of us carry the scars and wounds for the rest of our lives. When there is a lack of real communication and education it can be a dismal time for our beautiful young adventurers, the young men and women of tomorrow. Amrita's book helps them to find their path and bridges the gap between where they have been and where they are going. This book gives young people the foundation on which to base their sense of self. It offers a place for them to consider and explore their innermost feelings - to find their ideas and ideals in an inspiring and practical way. They are given not only facts but also the mythical and spiritual resonances that allow them to truly connect to their real selves.

This book provides a necessary tool for young people today. It helps them to navigate their way through the rapids of ever changing world politics, a loss of intimacy on many levels and a society based on materialism and the advertisers' dollar. What is happening is likely to befuddle and derail even the most level headed among us. I believe this terrific book will help many, many young people understand the truth. Find their own truth and give them the courage to live it."
Antoinette Sampson, author The Peace Angels

"GETTING REAL… about growing up! is a valuable resource. It is a rich and heart-felt guide to the challenges adolescents face in this millennium. It provides young people with a wealth of information and activities for exploring their identities, connecting with themselves, their peers and their communities.

I like the way it speaks to young people at their level. It's the sort of book I would have liked to have had as a teenager."
Peter Chown, Adolescent Psychologist

ABOUT THIS BOOK

GETTING REAL... about growing up! takes you on a Journey of self-discovery. It helps you identify who you are, your beliefs, thought patterns and personal issues. By working with this book you can gain clarity about your life and the Journey you are on.

GETTING REAL... about growing up!

- Helps you to find answers and to be clear about your direction.
- Encourages you to get real and to find out what you value.
- Supports you to express the freedom, passion and the joy of being alive.
- Gives maps for exploring where you are now and where you are going.
- Offers inspiration and new ways of thinking, feeling and looking at life.
- Encourages you through rough times.
- Invites you to accept, love, recognise, acknowledge and support yourself.
- Assists you to recognise that you are part of a much bigger picture.

GETTING REAL... about growing up! talks about change. It is an invitation to see beyond the conditions of your life and what it has made of you. It can assist you to remove the shells that hide your true Nature. Accepting yourself exactly as you are, in this moment, is a big step in becoming – becoming your true potential. You are not being asked to change yourself as much as to allow this book to assist the process of your natural unfolding.

Imagine yourself like a computer. So much is possible interactively with a good one. Computers in some ways defy time and space. The hard drive is the equivalent of your body/mind. Your cellular memory banks store everything that you've said and has been said to you. All of your life's experiences, senses, feelings, thoughts and ideas are saved. The software is your programming and is determined by your family, school, culture and your life experiences. It's all there, well stored!

GETTING REAL... about growing up! can allow you to retrieve out-dated files and erase what is no longer useful to you. You can clean up your hard drive. It can assist you to install more memory and new software and expand your capabilities. You can choose to upgrade your software – your inherited beliefs, the roles you play, your relationships and the way you think and function in the world. This book is an interactive tool! It offers practical things you can do. If you work with it, the re-programming can provide new information and insight that could be valuable for the rest of your life.

There is something hidden in life that is invisible to the eye but not to the heart. It cannot be seen but it is always there. Some call it Spirit, the Force, Power, God, Great Intelligence – you can call it whatever you like. This Power makes the World work. You may not tune in to it. But like a computer, if you don't plug it in to electricity it does not work for you. It does not mean that the Power is not there. You can only experience this Power if you connect! When you make this connection you can experience the Mystery of Life. This book can help you to do this.

GETTING REAL... about growing up! explores gender, your sexuality and the intimate relationships you create as you grow up. It deals with issues of life and death, of separation, divorce, drug and alcohol abuse. It brings society's taboos into the open – homosexuality, suicide, menstruation, sexual abuse and death.

GETTING REAL... about growing up! if you are an adult, invites you to travel back in time and imagine yourself as a teenager. Re-engage in your adolescent experience. Acknowledge that what you went through to become who you are now, served you! Forgive yourself for any mis-takes you may have made while learning about growing up. Using this book you can reclaim parts of yourself that were not recognised by those around you. You can celebrate your Journey NOW into adulthood.

GETTING REAL… about growing up! invites you to read with an open mind and to listen to the whispers of your own heart. The power of this book is not so much in the words as they are written but in what is hidden behind them. It's in the sense and feel of what is being said. If my language seems unusual, perhaps you could feel it rather than think it. Allow it to speak to your heart more than your head. This may make it easier to understand. I ask that as you read, your heart softens and your mind opens to the true expression of yourself in this wondrous World in which you live.

GETTING REAL… about growing up! is my expression. You may at times agree with and at other times doubt the things I say. Great! These are my thoughts at this time – they may change. Use the book to find out what your own beliefs, values and ideas are and to confirm what you already know. You are your own expert. My invitation is for you to listen and believe in yourself.

GETTING REAL… about growing up! is a tool that can lead you to what is true for you.

GETTING REAL… about growing up! challenges you to look within and connect to the Greater Mystery. The winds of change are blowing. If you are connected to who you are and to your heart you could live in a new World in your time.

You can read this book from start to finish. That may be too much to take in. You may prefer to look at the sections that are relevant to you or just pick it up and open it randomly. Whatever works best. You may like to have a Journal, a notebook and pen close by and do the suggested writing. This can help you gain understanding and clarity about yourself and what your life has made of you.

MY STORY is told throughout the book – it looks like this.

I would like to tell you about writing GETTING REAL… about growing up! It felt like I've been in otherworldly places for many months as the words and feelings emerged from my depth. I've found the resources, been supported by many wonderful people and followed the signs along the way. Following my passion, I've experienced despair as well as utter joy. My heart was torn open as I wrote about suicide, sexual abuse and addiction – things that threaten and harm young people. I wish these things were not a part of my world – or yours.

As I listen closely to the guidance I receive, incredible magic and power is available to me. So in the vulnerability and rawness that I felt then and toward the end of the writing, the fulfilment, I am learning that life has its way with me. If I can let go enough, I am shown new directions and new ways to move forward.

Now, lighter, as the creative process completes itself, I savour the gift of my expression and the sharing of it with you as you read. Writing this book has grown me up some more. It has revealed my gifts and aspects of myself that I was not fully aware of. Perhaps it can do the same for you.

If you find more of yourself as you read, we will both have gained.

My wish is that the magic woven within these pages allows you to GET REAL and to be who you really are.

To find your wings and fly!

This book is an offering from my heart to you and to the World.

Author's note: I self-published **IT COULD BE DIFFERENT – A self-help book for teenagers** in 1991. Some of the valuable material from that book has been expanded in **GETTING REAL… about growing up!**

About our World: you may notice that at times **world** is spelled with a capital letter. This is done to emphasise that a new World is possible in our lifetime.

IN GRATITUDE

GETTING REAL... about growing up! is written with a deep sense of gratitude to all the thousands of teenagers who have touched my life. For the hope and inspiration I gained from them and for the heart-bursting experiences that I've had through my work with them.

I am grateful for the pictures, stories and poems that appear. I hope those of you who feature in the book feel proud. I ask for your consent here if I could not ask you personally. Some names have been changed to protect privacy. In offering this book I have no wish to hurt or offend anyone. If you are not happy about your material or pictures being included please let me know.

I thank my mother, Sylvia and father, Jim for the gift of my life.

My sister, Jan and her family, my brother Clive and sisters Pauline, Wendy and Linda for sharing the experience of growing up in our family. And Jack, my stepfather.

I am deeply grateful to those who have made **GETTING REAL... about growing up!** possible. Jonathan, whose dedication to the integrity of the text and it's maturing deserves first mention in the list of people who have helped in its creation. Through thousands of hours of editing, he helped polish the crystal. He added his gift with words and his patience with me, in the creative process.

I thank Brian Priest of The Oracle Press for his encouragement as I began the book and his involvement in the creative process. Also to Marcel Priest who brought the book to life through his talent as a graphic artist and designer. To Robin Ellis for fine-tuning and refining the book. Christabelle Baranay and Kanan for the gift they gave of wonderful images and photographs. Also Libby Renney, Ian Webster and Jennifer Davies for encouraging me to begin and then keep going. I am grateful to Sandra Black from Southern Cross University for helping me to see the book more clearly. I'd like to thank the students of Cape Byron Rudolf Steiner School for their photographs on the front cover.

Robin and Paul Blainey, Pauline McKelvie, Les Joyce, Michael Sanders, Philip Watt and Trevor Jackson for making it possible to publish It Could Be Different the book that pre-seeded this one.

Friends who have been there for me to love, be loved by and lean on at times – James, Bronte and their daughters Cassie and Morgan, Lisa Bingham, Sylvia Longstaff, Alexandra Pope, Andrew Williams, Mary and Alan Earle, Sally and Brian Morgan, Greg Croaker, Richard Champion, Sharon and Steve, and Jacob and Julia. The Gain-Emery family, Jackie and Hari Stewart, Hela, Maeva and Dean and David Whistler. I thank the core group in Byron Bay – Ross, Laura-Doe, Cynthia, Jacinta, Jude and Jonathan, Saden, Nitzan and Petra who offered me ongoing support and helped me keep my heart open.

To those who have been my teachers – John Mee, Tony Hunt and Eddie Farquar from teacher training college for unfreezing me through drama and dance classes. Hans Poulsen for his gift of music and song. He awakened the singer in me. Tamara Slayton for her stories which inspired me to write my own. Sri Goenka for his love and compassion for all humanity. David Deida for showing me the way of spiritualised sexual relationships between men and women.

I'd like to thank all those who have taken me into their homes and hearts as I travelled around Australia and the World. I have family and community everywhere I go.

And lastly to the Source of All Life, which is a constant well I drink from for encouragement and inspiration. For the en-lightenment of my way.

With all that I have gathered from the people who cross my path and the experiences of my life I am able to share myself in this book.

FIRST WORDS

Growing up can be an exciting time. It's an adventure! There are ups and downs, successes and failures, joys and sorrows. Life offers a mixed bag of goodies.

Through teenage years there are many challenges to be faced. These challenges provide us with growth experiences that make us who we are. Life is a great teacher! It can sometimes be a school of hard knocks. Even when we rise above the conditions and circumstances that keep us down, other lessons confront us that we would rather not see or deal with. **This is how we grow.**

Life is a Mystery School, there is so much to discover, to dance, sing and celebrate about. It is a Miracle! Miracles can happen in every moment. When we allow ourselves to let go into the **BIGNESS** of it all, it can truly support us. It gives us all that is necessary to fulfil our purpose for being here and bring our dreams and visions into reality. This is how we expand and connect with the Universal Law of Love that is at the back of everything.

It is useful to learn how to look after and nourish who we really are and to focus on the good things about ourselves. If we can love ourselves and those around us, we can transform life on Earth as we have known it. Love with awareness gently washes away that which no longer serves our growth and then our lives evolve.

Life is also a Journey. Look for the signposts along the way. They give directions that help to make the way clear. Ask questions and wait for the answers. They come in the most surprising ways.

We create the future by our thoughts and our actions NOW! It is in our hands. The seeds we sow today provide us with the fruits of tomorrow. **GETTING REAL... about growing up!** is essential at this time. A new World is calling and its Soul whispers to our hearts.

What you get from these pages can help to create a vision and a purpose for your life. You can **FLY FREE** of all that is in your way. You can link together with others and bring more peace on Earth.

Hold on to your dreams for they are vital for ongoing life on Earth. Your dreams are the invisible threads that weave a better World.

Your dreams are like the stars. Let them shine brightly in the skies.

Your dreams are like the wind. Let them blow through your mind and carry the fragrance of Spring.

Your dreams are like a bubbling brook. Their song ripples on and on.

The power of your dreams is like the Sun – warming the Earth and everyone.

Dream your dreams – and imagine them done.

Just for fun!

It's time to celebrate GOODNESS – yours and mine.

We make a difference. Let's express our power, our joy and our love.

We can change the World.

IT'S AN ADVENTURE THAT STARTS NOW AND GOES ON FOREVER. IT CAN BE EXCITING!

ABOUT AMRITA

I was raised and educated in England. I am the eldest of six children and that brought with it a sense of responsibility for others. My father left when I was little. Life was pretty tough for many reasons. My mother loved us all but at times I could not feel her love. She was busy and had to spread her attention around.

The culture in which I lived did not assist me to grow up because there was no formal recognition of the stages I passed through.

There were no wise elders within my family or community that were available to show me the way. I've walked my Journey for most of the time, alone. I've had some help, but it could have been easier with more guidance. I've grown myself up to the extent that I have.

While training as a teacher in the 70's I discovered my passion for working with teenagers. In the groups that I facilitated, I quickly became aware of the difference it made in young peoples' lives when they had someone who listened to them and was there for them for a while. I was hooked.

When I qualified as a teacher at twenty-eight I moved to Australia. It was here that my Spiritual Journey began. Since then I have worked in schools, offered one-day workshops and ten-day residential Rites of Passage camps for young people and adults.

I explore Relationships and Sexuality, Gender Differences, Reclaiming our Rites and the rituals that make life more meaningful. The underlying focus of my work in groups is understanding, loving, self-awareness and spiritual connection in order for participants to be in harmony with themselves and the World.

By attending workshops and retreats facilitated by other people and running them myself, I have opened up and peeled away much that no longer serves me. I've experienced love and more love as my heart opened. Because of my experience and knowledge I am able to help others do the same. To see people recognise and value more of themselves is one of my greatest joys. I am grateful to every person who has crossed my path.

I follow my passion. It has many rewards. I have moved out of my family mould and also that of my culture. I have not worked in a regular job for over twenty years. It is an edge and sometimes there's little to hold on to. I find myself in a void. But that allows me to fly... free! I trust Life to support me.

I'm now over fifty and my life is a series of ups and downs, just like anyone else's. I now know that troubled waters do not run deep. Like the ocean when things get choppy on the surface, deep down it is undisturbed. There is stillness. At times I feel strong and powerful and at others, vulnerable and raw. Deep down I experience peace.

The advantage of my maturity is that I accept and love myself. I can also see more clearly and quickly the lessons I am offered and can embrace the changes. I celebrate the joys! I see through the things in life that can hold me back. To love, enjoy and celebrate – these are my main challenges. The stuff of my life has made me who I am and for that I am thankful.

As I become wiser, I recognise life for what it is – one big playground. Not to be taken too seriously but experienced for the learning. To walk Lightly on the Earth and to be grateful for this life is a blessing!

It is with my own personal life's experience and that of attending and running workshops for over twenty-five years that I write **GETTING REAL... about growing up!** It brings all the aspects of my passion, work and life together.

I know that change starts here, now with me, IN THIS MOMENT. It starts here, now with you also.

We can free ourselves of all that is in the way of being

truly magnificent!

about growing up! is the gift that I have to offer

Our deepest fear is not that we are inadequate.

Our deepest fear is that we are

powerful beyond measure.

It is our light, not our darkness,

that most frightens us.

We ask ourselves, who am I to be

brilliant, gorgeous, talented and fabulous.

– Nelson Mandela's Inaugural Speech 1994.

GETTING REAL...
your story

If, through reading this book, you experience **GETTING REAL... about growing up!** in any powerful way for yourself, or:

- you took a risk,
- released anything that was holding you back – hurts, grievances, untrue beliefs about yourself,
- challenged what was going on around you,
- gained more self-confidence,
- you began a Change Agent Club in your school,
- anything happened in your life that you think would inspire other young people...

WRITE ABOUT IT!

If you would like to see it published... **SEND IT TO ME**.

I plan to compile **TEENSPEAK – ABOUT GETTING REAL**!

This is to be a book of **your stories, poetry, photos, cartoons, anything**.

It will be like this one. Full of pictures and colours and yummm...

Any adults who have interesting stories about their adolescence can also send them in.

If you wish to comment on GETTING REAL... about growing up! or anything else, please do. I love to hear people's responses to my book.

Email to: info@amritahobbs.com

Check out the Website: www.amritahobbs.com

Or post your stories and poems to:
TeenSpeak
PO Box 76, Mullumbimby, NSW 2482, Australia.

What's in it?

OUR WORLD...

A Time of Transition

OUR WORLD is presently in a fragile condition of imbalance. We are constantly being made aware of this through the media. Issues that impact on the environment and affect the Earth, bombard us. What motivates the levels of destruction that we are facing now is greed – short-term rewards without ever considering long-term consequences, hatred, thoughtlessness, ignorance, self and planetary destructive behaviour and lack of caring. We have imposed our human will on the Earth and made a mess.

OUR WORLD has not been honoured. We do not live in harmony with our planet even though she keeps us alive.

OUR WORLD is full of beauty, trees, flowers, animals and insects, forests, mountains, lakes and streams. The Earth is a wonderland. Open your eyes to see it. If you take notice, care for and respect her, she offers you so much. By observing Nature around you, seeing what there is to be seen, appreciating and joining it by holding on to its power and Life Force, you give yourself more Life. The more you choose to embrace what Life has to offer, the more vital you become.

OUR WORLD has a place for you in it. You can help maintain the beauty on Earth and assist Nature by making the World a better place to live in. You can plant trees. You can clear away rubbish from your life and your surroundings. You can also do this by taking care of your body, thinking uplifting thoughts and looking after your living environment.

OUR WORLD is swarming with exciting people. The different colours, cultures, religions, lifestyles offer a fascinating array of shared experiences. You can choose to open your heart and accept these differences. You can focus on what is good in the peoples of the Earth. You can contribute to the spiritual re-creation, regeneration and renewal of our World.

OUR WORLD is a place where you can take responsibility. You can use your energy and enthusiasm to bring about change for the better. A choice you can make for life is to turn negative thoughts and beliefs into life-giving ones – noticing what you have, rather than what you haven't.

OUR WORLD is created moment by moment, through your desires, thoughts, feelings and actions. These have an effect on everyone and everything around you. Focus on giving more to your family, your community and the Earth than you are taking from it. Give your best.

OUR WORLD is improved when you are confident and have strong good intentions. Listen to your inner knowing so that you can be in the right place at the right moment. There are no mistakes. If you consciously choose life, you can live in new and different ways.

OUR WORLD is experiencing a metamorphosis. It is in a process of transition, a state of flux and evolution, a time of alteration and change – like a tadpole turning into a frog. We can move out of our limited consciousness and our lives on this Earth can be transformed. This period of transition may be disturbing, chaotic or eruptive as we move from what is familiar into what is new.

OUR WORLD is constantly evolving. In the story of humanity there have been numerous other times of great transformation. This time is yet another. By being at peace and holding love in our hearts we contribute to the transformation of all life on planet Earth.

OUR WORLD is changed by our love, courage and clear vision. When we remain true to our inner knowing in our lives, all may be well as we move through these times. The metamorphosis is already happening. Many of us are experiencing it.

We Are the World

This article was written for a local newspaper by Leigh (13) and Angie (14).

"As a young person there are always other threats that seem much greater than growing up itself. Nuclear war, poverty, crime, drugs, political prisoners and our overall lack of compassion for every living thing. Closer to home each of us has our own struggles with growing up.

There is a lot packed into our teenage years. We go from childhood into a time when hormones start to take control. It all seems to happen so fast. We're changing physically and emotionally. We're taking on much more responsibility at home and dealing with the heavy load of schoolwork, peer group pressure and the continual question, "What are you going to do with your life?"

We're trying to set a good example for our younger brothers and sisters, choosing a career and the millions of other things on our minds that really have nothing to do with our relationship with Mother Earth.

With so much going on it's quite a relief to think that our elected officials are going to take care of all of those minor and major planetary concerns while we concentrate on growing up.

It's obvious now that not only are those people not supervising the care of our home as we trusted, but we, the peoples of the World, have and still are perpetuating this planetary destruction.

Now, as I look ahead at my so-called future I'm amazed at how the Earth is letting us know in so many ways that there has been a gross injustice by mankind. The many recent devastating floods, landslides and dramatic weather changes show the Earth's pain and how out of balance our ecosystem has become. By polluting the water we drink and swim in and the air we breathe, we have altered the Earth's atmosphere itself.

We are now in a time of global emergency. There are solutions to these problems, but all of them will take conscious effort by every human being to eliminate the things that are leading us to impending disaster."

...teenager
The whole typical nutty teenager thing

WHO ARE YOU AS A TEENAGER?

Adolescence is as significant to the development of the personality as the formative years of life – conception to five years of age. Much of your future behaviour, beliefs, self-concept and self-esteem are learned during these five years. The influences around you during childhood are powerful.

A teenager is someone who is between thirteen and twenty years of age. As a teenager you are going through a BIG CHANGE. Adolescence is an in-between stage. During this time you are finding out who you are and where you fit in the World. You are on your Journey to becoming an adult.

What you are going through is similar to what happens to a caterpillar. The caterpillar looks at the world from a limited point of view. As a child you did too! Children often don't think about who they are. They just are!

When the time comes for the caterpillar to transform itself, it makes a cocoon. This is like the adolescent stage of human development. The caterpillar is willing to let go completely of its life as it has known it. It allows its body to become like a soup – a mish-mash of cells preparing themselves to transform into a butterfly. This is called metamorphosis. At this stage the caterpillar is not aware that this is happening. Slowly, over time, the cells re-group and eventually they become the form of the butterfly. It is not until the struggle to get out of the cocoon has been won that the butterfly can fly.

The butterfly in this example is the equivalent of an adult. Adolescence is the struggle to make sense of the world around you and your place in it – to grow from a child to an adult.

If your upbringing has been generally unsupportive, which is true for some of you, it's during your teenage years that childhood influences can be turned around. During adolescence you can make radical changes in your beliefs, the way you see yourself and how you behave as a result of your upbringing. Like the caterpillar you are in the soup. Adolescence is a time, more powerful than most, when you metamorphosise.

Changes

There are a few reasons why this metamorphosis happens:

- Hormone activity is making the child into someone else.
- Your brain is going through a developmental growth spurt.
- As you become more independent, you break away from established family structures and make choices that free you of childhood influences.
- You become more aware about making your own choices and taking control of your life.
- As you develop new levels of understanding, it's easier to be open to new and different thoughts, ideas and influences.

If you have been hurt, damaged or wounded in any way during your childhood, you can help yourself by using personal processes and by seeking support from caring adults. You may also benefit from reading this book. Becoming aware of your options makes choice possible.

If you have had a happy and loving childhood, reading GETTING REAL…about growing up! may broaden your horizon. You can find out about how others experience their lives. You may gain new perspectives and clarity about who you are at this time in your life and glimpse a bigger picture.

When you pass through adolescence successfully you become a young adult. This next phase of your maturing can take up until the age of thirty. By this time you could be considered an adult.

"Mentally, emotionally and physically the human being is designed for a long childhood, followed by a short adolescence and then adulthood – the state of responsible, self-reliant wholeness. What we see children experiencing now, however, is an ever-shortened childhood, followed by a premature, prolonged adolescence from which ever fewer seem to be emerging."
– TE OF PIGLET, Benjamin Hoff.

Becoming Your Own Person

Adolescence is a time for establishing an identity that is separate from parents or guardians. This is sometimes marked by arguments, anxiety, separation, fights and the breaking of rules. You are becoming an individual. You are discovering who you are and what you value as a person. You are learning that you are not either your father or mother. This is a testing-out time in the family that can be painful for everyone. You are naturally testing the boundaries they set for you. That is how you strengthen your personality. Their job is to set limits, to guide and support you to mature. It's useful to learn how to negotiate with them so that you can all feel like you are winning.

Ideally, parents also protect you and keep you as safe as they can. This can be challenging for them if they have not been brought up well themselves or if you are not willing to co-operate. Flexibility and open communication between teenagers, parents or guardians can make the lives of everyone easier. There is a natural process in becoming your own person. These changes don't have to be confusing or traumatic – though they can be. If you understand the process you are going through it may make your transition smoother.

At this time, new relationships are being established with friends and the other gender, providing you with opportunities to go outside the boundaries of the family.

Note: I use **other gender** rather than the usual **opposite sex**. Gender is either male or female and one is not the opposite of the other.

High self-esteem helps! Knowing the good things about yourself allows you to meet the challenges of adolescence. If you don't feel good about yourself, you may miss some opportunities for growth and learning. There is a chance for learning in any situation, no matter how challenging it may seem at the time. If you look for the lessons and find them, instead of feeling like a victim, small and inadequate, you can benefit. Don't tell yourself you are not good enough – accept and be confident about who you are.

Looking Cool

A lot of energy goes into looking cool during adolescence. No one likes anyone else to know that she or he is feeling insecure. It's easy to believe that everyone else is fine and you are the only one feeling:

- uncomfortable,
- unsure of what to say or how to behave,
- unattractive at least or ugly at worst,
- dealing with pimples, odours, bodily changes,
- not clever enough, not good enough,
- like hiding who you are or wearing a mask to disguise how you are feeling inside.

Don't be deceived. The cool image is not usually true. Many young people have a hard time. Under the surface they may be shy, unsure, isolated and afraid. They may also be struggling with the enormity of the feelings of growing up.

Be aware that the hormonal and physical changes that are taking place in your body can be largely responsible for mood swings and feelings of uncertainty. Things settle down as you get older.

If you are confident you may be able to lend a hand to those who aren't. They could benefit from a kind gesture or support. If you lack confidence, work with the suggestions in this book. You may not be what unsupportive adults have led you to believe about yourself.

Self-Consciousness

As a child, you are not usually self-conscious. You just are! Between the ages of twelve and sixteen you may become more concerned with questions like: Who am I? How do I judge myself? What am I like? How do others see me? What might I become? If you have low self-esteem or judge yourself harshly this can be painful.

What is Your Essential Nature?

I use the term Essential Nature to describe your authentic and real self. When you are experiencing your Essential Nature, it's like something clicks inside you. You feel at ease with yourself, comfortable with who you are. You know deep-down that everything is okay. You are relaxed. You sense your place in the Mystery.

When you fully express your Essential Nature you feel connected within yourself and to everyone and everything else around you. You then express that quality of connection and harmony through your personality and the things you do in your life. When you accept yourself you can then live your potential and share your unique gifts with the World.

Your Essential Nature is often covered up because of the treatment and expectations of your parents, teachers and society. Sometimes in order to connect with your Essential Nature you may choose to clear out what is layered over it – this can be beliefs, family and societal conditioning and negativity from others. When people expect you to behave in ways that go against your own knowing, this can take you away from your Essential Nature.

If, during childhood you lost connection to who you really are, for whatever reasons, you can now choose to reconnect and live from that place in you. GETTING REAL…about growing up! explores many ways you can do this.

Take Your Time

The transition from child to adult is gradual over time. It can take many years. It is something that happens almost when you are not looking.

Between the ages of twelve and twenty-one you may be ready to:

- leave childhood, where most of you are sheltered, clothed and fed,
- move towards more independence and be given more freedom,
- be given and take more responsibility for your self,
- learn to become trustworthy,
- participate more in the day-to-day running of a family,
- explore in your relationships,
- begin to learn about intimacy and sexuality,
- discover your values around friendships, alcohol, drugs, sexuality and spirituality,
- find out what your gifts, talents and abilities are,
- go on to further education or find employment,
- move toward the bigger world of adulthood and responsibility, e.g. provide for yourself financially, create your own home.

Generally in this phase of life the adults around you expect more from you. You are beginning to understand that how you behave has consequences and that what you say has an effect. You can also learn about becoming accountable for your actions.

Because there is so much pressure during adolescence, both from within and without, life can become confusing. It is natural as a teenager to experience new things – from attending parties and concerts, to dating. Perhaps you are considering or being pressured into experimenting with alcohol, drugs and sex before you are ready.

Adolescence is about learning how to cope with all of these new experiences and finding out what does and doesn't work for you. You are constantly faced with new feelings and difficult decisions. At times it may be hard to hear your Essential Nature. Your friends and acquaintances may be trying to influence you. You may be tempted to go along with them which makes them feel good about what they're doing. If you do not stay aware, you may lose connection to your own knowing. It is empowering when you decide what you are ready for.

During adolescence you are not only confronting stressful situations, just as adults do, but you are also developing ways to cope. Finding ways to respond to stress is a crucial skill for adolescents. This often gets easier with practice. Look for ways to create less stress and attempt to be as easy on yourself as you can. Remember you are learning. Don't give yourself a hard time.

Later in adolescence is the time when life-changing decisions are made. What kind of employment do you choose? When to leave home? When to form an intimate relationship? Marry? Have children? What are your dreams and visions for your life?

The process of growing up can take until your thirties. There is a lot of learning to do and it doesn't happen overnight. There is no rush.

All of the experience and learning is necessary in order for your transition from child to adult to take place. There are many steps to take that are part of your Journey. Are you willing to take them and accept that whatever you are going through is valuable learning for life? You live in a complex world. You are making your way in unfamiliar territory.

"Without any intentional, fancy way of adjusting yourself, to express yourself freely as you are is the most important thing to make yourself happy and to make others happy."

– Suzuki Roshi.

Transition – Child to Adult

Adolescence is a time of transition – like travelling on a train. You have left one station behind and you are on your way to somewhere else. As an adolescent you are clearly no longer a child, though sometimes you behave like one and you are not yet an adult.

There is little formal guidance to assist some teenagers during this transitional stage. Adolescence can be a time of mixed and confused emotions, feelings and messages from parents, friends, self and your own body. For example, you are not yet ready to take care of yourself but may like to stay out late at parties. Your parents don't allow you to do this, so you fight. You may sometimes feel grown up and at others like a little kid.

One aim of GETTING REAL…about growing up! is to help you understand what is happening and to make your transition easier. If you have parents, relatives, teachers, or adults you respect and who respect you, you can turn to them for guidance. This may make your Journey into adulthood less confusing. When you are facing issues that are beyond you, reach out. As you grow older, adults may no longer make your decisions for you, but they can help you become more confident and able to make your own.

If there is no one around who can give you the kind of guidance you seek, you can prepare for the changes you are experiencing and educate yourself to the best of your ability. Reading this book and others like it is a great place to start. If your problem becomes serious, do not suffer alone. Reach out. Look for support from your friends, extended family, friendly neighbours, community, social workers or a Help Line.

Transformation

Transformation is when you radically change from one thing into another. Turning from a child into an adult is one kind of change. Transformation can include some kind of Initiation, a Rite of Passage or spiritual experience. Some examples of transformation are when mean and horrible people become caring ones, because of something that happens to them. A criminal may change into a saint. Saint Francis of Assisi experienced a transformation when he realised that his parents' wealth could not make him happy and that life was more than material possessions. He gave everything up and went to live in an abandoned monastery. From his transformation the Franciscan Order evolved.

Not all teenagers go through a transformation during adolescence. Some do! In the process of becoming an adult he or she becomes a different person. Miraculous changes in attitudes, behaviour and ways of relating can happen for young people who take steps to look at and gain understanding about who they are. Teenagers who are treading a dangerous path of self-destruction can halt mid-step and choose a different way.

Transformation involves making a significant change in the way you are in the world and the way you see it. It's like walking down a road in one direction – you see where you are going and everything appears to be obvious. When a deep transformation happens you find yourself no longer walking down the same road. You may not even think you are on the same planet. You are changed within yourself and hold a different personal and Worldview.

Transformation can be triggered by different kinds of events:

- A death of someone close – no longer having that person around impacts on your life and the way you live it.
- A powerful experience that takes you out of your every day existence and catapults you into new understanding.
- A life threatening illness, which could be a healing crisis, changes the way you relate to your body and life in general.
- A near death experience, which gives you an opportunity to view life in a more expanded way.
- A religious experience, or a spiritual guide or a close encounter with a person of power, who touches the core of your being and shifts you to another level of awareness.

Transformation is something that you can bring about for yourself. **Reading and working with the material in GETTING REAL... about growing up! may provide a transformational experience for you.**

Unfamiliar Territory

Adolescence is an exciting adventure. When you go into unfamiliar terriory it is useful to have a map to guide you. You may not always be offered appropriate maps. The maps of your ancestors may be past their use-by-date. The maps your grandparents used for growing up were more clearly defined. At a certain age, a male went to work, probably for the rest of his life. His role was to offer material security to his family and ensure its survival. The woman was expected to be the homemaker – to raise a family. That's perhaps over-simplified! These days we have complex social structures, making maps out of date that are only twenty to thirty years old.

With the old maps there was little emphasis on fulfilling yourself, or following your passion. Basic survival for most people was often the priority. These days you have many more options. New maps are certainly more appealing AND it can be easier to get lost. The road is not so concretely defined. You have more flexibility and personal choices to make. Without maps you learn by trial and error. You make up your own Journey.

It's easy to get LOST in life. It's okay to ask for guidance, support and new instructions. It's okay to take your time.

It's absolutely brilliant to forge new directions and create new maps.

The Butterfly

Growing up is a process that is natural. There are no short cuts, as this story demonstrates:

A man found a cocoon of a butterfly. One day a small opening appeared in it. He sat and watched the cocoon for several hours as the butterfly struggled to force its body through that little hole. Then it seemed to stop making any progress. It appeared as if it had gotten as far as it could and it could go no further. So the man thought he would help it. He took a pair of scissors and snipped off the remaining bit of the cocoon. The butterfly then emerged easily. But it had a swollen body and small, shrivelled wings.

The man continued to watch the butterfly because he expected that at any moment the wings would enlarge and expand to support the body, which would contract in time. Neither happened! In fact, the butterfly spent the rest of its life crawling around with a swollen body and shrivelled wings. It never was able to fly.

What the man in his kindness and haste did not understand was that the restricting cocoon and the struggle required for the butterfly to get through the tiny opening were Nature's way of forcing fluid from the body of the butterfly into its wings. Then it would be ready for flight once it achieved its freedom from the cocoon.

Sometimes struggles expand us into our lives. If we go through life without any obstacles, it could cripple us. We may not become as strong as our potential allows. **We may never fly!**

Stunted Growth

You may struggle to grow yourself up, especially if life has given you some extremely heavy knocks: physical, mental, emotional abuse, alcoholism, neglect or separation from natural parents, homelessness or anything else like these.

Some other conditions that may stunt your growth:

- Not being accepted and loved by parents can damage you deeply. They are your major points of reference and assist you in the process of discovering who you are.
- If parents are not affirming and reassuring you then you may lack self-confidence and feel insecure.
- Having an absent father or mother when you are small can cause anxiety, insecurity, isolation and confusion about your identity.
- Not being allowed to freely express yourself as a child. Suppression of your spontaneous life force and your Essential Nature can deeply hurt you.
- Not having a sense of place or belonging within a larger community.
- If you are not admired by older people you are being hurt and in some way neglected.
- Being put down, judged or criticised by your parents or others or not being good enough for them as you are can hurt deeply and distort your sense of self.
- Violence or any kind of abuse can seriously affect the way you live your life.
- Not having powerful role models about what being a male/female is. Either, because dad/mum is not around or because he/she is not a whole and adult person. It is damaging for teenagers not to be welcomed into their male or female communities.

If you were hurt as a child you may attract further hardship as you grow up. You may be picked on, become a bashed wife or be a man who ends up in violent situations. You may recreate the environment you experienced as a child when you become an adult until you have erased and cleared the memories out of your cells. This takes awareness and focus. You have the whole of your life in front of you to do this.

Are you ready to move forward? If you address your childhood wounds during puberty, it can make your life as an adult easier, happier and fulfilling. If your hurts are not addressed, then you may go about acting out your pain, doing all kinds of damage to yourself and those around you, sometimes for the rest of your life.

The result of healing your childhood experiences can bring a sense of relief, release and freedom. You may, if you had an unhappy time, be able to experience the happiness that you didn't as a child. With the right kind of assistance you can shift through things quickly. This could be in the form of a book like this one, a caring adult, meditation, a counsellor, group work or other helpful experiences or people.

TEENSPEAK

"Teenage years are about having fun! It's a time to get yourself sorted. Learning about life skills, about everything really. It's good being a teenager because I don't have adult responsibilities, I can enjoy it more and I can relax. School's been challenging for me. It's good to do some study but not too much. That sets me up for my life. My social life is fast. Keeping up with everybody, it's a fast life." – Alan (16)

"Everything seems pointless. I feel like a bug in a swimming pool – nothing solid or definite to hold onto in life, no one else but me, this mass of unknown substance going round and round. Going nowhere fast.

A massive clawing wave of depression comes over me, stinging my eyes. It seems as though no one understands. No one really knows me. Ironically, I don't even know myself.

How could Mum trivialise my feelings of nothing to live for – my cry for help? The most meaningful time of my life – searching for the answers but looking in all the wrong places – and she passes it off in one fell swoop – It's just a stage."
– Mia (15)

"Being a teenager isn't easy. When you think you are drowning, all you can see is the water. There are so many things you begin to think about and start having to deal with; so many social rules and regulations and trying to fit them in with your fears and paranoias can be far from gentle! We seem to see everyone as our aggressors, our captors and our cruel judges, regardless of their actual intention. 'I'm just thinking of your future welfare' becomes 'I am just going to cut off your toes and see if you can walk' and every time someone says 'It's for your own good' you could swear they just told you the whole world hates you.

We all need to remember to act out of love and not fear, because it is a difficult time for everyone. The teenagers who are struggling to break new ground and find their own footing, apart from their parents; and for the parents who are struggling to understand these new points of view, yet still trying to be proper parents." – Emma (16)

"I haven't been aware of myself totally changing. But the changes have brought me mixed emotions and made me very confused. I blow up at nothing. Cry about nothing. All mixed up! It's scary for me not having control of my emotions. It feels like I'm trapped in a room with the walls closing in on me. I'd like to break away and I can't do that. The confusion brings mainly anger and hurt. Usually I get angry at Mum. I let fling at her. While I do it I feel angry and then hurt and guilty afterwards. I've always had a bad temper but I don't have the control I had in the past. I feel really alone.

I've become numb to everything. I had an accident the other day and I felt numb. I've noticed that a lot in the last two years. I don't react like I used to. There's a shadow over my whole life. I feel separated from everything around me. This sense got stronger since I went to high school." – Natalie (13)

Change....

"Change is often gradual and I am not aware of it. From my experience at the camps with Amrita I was able to take away with me certain insights and understandings that still influence the way in which I view the world. The greatest times for me were the times of group sharing. Within the greater view of what a person was, it allowed a space in which to share grief and guilt, pain and anger. It was a process of learning to know how I was feeling. Finding out that others have felt the same things and that I was not alone in my pain. This was a real insight for me. Here were all these teenagers of various ages and from various social backgrounds and yet they all felt pain and fear and wanted love and joy. To a certain extent, on a basic level, we were all the same. There was strength in that, a sharing of recognition, love and support.

I wasn't fitting in with friends and lacked support at home. I found a group of people who respected a greater view of the Nature of the individual than is currently accepted in Western society. It was an experience of relating to people in a new way, a more open way, which recognised that people are not just minds walking around in bodies, but that they also have emotions, spirits, pasts and futures and must relate to parents, brothers, sisters and friends. The person is an integrated whole of many levels that all need nurturing.

It is that process of communicating that brings release and then greater understanding. For me, it was a catharsis, releasing hurts and pains I hadn't even acknowledged in myself, beginning that process of inner listening, becoming aware of my own inner state that eventually led to balance. I had an experience of being aware of my own feelings, which has since been the departure point for further growth and knowledge." – Peter (16)

Julie Henderson, author of THE LOVER WITHIN speaks:

"Human beings are in a unique position. We are conscious. And consciousness moves instantaneously. In the moment of thought – what is thought, happens. But we are also embodied and bodies are slower. They move at the pace of heartbeats and water flow. They move like land adjusting itself. Like the inner pressures of the Earth. So our problem is that we are always changing faster than we can change. Especially when we are quite young and then again when we are adolescent. Then again at any time when we are genuinely engaging our spiritual growth. At these times we change even more rapidly than usual. The swiftness of our change, meeting the slowness of our change, is like waves beating on rocks or lightning striking the Earth. So it can be quite startling and uncomfortable. But change is also magnificent.

Over the slow course of a lifetime, incredible things are possible. In our minds we want to get it all done now and in our minds we can. But because minds change so rapidly, they change back again, so as anybody can remember and recognise, one moment we can feel grown up, whatever that means and the next moment we can feel seven years old. Even though it's frustrating that we can't change everything right away, we should also be glad because the body is like an anchor. The changes we make with our body are stable. They change slowly like mountains and we can rely on them.

Adolescence is a time when you are changing, fast! It's like running so fast; it feels like you're going to trip. The body is doing everything it can to keep up. What happens is that the brain is using about ten times as much fuel during this time to support the changes. It's the same as riding a surfboard or a wild horse. If you can remain balanced and stay relaxed, everything goes well. And even if you fall off, it's not such a big deal – but it feels like it.

Sometimes it's hard to be patient with change. But if we couldn't change we would be in worse straits. It's not possible not to change. Embryos wouldn't become babies; children would never grow wise; adolescents wouldn't become adults; no one would ever fall in love."

Dealing with Depression

It is normal during adolescence to experience mood swings as you grow and change. At times you may feel up, at others down and unsure of yourself. However if you suffer from the following symptoms over an extended period it may be that you are depressed.

You may:

- feel sad a lot of the time, feel hopeless and become frustrated,
- be slumped over and find it difficult to face life's experiences,
- be unable to concentrate,
- have lost interest in activities that you normally enjoy,
- lack motivation about schoolwork or life in general,
- be distancing yourself from family and friends,
- be sleeping more than is usual,
- become anti-social or aggressive,
- feel unwell as a result of long-term depression.

There could be any number of reasons for feeling the way you do. If this goes on for any length of time it may lower your self-esteem and interrupt your studies at school. It is possible for you to get out of any black hole you may find yourself in. Do not suffer alone – speak up, find help and allow others to support you. Talking can create change. For more serious depression seek professional help – a school counsellor, a supportive adult or contact your local community health service, or check out www.reachout.com.au.

Open Communication

If you are prepared to accept what's going on for you, there are ways you can help yourself. One way to gain support is to talk to those closest to you about your feelings and fears. Communication creates closer relationships. Your friends are going through changes similar to you. Your parents already have. Start by sharing with people who you really trust.

Life becomes enriched when you can share your deep feelings with others. You can experience yourself FREE! At this time, things in your life are changing so fast that you have the perfect opportunity to be radically different in your intimate relationships.

Approaching parents or friends tentatively but openly allows them to see that you are vulnerable and opens the door for real closeness. If you're really scared, practice in your mind or in the mirror or talk to a cushion before approaching them. The chances are they may be really grateful if you do.

Here are some examples of how to start meaningful and honest conversations:

"Mum… I've got something on my mind that I'd like to share with you. I'm a bit scared so don't laugh when I tell you…"

"Dad, you've been through puberty and I'd like to know what it was like for you. I've talked to Mum about it, but being a woman she doesn't quite understand what it's like for me…"

"Jamie, I know boys don't often talk seriously to one another about what's going on inside… I think that girls do… I'm a bit scared about my feelings for Jenny and I'd really like a friend to talk it over with. Can you help?"

Allow people to get to know the REAL you. Be courageous – speak up! When you do, it releases a lot of the tension that you feel about yourself and what's happening for you.

The Importance of Friendship

Friendships are vitally important during adolescence. They create a bridge from one world to another. As you move away from the family, the friendships that are formed during adolescence are what carry you through this stage of development.

As a teenager you begin to redefine yourself through your friendships. The people you mix with and the quality of your relationships are important for your growth. Friendship is essential for your well being. When you have a few special people in your life they help you to maintain your sense of connectedness and belonging in the World.

The strength you gain in your relationships can see you through hardships. Sharing with friends can also give you boundless joy and times of celebration.

Real friends can:

- be fun to be around,
- help you to see yourself more clearly, encourage you to be real and give you useful feedback,
- give you a solid foundation,
- be people to turn to, be supportive and loving, whatever you are going through,
- comfort you when you are down.

Sometimes your relationships become distorted when you:

- don't like or love yourself enough,
- expect others to fill the gap in your life and heart. Others are not able to do this,
- are not willing to take responsibility. You expect people to give to you, but don't give anything back,
- give too much and give yourself away too easily without receiving anything in return,
- let people down. By not following through on your word, you become untrustworthy. This can hurt others as well as yourself,
- expect a friend to meet all of your emotional and social demands. This creates pressure and doesn't allow growth. It destroys love between friends,
- are jealous and possessive. You expect your friend to be 'friends' only with you – excluding others. This is isolating and strangles your friendship.

Your Friends

Are the people you are spending your time with TRUE FRIENDS? Answer the following questions to find out by writing Yes or No in your notebook.

THINGS TO DO!

Do your friends:

Accept you as you are?

Encourage you when you choose to behave differently to them?

Support you to make positive changes in your life?

Bitch/gossip/grumble about you or others?

Have an understanding attitude when you've got something to say?

Put other people down to feel better about themselves?

Help you to feel good about yourself?

Have a positive attitude to life?

Support you when you are feeling down?

Say good things about themselves and you?

Put you first at times?

Generally care for you?

Love and accept you?

Stand by you when it matters?

Allow others to join the group?

Help others become better people?

Behave constructively?

Allow you to be honest with them?

Let you talk about your feelings?

Offer enjoyable company?

Count your score. If there are more No's than Yes's, it may be useful to consider what kind of friends you are spending your time with. Are these friends really valuing and honouring you?

"No man is an island entire of itself. All are a part of the continent, a part of the whole."

– John Donne.

THINGS TO DO!

Next Step:

Become clear about your friendships.

- Write a list of qualities that each of your friends has.

Look at it and ask yourself –

- Are these friends supporting me in my growth?
- Do my friends put me down because they don't agree with my beliefs or if I behave differently?
- Do I enjoy spending time with them? If not, decide either to talk to them about it, or spend less time with them.
- Make a list of positive qualities you'd like to have in a group of friends.

Other Suggestions –

- Draw a circle and place your name in the centre.
- Write the names of all your friends in or around that circle.
- Put those closest to you near to your name and people not so close, further away.

Take a look at your diagram and check out who your true friends are. See if there are people on the outer edges of your circle who could be closer to you or vice versa.
Make room for them in your life.

What Qualities are Valuable in Your Friendships?

Do your friends encourage you to make positive changes in your life, or do they allow you to stay stuck? By knowing what qualities you value in your relationships you are likely to attract them. If your present friends are not supporting you and you get clear about this they may move away. Don't get too concerned. There may be times of aloneness. When you can be strong enough to stand alone you draw to yourself other people who are also individuals.

Be confident that you can make new friends. Real friends mutually respect, share with, love and support each other. They accept you as you are. They encourage your growth and expansion.

**The ideal is not always possible.
Look for potential!**

Dare to be Different

Some people feel so desperate to be accepted by others that they are prepared, at times, to do anything and lose the connection with their own feelings and Essential Nature in order to fit in. By following others and not listening to yourself, you lose touch with the rhythms of your own Nature.

GETTING REAL... about growing up! challenges you to have the courage to be who you really are, rather than what the people you are with would like you to be. Be ready to stand by yourself if what is going on around you is not for you. Also be prepared to create waves if what is happening does not sit comfortably in your heart. Stand up against people who are behaving foolishly or harming themselves or others. If people are judging others or putting them down, speak up. If you don't think you can speak up – leave. Then you are no longer a follower but your own leader. You no longer rise in one voice with others but raise your own voice, speaking your own truth.

It is particularly challenging to stay true to yourself during teenage years. When you are moving away from identifying with your family it becomes crucial to find a place to fit in. You are ready to re-orientate yourself and are still looking for a place to belong. It may seem easier to be like everyone else in order to fit in. When you stand up and announce to the World that you are different, people may freak out. Friends who dare to be different – don't.

Are you willing to give the World the best of yourself, your insights, understanding and the gifts that are uniquely yours to give?

Have faith in yourself. Everyone is different.

Every person in the World is unique.

"As we have likely recognised by now, no two snowflakes, trees or animals are alike. No two people are the same, either. Everything has its own Inner Nature. Unlike other forms of life, though, people are easily led away from what's right for them, because people have Brain and Brain can be fooled. Inner Nature when relied on cannot be fooled. But many people do not look at it or listen to it and consequently do not understand themselves very much. Having little understanding of themselves, they have little respect for themselves and are therefore easily influenced by others."

– THE TAO OF POOH, Benjamin Hoff.

My Story

For years I lived alone near the forest, away from people. In Nature I could hear my own voice, find my own heart and reconnect with my Essential Nature.

I've stood alone a lot in my life and it's not an easy path.

I haven't had a conventional job for twenty years. I have followed my passion by doing the work I love. I've had a lot of freedom. I speak out and let people know how I am feeling. I create waves. I value my freedom. My spiritual life is more valuable to me than the material possessions I could accumulate.

In my earlier years I experienced self-doubt. I wondered whether to conform and keep my mouth shut. I often did in order to keep the peace.

As I've matured I've learned to stand up and to be true to myself. The price I paid has been worth every bit of daring to be different. I have mostly balanced those feelings with a growing sense of my own self-worth. I respect myself and appreciate my achievements. I still wobble and feel uncertain but not as much or for as long as I used to. Wobbling is a part of growth and I accept it. These days I have an inner strength and confidence. I have gathered wisdom.

TEENSPEAK

"I dare to be different by being friends with this guy that only has a couple of friends. The reason hardly no one likes him is because his family is not that well off. People don't like him because of the clothes he wears. They are not cool. But to me none of that worries me. I'm friends with him because he's a really nice guy with a great personality. I can talk to him about anything and it doesn't worry him." – Sharmane (15)

"I feel pressured sometimes to be like other people because there are some people that make you feel low because they seem to be better. But really they are not. They are the low ones."
– Angela (15)

"Peer pressure plays a big part in the way you act in your first year at high school. Eager to please everyone, I tried to fit into this new thing the best I could. I was frightened I'd do something wrong. I had plenty on my mind. Occupied! There was change all around me. The way you act is only part of the pressure of being thirteen. People get 'upped' if they are considered 'dags'. The desire to look good is strong. The pressure from others sometimes builds that desire which takes you away from your own true feelings. People don't want to be on their own. If you are wearing something or doing something that's not considered 'normal', you're talked about. Gossip! Hot gossip! But my life is turning. In future I want my World to be great, to have new friends and be myself. If I had my way there would be no gossips, no bitching about others, no judging just on how you look and act.

If everyone would give everyone a chance before they judge them the world for me right now would be better." – Jasmine (13)

"All my mates are into the drug scene at the moment. Out having a drink with just the boys and they start taking Ecstasy. I can't believe that they are doing it as if it's a normal thing. Going out to nightclubs and taking pills is not good. That's why I've separated out. I won't touch that stuff. I'm too scared of what the effects are going to be."
– Rick (18)

"I left school last year and thought that I should go in to a full time job and be like everyone else. Trying to make a lot of money – impress people – go after girls. I was more worried what my parents and other people thought rather than what I thought about myself. There is still a feeling of pressure on me from my old man. He's afraid I'll become one of the losers of society. What's a loser anyway? Being brought up in a wealthy suburb – everyone says that you have to be working full time and earning lots of money. So that's a lot of pressure if you are not doing something full on and being stressed out of your brain. Pressure helps to push you a little bit but I hate it. I want to go my own way. There are so many fake people. I just don't want to be like them.

Six months later I am feeling much more happy with what I am doing rather than what other people said." – Dan (18)

The pressure to conform can be tremendous during adolescence but when one person stands up and dares to be different at some level, it challenges everyone to question themselves.

Why This Pressure?

One reason people put pressure on each other to conform is to maintain their own level of comfort. BUT it's often painful if you abandon yourself to suit someone else.

Here are a few examples of where pressure may come from:

- Self – You think it's too risky to be who you are. You adapt your behaviour so that others like you. You are afraid of rejection, aloneness and are willing to do anything to belong.
- Parents – You believe it's easier for parents if you behave like them. Doing what you're told, going along with them and agreeing with what they say maintains the status quo. This creates a false sense of peace.
- Other Family Members – Grandparents, brothers or sisters may pressure you to stay as you have always been. It's sometimes uncomfortable for them as you change. They may try to keep you in the family mould.
- Friends – When you go along with the group and act cool, no one has to admit to fears, insecurity and doubts. Everyone can pretend that everything is fine. When this happens your time together becomes like a play – everyone acts out false roles. This can cause identity confusion.
- TV, Radio, Movies, Newspapers and Magazines – exposure to the media can put pressure on you materially. They sell fashion and gadgetry. They often present you with cardboard images and unreal people interacting socially in inadequate ways. The impact on your psyche if you watch a lot of TV is huge. Watch with awareness or not at all. What you read and watch is what you are unconsciously feeding your mind and emotions. This is impacting on your body/mind. Become selective about your visual and mental diet.
- Other Gender – You are meant to look attractive, do whatever it takes, starve yourself, paint your face, look cool, wear the right gear or be macho in order to be attractive to others. You may be buying into a false idea of what beauty and attractiveness are when you go along with this. Look beyond appearances and find out what you value.

"You're someone who is different, but who wants to be the same as everyone else. And that, in my view, is a serious illness."

"Is wanting to be different a serious illness?"

"It is if you force yourself to be the same as everyone else: it causes neurosis, psychosis and paranoia. It's a distortion of Nature. It goes against God's laws, for in all the world's woods and forests, He did not create a single leaf the same as another."

– VERONIKA DECIDES TO DIE, Paulo Coelho.

The Unreal Play of Life

When you go along with the above pressures you end up becoming actors in the unreal play of life. You lose yourself in a world of other peoples' perceptions, acting a part on the stage. A lack of awareness can keep you disconnected from your REAL self. Some people live out these unreal roles until they die.

Some of the roles:

- Peter and Penny People Pleaser – you turn yourself inside out to get it right at whatever the cost so that others like you.
- Colin Critic or Judge Jane – where you constantly make yourself wrong, stupid or something else. This freezes you into a corner. Lacking self-love and acceptance, you cannot see anything good in yourself and often not in others.
- Invisible Anna or Alan – you disappear by becoming small, you have no voice and believe you are not worth hearing or spending time with. This can make you miserable and you have a mousy sense of yourself and life.
- Natalie or Nick Nice One – you smile all the time and are without real character or depth, expressing nothing of real interest to a person of intelligence.

There are many more. These are examples of what you may become when you are not true to your Essential Nature. Are any of them familiar?

Clarify the roles you may be playing by writing them down or acting them out with a friend to help you become aware when you are not being REAL. Begin to take notice in your everyday life.

You are Not Invincible

Positive risk-taking behaviour is important and helps you create a stronger sense of who you are and your limits.

Some teenagers believe they can dance with death and win. Some do! Others die! Don't believe for a moment that you are indestructible. Bodies are fragile. We can't always presume that a person we say goodbye to one day will be there the next.

Be careful in your growing years. What happens to you now can affect you for the rest of your life. Drugs, alcohol, tobacco and any other harmful substances can have dangerous effects on your development, including the brain, the liver, kidneys, heart and lungs. You may behave rashly and have a serious accident, which damages your body. Can you imagine living for fifty or more years with a serious physical injury or mental illness? If you do anything to harm yourself, your quality of life can be seriously affected, including your relationships, your career and your family.

A life lived in fear is a life half lived

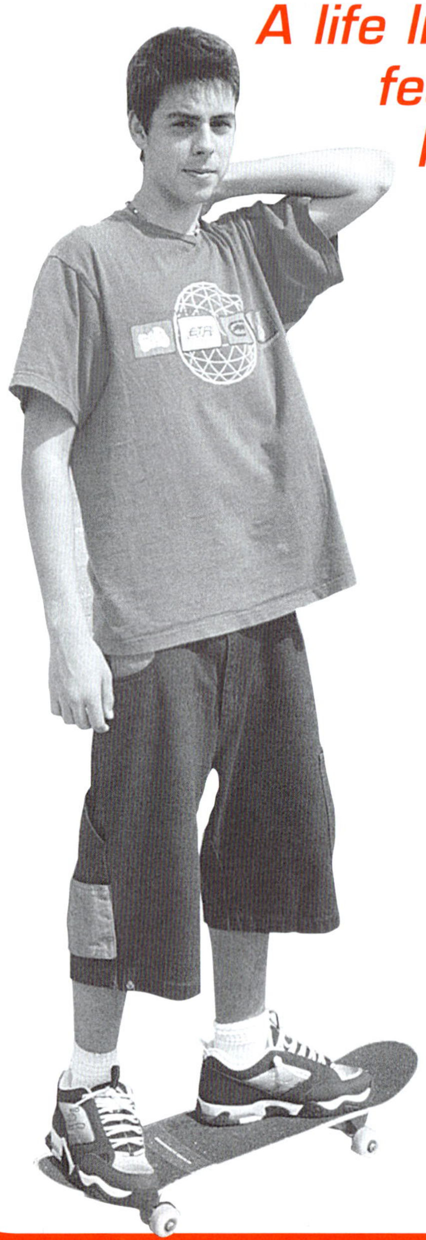

THINGS TO DO!

Imagine you have only one day to live. Visualise your funeral. Write your Eulogy – a paragraph or two that sums up the good things about you and your life. Who would be at your funeral? What would they say about you?

If you have only one day left to live, consider what there is to do. Are there things to say to people – apologies to make and appreciation to give? Do it! What could you do differently from your normal behaviour? Write your thoughts down.

Think about members of your family or your friends, choosing one person at a time. Imagine that tomorrow she or he will die. How are you relating to that person now? Why put people down and do things to harm yourself and others if you have only a short time to live? How would you prefer it to be? Ask yourself if this is the way to live the rest of your life.

Are you taking your life for granted?

Moving Beyond Fear

Some young people hurt themselves while searching for their identity and testing their strength. Going into unfamiliar territory can be frightening. But to become an alive, vital and an active human being it is good to stretch.

Risk-taking behaviour is a natural process of growing up. Over time you can develop your own wisdom about what to do and if you are capable of doing it. One of the things you learn while growing up is to expand your boundaries and your sense of yourself that has been a child. Be willing to take risks in order to grow. Your mind may sometimes attempt to hold you back. At other times it may push you too far. The right balance is when you can learn your lessons without harming yourself or others.

Fear can be a natural safety mechanism in some situations. At these times it is wise to listen to your fears and respond accordingly. It there is real danger, respond to your fear by taking care of yourself. At other times fear can hold you back from the experiences your life may be offering. If your fear is stopping you from living your life to the full – feel the fear and do it anyway. This allows you to do things you are ready to do but feel frightened to do.

Fear is experienced in the body. Never ignore it. Allow yourself to fully explore it. Some fears are imagined and so can be changed by looking at the situation logically. Once you've done that and if it's safe, go into the experience in spite of the fear. It can then transform into excitement.

How High Can You Fly?

Asking the following questions can support you to find the wings of your Spirit to chart the direction you are going in.

What kind of life can you imagine for yourself?

What are your gifts and how can you give them?

Do you hide your true self or express all of it?

Do you share your love or hide it away?

How can you best serve the World at this time?

When you connect with your Essential Nature, the true you, you become confident. You are open to receive guidance. You can have an understanding that makes it easier to live in the evolving World around you. The right people are drawn to you. All the support for your Journey becomes available to you. You find your place in the Mystery.

AIM LOW – BORING!

AIM HIGH – SOARING!

Rites of Passage Experiences

Johanna is a 15-year-old American, who now lives in Australia. She recently spent a year in Germany as an exchange student. She asked if she could interview me for a Year 11 School Project on Rites of Passage. I asked if I could interview her first. We had fun!

AMRITA INTERVIEWS JOHANNA

What do you consider a Rite of Passage to be?

It is a significant event or experience that marks my passage into a new stage of life. Something is changed in my outlook. When I went overseas, it was my Rite of Passage. I was alone there. It changed me in a way.

In what way did it change you?

It was like I had to go away from my family to find out how I fit in and what I could do. When I was with my family I couldn't change because everyone else was around me. When I arrived in Germany everyone was so happy to see me. When I met my host family I felt I already knew them. I became like one of their daughters. It was beautiful.

What is important for a Rite of Passage to occur?

I need to feel some sort of support from the people around me – family, friends or from within myself if I have difficulties. It offers a challenge to discover something within myself that I didn't know was there. It's also about being willing to take risks – going into a void to find out how I will handle it.

Was there a spiritual aspect to your Journey?

Yes! I was sitting in Sydney airport and there was a group of nuns – Sisters of the Sacred Heart. One of them came and started telling me about the pilgrimage she was making to Lourdes in France. At first I didn't realise she was talking to me. She was telling me about what it was like, always living in one place. She had never been out of Australia. She was so excited. She told me all the places she was going to visit. In my mind I saw Europe and all these little points of light – here she goes, there she goes. She wanted to do this before she died. This little seventy year-old lady just came and sat down next to me. So amazing! It felt really special – like the voice of God. It made me aware that I've got my whole life in front of me. Another special occasion was going to the Alps with my host family. We arrived at about eight at night. It was dark everywhere and it was so cold. I turned around and there was this huge black crag behind me. For a split second I felt this sense of the World as it is. How old it is. How it's all connected with everything. I felt less small, more a part of the whole picture. To see that there's all these things that are older and bigger and stronger than I am. But I was allowed to witness them. I felt accepted into the World as a whole. That was one of the most powerful moments of my year away.

Did you grow up as a result of your Rite of Passage?

I feel more diverse within myself. I have taken more responsibility and feel more independent. I can handle most situations. Wherever I go, I can make myself feel comfortable or at home. I was scared about going to Germany. When I got there all these old coats fell away. Nobody expected anything from me. I could be who I really am and didn't have to please someone else. It felt really liberating. I didn't have to think I couldn't do this or that, because everyone would be shocked. People could accept that was just a part of me. It was like a transition from my little Johanna, being the one that everyone cuddled, to feeling more mature and stronger within myself. When I was away I didn't feel different. When I was flying home I was so scared about seeing my parents again – I was shaking. When I first came back, all my thoughts were still in Germany. I didn't feel myself as a part of this place. Things at home hadn't changed. I felt how I'd changed and for a while it was really difficult. My family expected me to be just the way I was, so in the first three months we fought a lot. I felt really sad. One night I sat down and cried. I came to terms with what I had in Australia and also appreciated the experiences I'd had in Germany. If I have problems now I don't go directly to my parents, I try and work it out for myself. I feel more assured in myself that I can stand on my own two feet.

Amrita's Comment:

A Rite of Passage or Initiation takes you beyond your own edge. It is when something or someone takes you through a gateway into another aspect of yourself or your life. When you are conscious that it is happening it becomes a Rite of Passage. By creating Ritual your transitional experiences have more significance. Fighting with her parents and her tears were two ways Johanna integrated the new sense of herself into everyday life. These are examples of Johanna standing her new ground. The interview assisted her to acknowledge the power of her Journey, making it more significant.

JOHANNA INTERVIEWS AMRITA

What does a Rite of Passage mean to you?

It's been my way of **growing myself up.** It took me until I was 34 to realise that I wasn't a girl anymore. There was no one to tell me, or treat me otherwise. I was still being called a girl by friends and also at work. I was in a powerless and small place inside and outside myself. A major life Passage was when I left England. The following year, 1979, I experienced a spiritual awakening. Something deep within me was altered. At the time I wasn't conscious of what it was. So although it drastically changed my life, I didn't have any point of reference for it. I didn't know that these events could be marked with ritual. Part of me went through a death. I felt reborn. My whole life and the way I saw the World had changed.

What is a Rite of Passage?

A Rite of Passage marks a transition. It offers time away from everyday life and is an opportunity for reassessment, re-evaluation and regeneration. It's a movement from one phase of life or way of being, to another. This can be the transition from child to adult, single person to married, ending one aspect of a working life, acknowledging another. These events can be ritualised and time away can be taken to contemplate their significance. Emphasis can be placed beyond the personal on the big picture. It is not just the obtaining of a driver's licence or a young man shaving for the first time, though it can be. There is something spiritually significant about an experience for a Rite of Passage to be truly that. Something is consciously acknowledged and ritualised.

A true Rite of Passage or Initiation ceremony involves a number of different elements. My definition: **Conscious awareness of what the Passage is. Its significance. Awareness of where you are at the beginning and then at end of your Journey.** If you recognise what has changed, what allowed that to happen and ritualise it in some way, that helps make the experience real. It brings it back into your daily life. With understanding about what the liminal space (time between) is offering, you can be conscious of the benefit of your Rite of Passage. A Rite of Passage allows an embodiment of a spiritual experience in some way. An ordinary event does not usually qualify as a Rite of Passage. What takes place occurs on many levels – the physical, emotional and spiritual. If the experience goes deep enough there is an effect on levels that are also subconscious but which may become conscious at some future time.

Why did you start running Rites of Passage camps?

While running seven-day camps with teenagers it became clear there was something missing! Some teenagers seemed to be begging to be challenged, tested and strengthened. I sensed there was a way to support young people to move through adolescence with more understanding and awareness. A true Rite of Passage marks a transition. Adolescence is one of our biggest ones. Once I became aware of this I began facilitating ten-day Journeys for teenagers. These were clearly a Rite of Passage and for some an Initiation process. A Rite of Passage matures and readies young people for what they face during their transition. It also offers a signpost to where they are headed. It is useful to include Initiation and Ritual as an accepted part of growing up. These experiences are more powerful when there is family and community involvement and follow-up.

What changes have you seen in yourself since you have become Initiated?

The little me was wounded, damaged and unconscious of her spiritual connection. Every time I go through any kind of an Initiation I give aspects of myself back to myself. I am able to stand in my centre and power and to accept and love myself as woman to a greater extent. I take risks, live more fully and am more of myself, more and more and more. I have Initiated myself, at times through bleeding (menstruation), by isolating myself in the bush, by participating in rituals offered by others and by running my own workshops. Recently having gone through the change (menopause) I have gone even deeper into the process of maturing and reclaiming myself. At times I have been excruciatingly challenged as I faced my limiting beliefs and personal demons. By cutting away the illusion – the dross – my Essential Nature has become more visible, this has allowed me to become whole. By coming to the edge, jumping off and sometimes reluctantly going into the void, I have learned about life. This has allowed Spirit to work and shine through me.

How have Rites of Passage affected your lifestyle?

They have brought to my awareness many different levels of consciousness. When I take myself away from everyday life, space is created within me for something new to arise. Often I change direction at these Rites of Passage times. I am constantly led to create situations that allow this deepening process to occur. It feels like I've lived many lives in this one. I see Rites of Passage and Initiations as crucial for my spiritual awakening, deepening and evolving. I then translate this into my work. I co-create Rites of Passage for others that are appropriate within this culture.

Could Rites of Passage be a value system?

Yes. Rites of Passage and Initiation are an important part of culture. Through them people generally and young people in particular, can experience their sense of place and where they belong in the scheme of things. There can be confusion, isolation and disconnection for some young people that could change with appropriate Rites of Passage. They also support young people to mature. They enable them to take more responsibility for what's going on within and around them. With appropriate Rites of Passage we could support our children to mature both emotionally and spiritually. We could bring all of our goodness to each other and the World.

Rites of Passage assist individuals to connect consciously to their deeper, Essential Selves and allow an intimate relationship with Spirit and the Earth.

Are Rites of Passage like an education?

When a person is ready and willing, Rites of Passage can be a real education. They are an invitation into that which is beyond our personal sense of self. They can be an introduction, consciously to our Essential Nature and to Spirit.

With children the question, "Who am I", is not relevant because they just are. As a young person that kind of question becomes vital. Without asking appropriate questions young people can remain immature and disconnected. Moving through a Rite of Passage can bring an awareness of our capabilities and responsibilities. It paints a picture that shows we are conscious about who we are at this point in our lives and prepares us for the next phase.

It is helpful if there are guides – adults who can answer questions wisely. These people deserve respect. They have gained wisdom from their experiences of life or from spirit beings or God. For teenagers to sit in a circle and ask their questions is a great gift to them, to the adults present and to me. No one told me much that was useful to prepare me for menstruation or my first sexual experience, or about the challenges of leaving school. This was an enormous disadvantage and it left me floundering and vulnerable.

At what point in life are Rites of Passage most powerful?

Obviously birth is the first Rite of Passage and then the next is around seven or eight years old because at this time the child can lose the natural connection to Spirit. But within the context of moving into adolescence ten is an age for girls to have a Ritual in preparation for what's changing in their bodies and what happens when they menstruate.

The time between twelve and fifteen for both males and females is the time to acknowledge the physical, emotional, mental, social and spiritual changes they face. Rites of Passage help teenagers to embrace the Journey towards manhood and womanhood more easily. Leaving school, first sexual experience, changing life directions, marriage, pregnancy, menopause, retirement and death are all events that are well served by ceremonies, rituals or Rites of Passage processes. There are many more. We are lacking rituals that weave strong threads. These threads create rich tapestries to carry us through life into a fulfilled and satisfied spiritual maturity.

Are Rites of Passage still relevant?

More so than ever! A material focus in life is no longer enough. Many people have moved away from religion and feel disconnected. Others are bringing meaning into their lives and are reinventing the ways in which they pray. They are yearning to reconnect with the Sacred. When what seems ordinary is celebrated it becomes special. Absolutely everything constantly changes. Life is enriched when these changes are marked with Ritual.

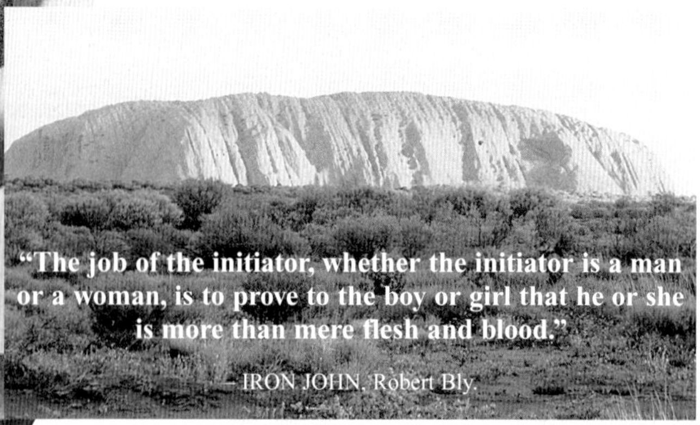

DYLAN'S JOURNEY

When you first came to the camp you said that your life was going downhill?

My life was ruled by TIME. Get up 7.30, get dressed, have breakfast, pack my bag, go to school, come home, do my homework. My life was just ruled by big time clocks. It got really stressful. I didn't need to be ruled by time like that. I also had parent problems.

Author's Note: Dylan was twelve and during a seven-day camp he had an extraordinary experience. Late one afternoon while we were walking he left the group and got lost. He waited for us to find him. When he realised we weren't coming he began a Journey that became his first step from boy to man. This unexpectedly became a Rite of Passage for him. Dylan's Journey involved walking along the beach and then a railway track. He created a situation where he was facing his fears. When we talked afterwards it became obvious that Dylan hadn't seen the consequences of his actions of leaving the group. He'd expected us to go back to find him, like his parents would. In the process of growing up, it was time for Dylan to learn about taking responsibility for himself, communicating intentions clearly and not expecting others to always take care of him. With Dylan, we saw this as an opportunity to create a ritual for him. He was ready to become more responsible for his choices. He could take this step into becoming a young man. We prepared the room with candles and played Dylan's favourite music. He was asked to stand away from the group and tell us what qualities from his childhood he was ready to leave behind. He symbolically shed an old skin.

What was it like when you got lost?

It was scary, because it was night-time. It's best to walk on the beach at night. It was very dark. I felt worried, so I sang. When you sing, it takes your worries away from you. It's a lot easier. I found a stick and swung that around. That helped too. At times I felt like someone was chasing me.

What was the Ritual like for you?

I walked towards a blue light and there were candles on each side. I said the things that I wanted to bring into manhood from my boyhood – wisdom, humour, love and skill. Everybody told me qualities that they wanted me to have in my manhood. It was a very special ceremony. It was moving and very beautiful. One thing I felt was energy going through me that I had to control. It was just going through me in spasms and I was shaking. The energy was coming from other people towards me. When I held hands with the others it really helped me to relieve it but it stayed with me. I learned to control it. A lot of energy gathered and it was going through everybody. I felt really powerful. I felt loved and that a lot of people really cared about me. I knew this before but not as strongly.

What did the Ritual mean to you?

It means a lot to me, but it's hard to verbally express it. The only way I can say it is LOVING ENERGY. It's going to be really good going back... It's going to make a great difference in my maturity.

POWER-LOVE
Dylan (12)

Everything we do seems so powerful.
Sometimes love overpowers me,
And makes me so blissful.
As if the main thing is Love,
As if I was a flying white dove.
Making peace by using my power.
Turning world leaders into flowers.
Turning the military into hippies.
Turning the navy into pippies.

Author's Note: Pippies are shellfish that live in the sand at the beach and are used for fish bait.

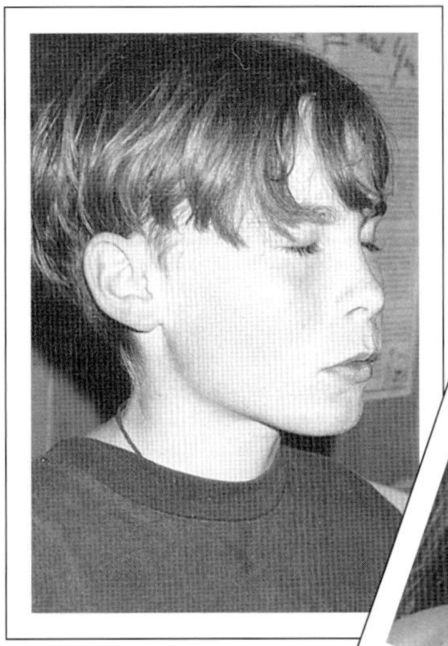

Changing Times, New Beginnings

The foundations of human life on Earth are being shaken. The old ways of warring against countries, fellow humans, the other gender, environment and self – are coming to an end. While we allow the din of humanity to drown out our inner knowing, our wisdom remains asleep. Nature does not support an unconscious, unfeeling humanity on the Earth.

It's easy to see why more people are getting sick. We have weakened our immune systems and now live with the consequences of that. We are killing ourselves with discordant relationships, alcohol abuse and doped-up minds. We are creating dis-eased bodies, numbing ourselves and pretending that the pain is not there.

There is a quickening – a radical shift taking place, assisting every good intention. Open your heart and support a Worldwide movement for peace. Spend time being still.

Ask your Essential Nature for help. It comes. Why? Because the time is ripe and you are Love, even though you may not be aware of it. Your Essential Nature is love expressing itself through you. The more you are connected the more love you have in your life.

It is time for a different attitude, a new stand to bring into being a World that we can be proud to live in.

Can you imagine GETTING REAL and

- safely expressing your true feelings and emotions in the moment they arise?
- living in a place where you love yourself, others and appreciate the gift of life?
- living life as a spiritual being having a human experience?
- realising your oneness with all Life?
- creating a way of life that preserves and nurtures all life forms on Earth?
- living in a World that is in harmony with natural and spiritual laws?

The support to bring about your personal and planetary transformation is available.

Can you call upon it and use it now for the good of others as well as yourself?

I AM – Lynne

I am one with all that is,
Any place is home.
And part of you, is part of me.
This world is my home, my country.
And I am where I'm meant to be,
To be right now, with all I see.
All is fine and all is sweet,
I am and I can live in harmony;
And make the magic and be free,
And heal my wings so I can fly,
Way beyond the sky.
I am one with all,
I am the waterfall,
I know I can,
'Cos I am, yes I am.

I celebrate, I celebrate all the good I can be.
I am the light, the light within you and me.
I am one with all that is,
And any place I can forgive.
For I am one with all and all is one with me.
I am one, for the world is my country,
I know I can for I am, I am.

HAVE A JOYFUL ADVENTURE, FELLOW TRAVELLER

SHINING SUN AND RUNNING WATER

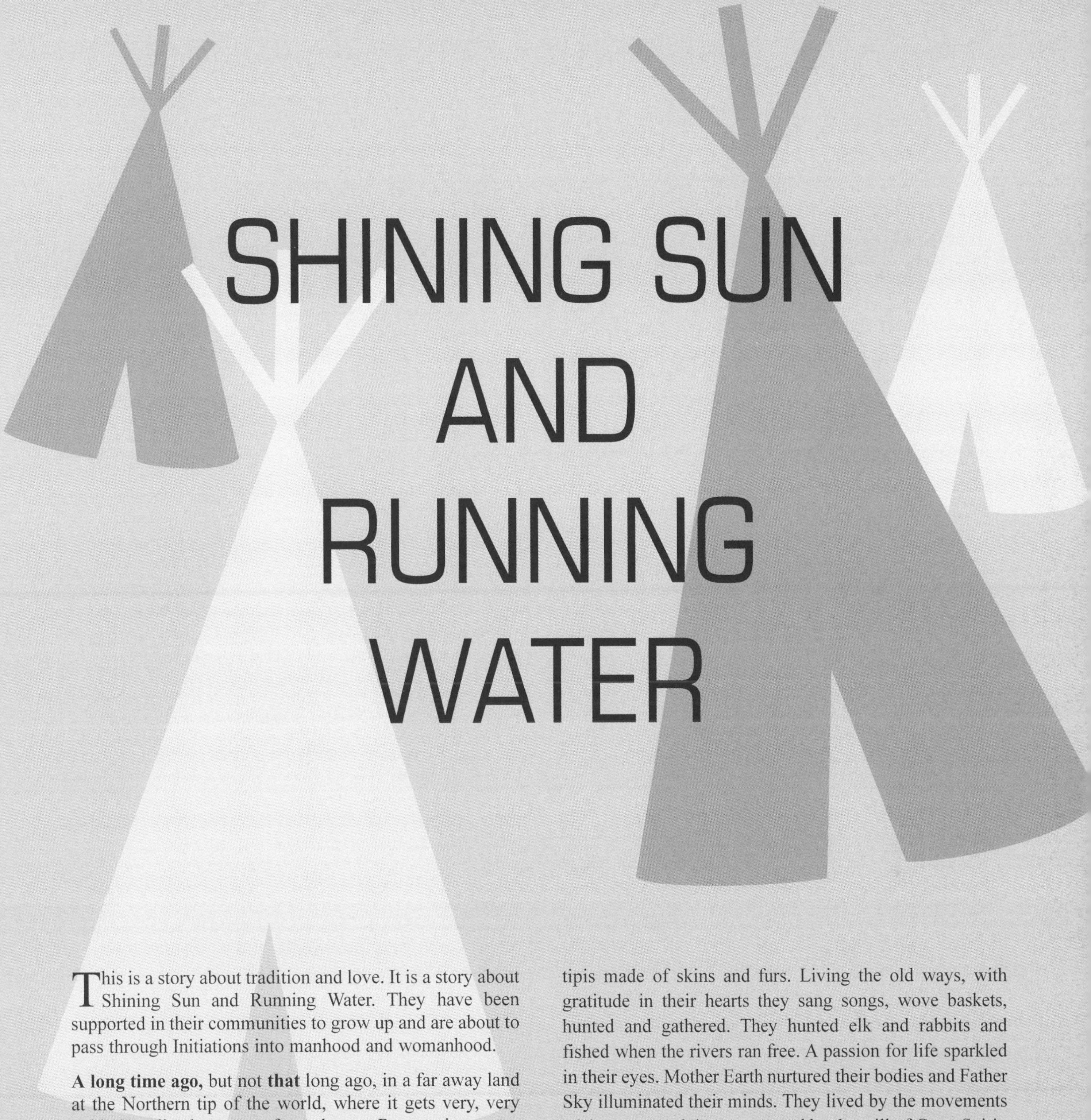

This is a story about tradition and love. It is a story about Shining Sun and Running Water. They have been supported in their communities to grow up and are about to pass through Initiations into manhood and womanhood.

A long time ago, but not **that** long ago, in a far away land at the Northern tip of the world, where it gets very, very cold, there lived a group of people on a Reservation.

The people were simple tribes-folk struggling to retain remnants of their old and wise ways. Many had left and lived comfortably in houses, working in offices or local factories. They became urban fringe-dwellers, drinking and gambling, with souls and spirits that yearned for the land of their birth and the richness of their ancestors.

The few who stayed on the Reservation lived out their days in mountainous regions. In winter the land wore a dazzling white dress and people huddled around central fireplaces. They maintained their lives, even in the freezing times, in tipis made of skins and furs. Living the old ways, with gratitude in their hearts they sang songs, wove baskets, hunted and gathered. They hunted elk and rabbits and fished when the rivers ran free. A passion for life sparkled in their eyes. Mother Earth nurtured their bodies and Father Sky illuminated their minds. They lived by the movements of the moon and the seasons and by the will of Great Spirit.

On the Northern edge of the Reservation two villages had lived side by side for many generations. Only during Summer Camps did they come together for the Sun Dance. Little was more important to the tribes-people than their children and the growing times they passed through.

The old ways made sure that the young were honoured. They were taught by the elders and prepared for their Journey from child to adult. Celebration, ceremony and ritual marked this special time.

Shining Sun was born only hours after the Spring rains had stopped – hence his name. As he grew up, he lived up to it, singing or humming to himself as he moved around the village, warming the hearts of everyone. He was just a boy, doing what boys do. He did not think of the future and had no idea about his destiny. Life lived and danced through him, adding to all of life a sense of joy and freedom. The world was his playground.

At times Shining Sun and the other boys were allowed to join fathers, uncles and the men of the village. They gathered in circles, telling their stories and sharing knowledge. These were special times that the boys treasured. The men were strong and solid. The boys felt safe knowing they were there.

Things were about to change for Shining Sun and he had no idea what was in store for him. That's how it was with the people. Knowing the power of surprise they did not tell their children what to expect during times of Initiation as they moved quickly from childhood into puberty.

Full moon was the time Shining Sun loved best of all. On warm nights he lay under the stars, staying close to the village. Wolves howled and bears grizzled as night deepened.

Every now and again a teenage boy disappeared – taken by the men from the village. The younger boys didn't know what happened. They noticed that when the boy came back he slept with the single men on the edge of the encampment. He didn't return to his family tipi for many moons.

One morning, just before dawn, Shining Sun heard heavy footsteps outside his family tipi. The flap close to his head was dragged open. Men appeared – looking stern and hard. He was shocked! They were wearing face paint and that worried him. He had no time to think. Before he could blink, he was being dragged away.

His mother stirred as he called out to her. Rushing, she grabbed Shining Sun's foot, screaming, "Stop, stop! Let him go." But the men won the battle for the boy. Putting a sack over his head, they took him away.

Shining Sun, shaking from head to foot, was cold, frightened and confused. What was going on? What will they do to me, he wondered. He had never been so scared in his life. His lip trembled. Afraid, he felt like crying. So cry he did and loudly too. The men took no notice of him. This frightened him even more.

After travelling some distance, the men stopped. They left him in a heap on the Earth. She comforted him. He heard them gathering wood and lighting a fire. Shivering shamelessly by now, he was grateful. A kindly old man took the sack from his head and led him to the fireside. Shining Sun looked around. He saw a circle of men looking very solemnly at him. Alarmed, he realised his father was not one of them.

This was The Council. Silently, they sat for an awfully long time. After what seemed like hours, the Elder Man spoke, "Shining Sun, your time has come. You are showing signs of your coming manhood. We cannot leave you to be spoiled in your mother's tipi. It's your time to stay with the men until your work is done. Great Spirit reveals your fate. We do not know what your Journey holds for you. We wish you courage and bravery."

Shining Sun felt anything but brave. He felt even smaller than the ant crawling across his foot. Childhood's freedom ebbed from his soul. With dread, he knew this was serious men's business. The men camped together in the forest over the next few days. Shining Sun was not allowed to eat. He sensed he was being prepared – for what, he did not know.

Early in the mornings, the young, fit men shook him awake. Ordering him to follow, they began running, running, running! He followed, sweating and panting. Days later, when he dipped himself naked into the stinging water of the river, he noticed that muscles were developing on his body. He was seeing himself becoming a man. If his reckoning was right he had walked on the Earth for more than fourteen years.

After many night skies, Shining Sun was led once again to The Council. They informed him that this was his last night with them. At dawn the next day he was to face his fate.

It was time for the men to share with Shining Sun some of what they had learned about becoming a man. They told him of the changes happening to him physically and in other ways. They told him that his male organ gets bigger, that hair covers his body and his voice breaks. The men told him of joining with woman and warned him to be aware of the preciousness of his seed. Not to waste it thoughtlessly. They told him men who waste their seed, waste their life force. When men do not feel love and respect in joining they dishonour all of Creation. They said that to love a woman and share his body with her body is a sacred act of Great Spirit's love.

Teaching him their law they reminded him that any action, word or deed affects the next seven generations. He was told that when the first seed of his manhood landed on the Earth, his Soul's purpose is activated. The reason for his Earth Walk is set in motion and he now walks the Mother as a man.

The men shared stories of their challenges as they had changed themselves into men from boys. They said some boys never truly become men. They stay immature until they go back to Great Spirit. They instructed him to thank his ancestors at this Initiation time and to be grateful to the men-folk of his village.

They said that guidance from the Elders is necessary at this time. That after his Initiation the people would call him a man and expect him to be the man he was becoming. This was serious men's business indeed. That night there was a great deal for Shining Sun to consider.

His sleep was half-awake of dream images of his ancestors and the webs they weave through life. Riding on horseback, hunting buffalo, celebrating the coming of Spring and gathering in for Winter. His ancestors felt close.

Next morning, before another soul stirred, he was fully awake, expectant!

The oldest man came for him and Shining Sun followed. Without speaking, they travelled a great distance into the wilderness. Walking for most of the day, every so often the old man stopped and listened. Passing through forests and fast flowing rivers they came to the foot of a mountain.

The old man once again looked for signs. Spirit whispers. Something! Out of nowhere an Eagle flew past them. This was the omen – the old man smiled, "Shining Sun, Son of Dark Cloud, you have been blessed on your Journey by the winged ones. Great Spirit has sent you Eagle. Stay here alone, without food or water and cry to Great Spirit for your Vision. You will know when your time is done. I leave you to your fate."

Wandering the wilderness for days and nights, following the signs Great Spirit sent him, Shining Sun battled with himself. Night Owl, his only witness, watched over him. Sleeping little, his demons haunted him. Nature spirits tested him! Who knows what creatures visited him in the dark nights that followed? Who knows what visions he saw? What messages and understanding about his life he received from Great Spirit? What knowing of his purpose came to his heart? **These things are personal to a boy becoming man.**

One intense night of dreaming, he fought with death! He wrestled with the darkness of the Spirit world and after facing his symbolic death, woke up to find himself alive! Shining Sun knew his quest was almost over. He was changed and had come to know himself. He sat with resolve, strong and fully alert. Waiting! Before noon he saw dust rising in the distance. Running Elk, his oldest brother, appeared on a black stallion. He hauled the weakened Shining Sun onto the horse's back. Without words, flying with the wind at their backs, they headed back to camp. Shining Sun held on, half asleep. All that night and the following day he slept. We leave him close to his dreams and the truth of his Vision.

We follow another weaving thread, in another place, about the same time.

As the mountain snows melted and Spring came to the other village, we meet Running Water. Pretty as a picture, with pink cheeks and shining black hair. She is a girl of intelligence and maturity for her thirteen years. For almost a year she has been listening to the stories of the grey-haired ones as they gently prepare her for her changes.

Her changing body looks strange to her. Plumper, she also has two small peaks where her chest had been flat and a thin clump of hair where there was none before. Although she knows what to expect, she is also a little afraid.

"The Mystery is a powerful place to be!" Aunt Howling Wolf told her: "Women gotta trust in the Mystery. Great Spirit's wisdom is wondrous. But as a woman you gotta be prepared to let go, get out of your head and stop tryin' to control things. 'Cos you can't, your body won't let you. The Mystery moves in you! It takes over and the moon will pull at you and your belly calls you home. But you gotta let go and listen to what she's tellin' you."

Running Water had a sense she knew what her Aunt meant but at the same time she had no idea. It was a funny sort of in-between place to be. What she did know was that things were moving in her. She was crying a lot and losing her temper. This shocked her. When her emotions took over, the older women looked knowingly at each other, for they could read the signs. They had seen it all before and experienced it themselves. They lovingly watched and waited, for they knew her time was almost upon her.

Running Water was told, "Your body sheds the lining of your womb when you bleed." She thought that was strange! She expected to see the redness from between her legs leave her body and was curious to find out what it felt like.

The women told her to watch carefully. They said, "Usually a special dream comes just before your first body bleed. Great Spirit sends you a vision. It shows you the reason for your Earth Walk."

When she considered it, Running Water decided it was good to be a girl. Not only because of her blood but also because she could give birth. She had a natural connection to the Mystery. At least she didn't have to go into the wilderness like the boys! She could stay by the hearth and drink warm teas from the herbs and bushes that grew close by.

The weather was warming up! Emotionally she was scattered like the wind. The signs were obvious. The women felt her movement in their waters. She had a queer feeling in her belly and could tell by the way the women looked at her that at any minute her flood gates could open and the blood pour out over everything. The women told her it doesn't happen like this but that is what she feared. She stayed in the Moon-Lodge that night. The Moon-Lodge was a resting-place for all the women at their Moon-time. They looked after one another with great care. They welcomed the Mystery of their women's bodies and knew they were full of power.

And she dreamt! She entered a magical garden grove of beautiful flowers which were being fed by a Red River. She saw a beautiful woman wearing a deerskin dress and raven black hair hanging to her waist. Behind the woman sat the biggest Eagle she had ever seen. It was as tall as she was. Running Water gazed at the dark brownness of the woman before her and when she looked closely into her beautiful face she recognised something, "I am you, as woman. You will travel far, shining your love and light and singing a song of freedom to the women of the Earth. Your message to woman is of beauty, harmony and powerful relationship to HER Self. You teach about HER sacred union with man. Eagle is your guardian, revealing the higher purpose of the challenges you face. Your service opens the hearts of many and your Journey is long."

The image faded and Running Water stirred in her sleep. The first light of dawn, alive with birdsong, woke her from her dreaming. She became aware of an unfamiliar trickling, a warmth between her legs. She knew she was embarking on her Journey to womanhood.

The women in the Moon-Lodge stirred. They prepared a warm hyssop bath for her and brought a red garment in honour of her first blood. Going about their business, they sang sweet songs of the Journey from girl to woman and told stories from Running Water's life.

We leave Running Water resting in the Moon-Lodge and we move forward.

Her family planned to announce at Summer Camp that Running Water's Journey into womanhood had begun. Other villages were invited to come and celebrate her. The men would go on the biggest hunt of the year. There was much to be done.

Over the next two moons, Running Water was being prepared. As soon as the river warmed up, she was tied with a long rope to a log on the bank and thrown into the water. To strengthen her body she had to swim against the current for many hours. When she complained that this was too long, the women said, "Tut-tut, tut! Running Water, you are to travel far. If you give birth your body must be strong." A deerskin dress was beaded ready for the celebration.

Three moons after her first blood, people gathered from many villages. Amidst great excitement, Running Water was once again sent to the Moon-Lodge to prepare herself for the Ritual. She missed the fun and games.

We leave her there for now.

We find Shining Sun staying in the men's tent at Summer Camp. It's been a long walk from his village. He has grown up since his Vision Quest in the wilderness. When he looks closely he sees wispy hair on his face. It makes him laugh!

He was with the men at the ceremonies! The men stood still – their backs straight. They looked fierce! They were present, attentive to everything that went on around them. No day-dreaming! Relaxed, yet fully alert! Shining Sun felt strange being with them, but also excited.

Imagine being there now. Campfires and lots to eat with old friends. The women sitting on the ground nursing their babies. The old folks on logs have the best view! Everyone else chatting and making themselves comfortable. Children running wild as they always do.

The men – what a sight! Shining Sun could feel their power adding to his own strength, as he stood with them.

The Ceremonies took hours. Late in the afternoon Running Water, wrapped in a blanket, was presented to the circle. Her mother announced that her Initiation was about to begin – she was to face the river. An old grey one took her to the dugout canoe on the river. They rowed downstream for some time.

Running Water prayed to Great Spirit for strength. She knew this was one of her greatest challenges. It seemed they had gone downstream for miles when the old woman finally nodded. Running Water knew what to do. She took off the blanket and dived into the water. She swam upstream, harder and harder. She faced the current that could have swept her away. Now grateful for the hours of training, she thought, "I can make it if I keep going strong". Nearer and nearer she could see the fires burning and people cheered her on. Her body trembled from head to foot as she crawled onto the shore. The roaring cheer almost deafened her. Someone brought her a blanket and led her to the fire. Weak at the knees and shivering she looked around at the people. They were cheering, hollering and feeling very proud of her. She glowed!

Her father said, **"A girl went down the river – a woman came back!"** The crowd erupted! People moved towards her, bringing gifts in honour and celebration. Some of the gifts were for when she had her own tipi. For now she had passed through an Initiation gateway and could marry when she was ready.

Poor Shining Sun, standing stock still for all that time with the men. When he first saw Running Water his temperature shot up. He turned bright red. He felt a stirring in his loins! This was the first time anything like this had happened to him! He was sure everyone had noticed!

He could not take his eyes off her. Her eyes were bright and her heart was open – radiant! He wished he could die. But he could not take his eyes off her, not even to miss a single blink. As she thanked people, he caught her eye. He blushed to the roots of his hair and back again. Did she notice?

We move forward in the story.

During the next season, Shining Sun sat under a crop of overhanging rocks close to Running Water's village. He could not forget her! He went to this place seeking stillness and for comfort. He was moving away from all that had been familiar and safe to him.

Another day, Running Water walked in the woods. She found a crop of overhanging rocks. There was a special feel about the place. She sat for hours and yearned to give the love of her open heart.

For the rest of that Summer both Shining Sun and Running Water went to that special place to be alone and dream.

They never once met!

Winter set in. Tipis were covered in snow. People stayed close to their own hearths, resting and preparing for the turning tide of Spring. Shining Sun looked forward to being out in the wilds, dreaming of Running Water.

Running Water yearned expectantly, for the new life of Spring.

Both imagined their special place.

It was their destiny to meet and meet they did! How long did that take? We leave that in the hands of Time and the Great Mystery. Ending the story where we began…

A long time ago, but not **that** long ago, in a far away land at the Northern tip of the world, there lived a boy who was becoming a man and only a whisper away, a girl who was becoming a woman...

Nature waited to celebrate their meeting!

As a young person, you are on your Journey from boy to man, girl to woman. In most modern cultures the old ones no longer take boys into the wilderness or girls into the Moon-Lodge. Sometimes they don't tell you about the changes you can expect or about growing up.

You can find out for yourself. Or if you are lucky, a grey-haired one might cross your path!

WHO ARE YOU?

Who Am I? is a question that has been examined through the ages.

Are you your body? Or is your body like the clothes you wear – discarded when it's worn out and it's time to move on? Are you your thoughts? Or are thoughts only what you are thinking? Not who you are? Are you your feelings?

Only you can answer the question Who Am I? for yourself. No one can tell you.

One of the main purposes of this book is to assist you to discover that for yourself. GETTING REAL... about growing up! also supports you to be aware of your personality and social self, living on the Earth. It takes you one step further, aiding you to uncover who you truly are when connected to your Essential Nature.

Your Essential Nature may be hidden, buried, discarded or, at worst, seems to be destroyed. This happens when the people around you and the conditions in which you are brought up, do not support, nurture and encourage who you really are. When your Essential Nature is not recognised or valued in ways that allow you to flower it may be hidden under self-protective layers and masks.

When you are able to connect with what is Essentially you, you can live life fully and freely. When you allow the purity of your Essential Nature its expression, your gifts are given to the World.

"In giving the gift of ourselves back to ourselves, in affirming and trusting who we are, we uncover a universe that can never be contained within the pages of a book."
– TO LOVE IS TO BE HAPPY WITH, Barry Kaufman.

How Have You Become?

What experiences have formulated the sense you have of yourself? Who or what gives value to you? All your social interactions, sensations and responses to your life's experiences affect the idea you have of yourself. All your perceptions of the world are recorded in your brain as well as in the cellular memory banks of your body.

"A child's life is like a piece of paper on which every passer-by leaves a mark."

– Ancient Chinese Proverb.

The influence of your parents and the emotional environment in which you are brought up partly forms who you become. If your parents are mature, stable, well-balanced and wise people, they can give your sense of ME, of who you are, some solid foundations. If that is the case you flourish and express your Essential Nature naturally. You easily achieve, make friends, have fun and may move through the challenges you face during adolescence and life generally, in a relatively easy way.

If you have had a supportive family in which to grow, you have been blessed. GETTING REAL… about growing up! can help you become more self-aware. It encourages you to think about who you are and who you are becoming.

If you've had a healthy environment as you have grown up, you may take it for granted. While reading you may realise that others have not been as fortunate as you. If you have not been taken care of properly, you now can take some responsibility for your own life and choose to recreate your own sense of who you are.

By doing the exercises offered in this book, you can become confident and reconnect with your Essential Nature if you have lost that connection. It is possible! It can be challenging and…

it can be fun and freeing!

If you are willing to go beyond the experiences of your childhood and the belief that you are only a body that has thoughts and feelings, you can begin to see yourself as part of a much bigger picture.

Is it possible:

That you are a spiritual being who made a contract when you came here?

That you have certain lessons to learn and a job to do?

That on a Soul level, there are reasons for you to be here?

That you chose to be in your family to work out unfinished business, to pay back old debts or learn valuable lessons?

To take more responsibility, you can acknowledge, that for reasons you may not be aware of, you chose your present circumstances to learn from. That's a great place to start. If you don't do this, you may feel like a victim of the circumstances of your life. This may not allow any desirable changes to take place for you. If this sounds a bit weird, hold on! There is more about this later in the book. It may become clear and open up new possibilities for you and the times you are living in.

Are You an Indigo Child?

Many Indigo Children are gifted souls.

"We know that Indigo Children are born wearing their God-given gifts on their sleeves. Many of them are natural born philosophers who think about the meaning of life and how to save the planet. They are gifted scientists, inventors and artists. Yet our society, built upon the old energy, is smothering the gifts of the Indigo Children."
– Doreen Virtue quoted in THE INDIGO CHILDREN, Lee Carroll and Jan Tober.

If you are an Indigo Child, you value yourself because you know who you are and you believe in yourself. You may get bored easily and are frustrated by situations that are repetitive and are not creative. You have lots of energy and can be very sensitive. You like to do things in new and better ways. You may seem antisocial, unless you are with other Indigo Children. You are fearless and do not respond to guilt-inducing discipline techniques in school or at home.

Your nervous system is wired for the high-tech possibilities of the next few decades – processing and acting upon huge amounts of information in very short spaces of time. You can be described as creative, independent, brilliant and self-governing. Unfortunately, it also means you do not fit in with today's education systems, which may seem as unfulfilling as a discarded old piece of rag. You thrive with understanding, support, creativity and patience.

Many Indigo Children are being falsely labelled with Attention Deficit Hyperactive Disorder (ADHD) or Attention Deficit Disorder (ADD).

For some children who have a chemical imbalance it may help stabilise their behaviour to take prescribed drugs allowing them to participate in their world.

It is shameful that some children are mis-diagnosed as hyperactive, dyslexic or suffering from neurological disorders and given drugs to make them controllable.

If you think you are an Indigo Child you could check out this Website and ask your parents to:
www.indigochildren.com

WHO AM I?

Karensa (14)

Tears are falling,
There's sorrow in the heart.
Not for what's past, but for what's coming.
Not for the old, but for the new.

Arise the pain,
Shoot forth the anger,
Flung far with no return.

Forever gone; none within.
The flame of courage rekindled;
The fire of hope burns bright.
Released are the tears,
A smile is born.

Strangers approach, friendly faces,
giving strength,
The open arms and loving hearts.

Caring and sharing, forgiving are we;
You and I, hand in hand.
Together we are learning.
United we believe.
As one we live, as one we love.

No longer lost, no longer alone.
I am whole I am complete.
I am beautiful, I am ME.

Self-Esteem and why it is important

Self-esteem is one way you can measure how you feel about yourself. It is important that you learn to nurture positive thoughts about yourself to maintain it. If you have not been nurtured or have been given lots of negative messages, the chances are your self-esteem is low.

If you have low self-esteem you may:

- not like yourself,
- be unaware that you do not value who you are,
- believe you can't achieve good results at school or elsewhere,
- live in a world that does not work for you,
- harm yourself by abusing drugs and alcohol,
- become self-destructive in other ways.

Low self-esteem often makes people do things for the wrong reasons.

If you have low self-esteem you may think you have to prove you are worthwhile. Inside you don't believe it. If you know you're okay there's nothing to prove. If you trust yourself you do things for honest reasons. It's not really honest to do good deeds that are a cover up for feeling bad about yourself.

Possibly 85% of people in our society have low self-esteem. **Think about that!** Even millionaires, sports idols, top executives, pop stars, teachers and parents. It may look like they have everything going for them, but inside they may not like themselves, are depressed or suicidal.

How many people do you know who really love and regard themselves highly?

"Self-esteem is one of the most important things in life. Being comfortable with yourself, talking to other people and getting on in life – you need it for absolutely everything. My self-esteem is not as high as I want it to be. I could be more confident. When I am, my self-esteem rises. I want to live a successful life, so I'm working on it." – Alan (16).

"This girl has to be perfect. Every hair in place and she puts people down who are not perfect. She can ruin the self-esteem of others. Takes it out on them. That's not very fair. When people are bitchy to other people it usually means that they are insecure about themselves." – Chelsea (14).

"If you say bad things about other people you are trying to raise your self-esteem, but you are just lowering it. If you say good things about other people, you feel better about yourself." – Angie (14).

The beliefs you hold about yourself are powerful. With attention and effort you can change those that don't work for you.

Developing a Positive Sense of Self

Your self-concept is made up of all the beliefs and attitudes you have about yourself. These determine who you think you are and what you become. Do you have a positive self-concept?

THINGS TO DO!

Write down the statements that describe you in your notebook:

I am happy. I am sick. I am good. I am beautiful.
I'm a loser. I'm a winner. I am dumb. I am fine.
I'm OK. I am bad. I am clumsy. I am a gossip.
I'm anxious. I'm boring. I'm a mess. I'm cool.
I am successful. I'm a failure. I'm lovable. I'm sexy.
I am sad. I'm smart. I'm a good student. I'm ugly.
I'm a good person. I'm a slow learner. I'm not OK.

How do you score? Half are uplifting, the others are not.

What have you made of yourself?

Adapted from 100 WAYS TO ENHANCE SELF-CONCEPT IN THE CLASSROOM – Jack Canfield and Harold Wells.

Most people like and are attracted to people who have high self-esteem. They express inner qualities we admire. By discovering your Essential Nature you become self-confident. What are the thoughts that stop you being your true self? Some examples: I'm dumb – Nobody likes me – My hair is always a mess – I'm no good at soccer.

THINGS TO DO!

Next Step:

Use a double page in your notebook.

- Write a list of all the things you don't like about yourself on the left-hand page.
- On the right, list all the things you like and love about yourself.

Are they equal? If not, what does this say about how you think and feel about yourself?

- Examine the negatives carefully. Cross out any that are obviously not true about you.

To take this exercise further –

- Look at the negative statements you didn't cross out. Are any of them repeated? Do any still have a lot of charge (a strong emotional reaction)? Write them down again on the left-hand page now.
- On the opposite page, change all these statements into ones that make you feel better about yourself.

Like this –

Nobody likes me – I am lovable just as I am.
I'm useless – I am good at everything I do.
I don't like my legs – My body is just perfect the way it is.

- For statements that had the most **charge**, write a sentence or two that includes an affirmation – that is, a positive statement about yourself.
- Make sure that everything you have now written is positive.

For example – I love myself. My body is vibrant, healthy and beautiful.

- Read your new list out loud. You could look in the mirror while doing that. How does that make you feel?
- You can draw a picture that reflects that feeling, write your affirmation on it and put it on your bedroom wall. Everything helps. See page 88 for more on Affirmations.

What pictures have others painted of you? Turn to the next double page:

- Think about what your parents, teachers and friends say about you.
- Write down all the not very nice and negative things on the left-hand page.
- On the right-hand page write all the positive things. Examine them and consider what these verbal messages are doing for your self- esteem.

You can do this exercise again after you have read the rest of the book and see how your self-concept changes.

Projecting Negative Feelings

Sometimes people may say things to you that are more about them, than about you. For example - "Are you all right? You don't look too good…" when the person speaking does not feel well. "When she threatened us, you were afraid weren't you?" When it was him who didn't own up to his own fear.

OR, "He's always so angry, it really pisses me off!" When in fact the person speaking is angry. Not seeing her own anger, she blames or labels the other as the angry one.

When people are projecting their feelings onto others, they are seeing aspects of their personality they do not recognise. They may have a blind spot. It is their disowned shadow reflected back at them. They may not be seeing the YOU that you are. This is called projection.

THINGS TO DO!

Another Step:

- Go back to your list of negative statements and ask yourself: Is this really true about me? Am I believing the messages I'm getting from other people, or is it true about the person who says it to me? Cross out all the statements on the left-hand page if you don't believe they are true of you now.
- Ask yourself about the ones that are left:

  Is this how I appear?
  Is this how I choose to be?
  Am I creating supportive relationships by behaving or being this way?
  Is this working for me or is it alienating people?

An example: You are a person that shouts a lot. People shy away from your overbearing approach. As the shouter you may decide to talk more softly so that people enjoy being with you.

- Examine yourself: You can change your behaviour at any time. To do this you can change any of the statements you have written down about yourself. Make them into statements you would like people to be making about you.

When your perception of yourself changes, other people see you differently.

Projecting Thoughts

Sometimes we think we know what other people are thinking OR we imagine all kinds of things they may be thinking about us. The only way to truly know what others are thinking is to ask them. Make sure you are not projecting your thoughts onto them. When you ask what is going on for them, check in with your body to see if what they say feels right to you. Don't presume you know what others are thinking. It causes a lot of conflict. You are not a mind reader and neither are they.

People as Mirrors

Some of us may believe that we are victims of whatever is going on around us. There's an alternative way of looking at things. Sometimes people come into our lives and like mirrors reflect parts of ourselves that we don't easily see – good things we don't accept or things we are denying. What we have difficulty with on the outside can be a reflection of what is happening inside of us.

If what people do **really** irritates you – take a close look.

Are the people around you angry or selfish?
Are they aggravating you?
Is there something about them you don't like?
If people abuse you, take a look and see where you abuse yourself.
If you have no friends, ask yourself what this is showing you about yourself?
Are you unsure of yourself and afraid no one likes you?
Is it that you don't like yourself?
Maybe you're not a friend to yourself.
Are you making enough effort to meet people?

These things and others could be telling you that you are not fully aware of all aspects of yourself. Explore them and become aware of what you are doing. If not, you can do something to change that.

If things go well for you and you have good friends and people love you, the chances are that you have a very positive sense of yourself.

When what's going on **inside** of you changes, things on the outside can.

Owning Your Shadow

It is important not to deny aspects of your personality that you do not like – the miserable, bitchy, bragging part of you or whatever your shadow qualities may be. You are multi-faceted. The shadow sides of your nature add richness and depth to your character. The question is: What do you do with them? If they dominate your personality you may not care about yourself. It's okay that they are there – you are human. You may not feel good all of the time.

It's not healthy though if your thoughts about yourself are unloving more often than not. Thinking negatively about yourself can make you ill or depressed. See if this is the case for you and find a balance.

If you get to eat only sugar every day you soon tire of it. The shadow side of your nature is the salt that balances that out. What aspects of you live in the shadows? What parts of you hide? Can you bring them out into the open, love and accept them?

"Sooner or later, we are bound to discover some things about ourselves that we don't like. But once we see they're there, we can decide what we want to do with them. Do we want to get rid of them completely, change them into other things, or use them in beneficial ways?"

– THE TAO OF POOH, Benjamin Hoff.

Wearing Protective Shells

You may be wearing a shell that is protecting you from the outside world. You may have been badly hurt as a child, lost someone dear to you or been abandoned in some way by either friends or family. This may not allow you to create the quality of friendships you deserve. If this is not true for you, it may be true for one or more of your friends. Don't be deceived by this outer shell – look deeper.

If you are protecting yourself:

- Breathe into your heart. Imagine it opening like a flower. As you breathe, allow feelings to arise. Let any tears flow.
- Soften your armour by feeling into your body. Notice if you are numb or tense. Notice where? Focus on this and breathe into that part of your body. Give it permission to relax and release.
- Find some form of exercise which helps you open up – Aikido, Tai Chi and Yoga, dancing or anything that appeals to you.
- See if it is possible to visit a massage therapist or body worker. If your parents are not open to this, do it as soon as you can when you become independent. If you have a close friend you feel safe with, you could exchange massages. There are suggestions in the book on how to do this.

If you know people who are protecting themselves, it is possible to see through the shells they hide behind. You can become aware and sensitive to what is going on for them.

Check out what their behaviour is telling you. Check in with your body. Imagine yourself looking and feeling with your inner eye, like a laser beam. Sense if they are holding tension. Ask if you can give them a hug or touch them gently on the arm. Touch can be re-assuring. Offer them a massage. Ask questions. Listen to what they say, show concern and most importantly, love them.

Be kind and loving toward the tough ones. Often the people with the hardest, toughest exterior have the softest marshmallow centre.

Be careful: If you are over-sensitive, you may feel and pick up other people's pain. This could cause you distress if you do not know how to deal with it. If you are like this, it is useful to develop skills and strategies to protect yourself. If you are going through a vulnerable time or not coping very well, you can stay aware of what's going on around you. It may be useful to avoid difficult situations as a way of looking after yourself.

Developing Strength of Character

Character development occurs when you are being rubbed up against or tested by life. It happens when things don't go smoothly or stretch you beyond your comfort zones.

Character development does not happen when you:

- are not challenged to keep your word,
- are not being honest with yourself and others,
- always get your own way.

Or if you:

- don't have to contribute to household chores when you don't feel like it,
- take what is not yours,
- are disrespectful and abusive to others,
- sulk and are moody when you don't win or get what you expected,
- make agreements and break them.

You may end up being a person who has a weak character if more than three or four of these points are true about you. You may become someone who does not activate your will, has no resolve, may not be trustworthy or honourable. However, you can strengthen the sense of yourself and change behaviour that is not expressing who you truly are.

An example: Your friends plan to break the law. You know they are taking a risk and you would rather not or are afraid of going along with them. Say NO! Use all the strength you have, give them your reasons and leave as quickly as you can. Don't allow them to persuade you to stay.

THINGS TO DO!

- When you are with your friends, watch yourself. Have one eye on your behaviour. Ask yourself: Is this the real me acting or am I being influenced by others? Check out whether you are motivated by insecurity, trying to please or by fear. You know what is not true when you feel uncomfortable inside. As you become more aware, this becomes easier to recognise.
- Write in your Journal the successes you have when you disconnect from the pressures you experience from friends.
- Give yourself pats on the back. When you intend to be strong in yourself, your efforts pay off.
- Take yourself away from people for some time each day. Sit in a quiet place where no one can disturb you. Relax, be still, ask for guidance about anything that is on your mind – listen. It may take a little while for your inner ear to open, but if you are willing and persevere, you can hear.
- Draw a picture of your powerful self. Write on the back, or in your Journal, all the characteristics that you intend to strengthen or develop. Put it on your bedroom wall as a reminder.

Suggestions to help you strengthen your character.

Be True to Your Word

Do your best to honour your word and be respectful to others with what you say.

- If you make an agreement to do something – Do it! If you find it's impossible, or you change your mind, communicate that to the person. Make another arrangement.
- When you are true to your word and follow through, you develop a sense that you are trustworthy.
- Others can trust you because you are an honest, honourable and dependable person.

Become aware of the power of your words!

Use Your Speech as a Gift to Others

Some people put others down rather than say uplifting things. As you become sensitive to the damage this causes, you may stop yourself and others doing this. Put-downs are hurtful! Can you use your speech to improve the quality of life for yourself and those around you?

You can:

- speak of your gratitude to your friends and parents,
- encourage someone who is shy or fed-up,
- give thanks for your health, youth and vitality, your very life,
- share new and uplifting ideas with your friends.

There are a lot of confused people in the world. Sometimes, it only takes one person to get clear and confident for a whole group to change.

You could be that person!

NO – A Big, Small Word

It's useful to start practising saying NO! now. When your friends ask you to do something, say NO just to see how they react. Check out how it feels for you. Say NO sometimes to things that you like to be involved in, just to test your strength. Say **NO** before saying YES to things that may get you into trouble with the law or before you do something that hurts yourself or someone else.

- Write down how you feel when you say NO in your Journal so that you can check your progress.
- Applaud your successes when you say NO to something you choose not to be involved in, which before reading this book, you may have gone along with. You can speak your truth knowing that you have every right to be you.

As you gain more confidence in yourself, say NO and explain why you are refusing to be involved in any harmful activity.

It is Your Choice!

You have the power of choice in your life. It can be a life changing power. In everything you do you either honour, love and respect who you are – or you don't.

One way leads to inner peace and harmony, which does not solely depend on people outside of yourself. The other creates a disconnection from your Essential Nature. Do you love yourself enough not to hurt yourself, others or the Earth? Do you choose to be with your friends when they behave badly or when they set about destroying what they have?

Are you brave enough to act now? Can you face the challenges of being who you are? Are you willing to love yourself enough and then give and share the best of yourself?

Complete Things and Order Your Environment

It helps to keep the mind clear when you finish things that you've started – in your relationships, with jobs around the house or with your schoolwork. The more you finish off, the more spacious inside and free you become.

"All humans are spirits only visiting this world. All spirits are forever beings. All encounters with other people are experiences and all experiences are forever connections. Real People close the circle of each experience. We do not leave ends frayed as Mutants do. If you walk away with bad feelings in your heart for another person and that circle is not closed, it will be repeated later in your life. You will not suffer once but over and over until you learn. It is good to observe and learn and become wiser from what has happened. It is good to give thanks, as you say, to bless it, and walk away in peace."

– MUTANT MESSAGES DOWNUNDER, Marlo Morgan.

Decisiveness

Being unsure and undecided can waste a great deal of energy. It can create confusion and inaction. It is a hard place to be. Even with what seems like the biggest decisions it is best to take some action.

THINGS TO DO!

Do this process for clarity:

- Get a large piece of paper and divide it into four squares.
- In each square write one of the following statements:

  Who am I and where am I going?

  What obstacles am I facing?

  What inner qualities can I develop to overcome these obstacles?

  What actions can I take to move forward in my life right now?
- In each box write in words and/or draw a picture symbolising each of these aspects.
- In your notebook write in more detail about these questions and about the way you plan your life to be.

This may help you move forward and maintain focus.

Adapted from 100 WAYS TO ENHANCE SELF-CONCEPT IN THE CLASSROOM, Jack Canfield and Harold Wells.

Spending time alone in Nature and playing trust games can also strengthen your character.

Accountability Versus Apology

The word SORRY is often misused. You may see children hanging their heads in shame when parents are telling them off for doing something that has upset them. They are told to say, sorry. You may remember this happening to you. You may not have done anything wrong in your own eyes. This sorry word can be confusing.

Words can be cheap. Saying sorry may at times be too easy! You can say sorry and not mean it. You can tell white lies to get off easy. There is another way that is empowering and is in fact more meaningful.

A suggestion:

If you hurt others or damage their property and you regret it, be willing to own up to it with them. Rather than simply be apologetic, make it up to them. For example – you have a date with your girlfriend and you are an hour late. She has waited for you, worrying about your safety, wondering where you are. In fact she's wasted an hour of her time. Instead of saying SORRY, do something to make up that hour. It could be to clean her bedroom or give her a massage.

If you damage someone's property, be willing to replace it or get it fixed. You are becoming more responsible and thoughtful when you do this.

Actions speak louder than words!

'I' Statements

Making 'I' statements improves communication and empowers you. Making 'I' statements helps develop a strong sense of identity. Saying 'I' brings your feelings and experiences back to where they belong.

Most people talk like this:

"You know what it's like when your parents go and leave you alone, you feel angry."

An empowering way to say this is:

"When my parents go out and leave me alone I feel really angry. Is it like that for you?"

Another example:

"Sometimes when you get hurt inside you feel like running away and hiding, especially when you think your friends are laughing at you."

How about this way:

"Sometimes when I think my friends are laughing at me, it hurts and I feel like running away."

Or: "When you think everything is going OK you get a setback."

You could say:

"When I think everything is going OK, I get a setback. I can have a look at what beliefs I have that are creating this."

Can you see how much clearer this is? It brings the experience back to you rather than all the other 'you's' out there. Practice making 'I' statements with a friend. First say 'you's', then change them into 'I's'. Make them as ridiculous as you like. Experience the difference as you practise this. If you are doing this exercise alone write down your examples and then speak them out loud.

Sacrifice Boredom

Boredom comes about through inactivity, lack of motivation or relying on something outside of yourself to stimulate you. If you experience boredom, it could be because you've been constantly entertained or are not at peace with yourself.

Some people waste their time, both in school and in their lives, feeling bored:

They complain there is nothing to do and blame others for their lack of interest or activity.

They have no curiosity about life.

They miss opportunities for growth and learning.

They acquire no self-discipline.

"In order to live freely and happily, you must sacrifice boredom. It is not always an easy sacrifice."
– ILLUSIONS, Richard Bach.

You can sacrifice boredom by:

- paying attention and applying yourself in your present activity,
- being interested and by staying alert,
- making different choices,
- deciding to embrace your life as an adventurer, a warrior.

The quality of your experience is your responsibility.

If you take charge of your life you may be amazed at the difference it makes to the way you feel about yourself.

"If you can't get enthusiastic about what you are doing, it's time to get alarmed – something is wrong. Compete with yourself, set your teeth and dive into the job of breaking your own record of achievements. Enthusiasm is not kept up automatically. It must be nourished with new actions, new aspirations, new efforts and new vision. It is your own fault if your enthusiasm has gone – you have failed to feed it. If you want to turn hours into minutes, renew your enthusiasm." – Ian Bassett, Area Commissioner, SCOUTS.

Observe Yourself

Make a commitment to spend half an hour every day being keenly aware of your speech, actions and behaviour. Well, at least ten minutes! Extend this time, as it becomes easier for you.

This strengthens your ability to witness what goes on around you rather than getting lost in the scene. If you can distance yourself from outside events, it may help you to become objective about your experiences of life.

"As a spectator you can see clearly, the participants are often lost in the maze."

– THE BOOK OF CHANGES AND THE UNCHANGING TRUTH, Taoist Master Ni, Hua Ching.

Make Feelings Fashionable

Without intelligent feeling responses you are living a half-life, which can be grey and empty. During adolescence do your best to stay in touch with your feelings. If you have disconnected from them or have gone numb because of childhood experiences, or for any other reason, it's important to re-connect as soon as you can and feel again. This helps to create a sense of identity that is whole. You then can express yourself differently, with depth and variety. When you are conscious of your feelings, you are able to communicate intimately with others.

Feelings are not emphasised in our culture. Much of our daily lives cuts us off from them. People around us may not value feelings, so over time we stop paying attention to them. Violence in movies, distressing media coverage on television and noisy, disturbing environments deaden feelings.

Feelings are a key to making you a whole and healthy individual. Feeling your feelings offers you a rich and full life.

Are you willing to make feeling choices in order to stay sensitive in this World?

LET OUT YOUR FEELINGS

Sky (14)

Don't mope around, don't be so blue,
I just know what you're going through.
Open your eyes and look around,
At the trees, flowers in the ground.
You'll see this is the world we live in,
That you can change.
Enjoy all the love you can,
Although this world is strange.

So let out your feelings,
And open up your hearts;
You will end up where you started,
Right back at the start.
Don't mope around, don't be so blue,
I know just what you're going through.

And this is the world we live in,
But I think you can change.
We enjoy what we're giving,
And I know that may sound strange.

When you give, you start to live,
When you give, you start to live.

So let's give and start to live.
So let's give in a powerful way.
Let's give, let's give,
And start to live.

Identifying Feelings

In some educational institutions the emphasis is on the intellect, measurable knowledge and a good memory. Constant exposure to information, facts and figures without reference to feelings and emotions creates imbalance. When you are not in touch with your feelings, you become disconnected from sensory and emotional experiences.

You think about things rather than feel your responses.

Your thoughts can easily deceive you. It's sometimes easier to allow them to take over your life's experience. It can be less painful and also less joyful. You are often taught to override your feelings and allow your logical thoughts to dominate. This does not always serve you. If you allow your thoughts to take over you can become confused because they may be telling you something that is the opposite of how you feel.

You can practice identifying your feelings by becoming aware of them. They arise from experiences or thoughts you have and are felt in your body. Some feelings are: anger, hurt, pain, despair, joy, confusion, happiness, sorrow, dejection, loneliness, awe, wonder, disillusionment, excitement, bliss. Feelings are expressed through the body and usually can be identified and named. When you learn to identify what is going on for you at a feeling level, communication with others becomes easier.

"By going along with feelings, you unify your emotional, mental and bodily states. When you try to fight or deny them, you divorce yourself from the REALITY of your being."

– THE NATURE OF PERSONAL REALITY, Jane Roberts.

THINGS TO DO!

Think of and write down an issue you are facing. For example – you are being bullied or teased at school. Your thoughts may tell you: Don't say or do anything about it because it only makes things worse.

The feeling responses you are having are obviously different to these thoughts. You may have a variety of different feelings going on inside – hurt, anger, pain, isolation, feeling over-powered and perhaps also sadness. Either write in your notebook or talk with a friend:

- Make a verbal statement about what is happening by repeating the following –

  This is how it IS for me..... Complete this sentence. For example:

  I am being bullied by people at school. They attack me in the playground when my friends are not around. I am scared and don't fight back. I really hate it when that happens because I don't know what to do about it.
- **This is how I FEEL about it.....** Now get clear about how you are feeling. For example:

  I am feeling hurt and angry. I also feel really pissed off that I am being picked on like this.
- **This is WHY I'm feeling like this.....** Now become clear about the why of your feelings.

  Go on to explore:

  Because – when you bully/tease me I feel powerless. I can't fight back. I feel small and picked on by you and that hurts.
- **This is what I ASK.....** The next and perhaps the most powerful part of the process is to say or write something like: I ask you to leave me alone. Please stop bullying/teasing me. I have a right to enjoy my time at school.
- **Allow yourself to receive what you asked for.** You can have it! Imagine getting it. Do this through visualisation if you are doing this process alone. If you are speaking directly to the persons concerned, allow them the space to give you what you ask for.

In a situation where people are bullying or teasing you, they may not listen. Can you imagine yourself being strong enough to stand up for yourself? This may change what is going on in the playground. You have begun to take back your power in the situation.

BE BRAVE! If you are facing an issue with people you trust, do this process directly with them. Discover the power of clear, direct communication. If not, practice in the mirror or with another friend. It can help!

If you are able to practise communicating like this, you may be amazed at how quickly your relationship with yourself and others changes.

You can trust your body's knowing and feelings. Learn to listen to what it is saying to you.

Self-Love

Any aspects of our lives that are not working or are not in harmony can be healed through loving ourselves.

In what ways do you express love for yourself?
Do you congratulate yourself when you do something well?
Do you take care of yourself?
Do you listen to your favourite music, take your dog for a walk, ring up a friend, or give yourself a massage?

- Write a list of ways that you do love yourself. Add things you can do to give more love to yourself.
- Write down all the things you really enjoy doing. Check in when did you last do them? Do some of the things on your list now and whenever you feel like it. Do loving things for yourself as often as possible.
- Look straight into your eyes in a mirror and say, I love you. Feel your reaction to this. Notice if it makes you feel uncomfortable. If it does, accept that for now. Practise this and feel increasing love for yourself.
- Spend time saying, while sitting quietly, I love myself, every day. Feel this move through your body and experience any sensations inside you – warmth, tingling, moving and a filling up.

In spite of anything that anyone has ever said to you and the ways that you may not have been loved and not nurtured or if you have been treated badly

– you are lovable and OK just the way you are.

THIS IS USEFUL:

If you don't like yourself

…or don't see what's good about yourself...

listen to the good things other people say about you and believe them!

It may shock you to realise that other people have wonderful things to say about you! Take notice. By checking into your own feelings to see if what they are saying is genuine, you can change the false self-image you have developed from your childhood and other experiences.

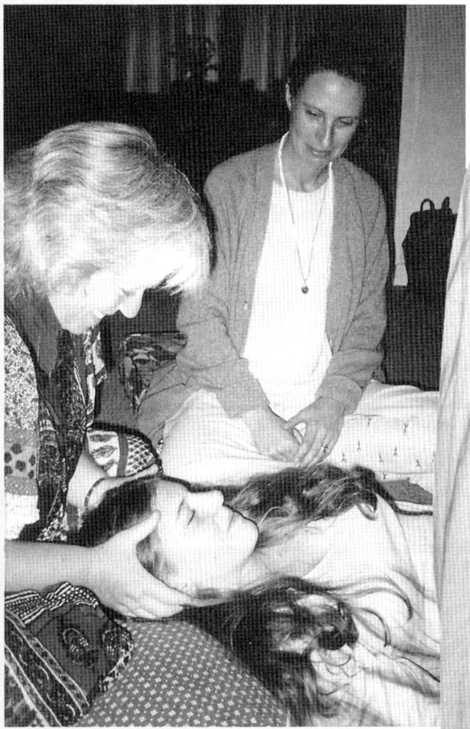

Awakening the Heart

The Heart, as I speak about it here, is not the organ pumping blood through your body. It is situated in the middle of your chest to the right of your heart organ. It is sometimes called the Heart Centre or the Heart Chakra. Just as blood is pumped through your veins to keep you alive, so the flow of love from your Heart Centre increases your energy and power. If you are experiencing love, your Heart Centre sends out a vibration that is peaceful, loving, calming and delicious.

A Heart Meditation

- Close your eyes.
- Focus on your Heart Centre in the middle of your chest and feel any sensations that arise there.
- Keep some of your attention on your breathing.
- Imagine that you are filling up your Heart Centre with love. You can do that by imagining a colour moving into your Heart OR just by feeling it being filled up with loving energy.
- Expand that feeling of love to the whole of your body. Feel your love getting bigger.
- Now expand that feeling to your family and then to anyone else you love.
- Think of people you have differences with or who have hurt you or damaged the world. Send love to them.
- Keep expanding that sense of love you feel to the town you live in, the country and the rest of the planet – it can touch everyone with love wherever they are.
- Stay connected to the feelings you have in your Heart Centre as you gradually open your eyes and move back into the activities of your day.

You become less selfish when you live with an Awakened Heart. You feel more love for yourself, those around you and for the World. You glow!

As more of us open our Heart Centres, we are naturally good to one another.

"And now, here is my secret, a very simple secret:
It is only with the heart that one can see rightly;
what is essential is invisible to the eyes."

– THE LITTLE PRINCE Antoine de Saint-Exupéry.

Be adventurous – see how easy it is to create love in your life...

A Heart Talk

Heart Talks give you a chance to work things out for yourself as well as in your relationships with others. They open up a loving space for connection and true intimacy. Communicating from your heart brings more honesty, understanding and feeling into your life. Through Heart Talks you can begin to sense your oneness with everyone and all of life.

How to have a Heart Talk

Find a quiet place for your Heart Talk. Close the door and take the phone off the hook or be in Nature.

Make sure everyone knows what a Heart Talk is.

- Heart Talks can happen between two or more people who are ready to share from their hearts. Sit facing your partner, or if in a group, in a close circle.
- Use a symbol of a heart. This can be cardboard or material (filled with beans or sand) in a heart shape or a rock or stick. The person holding it is the only one allowed to speak. That person receives the love and attention of the group.
- Other group members give him /her their undivided attention and are silent.

Make agreements:

- When holding the heart express only your true feelings.
- Don't analyse, criticise, rationalise, justify or speak about other people.
- Do not say anything about anyone else's sharing when it's your turn.
- Stay focussed on what is true for you and what you are saying.

Respect confidentiality, offer support, compassion and caring for the one sharing.

Before you begin:

- Hold hands and let go of thoughts about the outside world. Create a loving and safe space.
- Take the heart when ready. Share how you are feeling right now and then move on to other issues that come up. It's not always necessary to describe everything that has happened. Just relate enough information so that the people listening know what's going on for you.
- Maintain eye contact with your partner or members of the group. This creates a non-verbal link between you. When you have said all you wish to say, pass the heart on to the next person.
- If you are not ready to share, pass it on. The heart can go around several times until everyone feels finished.

Sometimes you may choose to focus on a subject that is of concern to you all – it could be family matters, sexuality, relationships or anything else.

The Heart Talk can end with hugs all round.

Adapted from THE LOVE CLUB MANUAL,
Baraka Educational Foundation.

If you do not feel love for yourself yet –
GETTING REAL... about growing up!
offers you clues.
There are other exercises later.

by sharing your feelings

A Journal Friend

Writing in a Journal is something that everyone can do. Using your Journal can reduce stress and tension about what is going on for you. It gives you time to make sense of it. It brings clarity, understanding and inspiration. It offers you time alone with your private thoughts, emotions and feelings. Journal writing allows you to become a witness of your experience – to stand back and not get caught up. It can help you to develop trust in yourself.

Write your emotions and feelings down.

Some feelings are: joy, happiness, excitement, love, fulfilment, peace … and on and on they go.

Some emotions are: anger, hatred, confusion, sadness, loneliness, grief, hurt, abandonment, frustration, let down. When you cut yourself off from feelings and emotions you experience disconnection, numbness, nothingness, apathy, boredom.

It is useful if you can **feel** and **sense** them as you write. Seeing them on paper can help you become more objective. It's best not to let them build up and overwhelm you. Expressing your emotions and feelings either through writing, talking or by some action you do, frees you up.

To get clear: Express your thoughts in writing, especially if it's difficult to talk with family members or your friends. You can write about any situation that concerns you. Getting thoughts out of your head and onto paper can bring clarity. It can also release communication blocks that seem impossible to move beyond.

For understanding: If you are facing complex issues or situations, write down all the details. Rather than just leaving them as thoughts swimming around inside your head, look at them from the outside.

If you are facing a difficult decision, write down the facts/issues/thoughts for and against it.

Receiving guidance and understanding: Writing thoughts down, then listening for guidance and inspiration opens up the channels for input from your Essential Nature or God. This might appear in your writing as if there is another voice in your head. This Voice may have been waiting to talk to you. It can offer support, insight and great wisdom. This may seem strange at first. You may be amazed by the messages you receive as your inner listening gets fine tuned.

You can draw pictures in your Journal. Use coloured pens and pencils. You can glue in mementos, photos of your friends or anything else. To go really big you could get yourself a scrapbook and make collages and pictures, write poetry and stories.

Your Journal can become an intimate friend. Keep it in a safe place to protect your privacy.

THE PATH OF LOVE

Peter (16)

Walking down the path of love,
Please forgive me if I stray.
For I am learning, I am learning
From the way, the way my heart shakes;
Learning from my mistakes.

Oh yeh! On we go... So, oh yeh, on we go.
While you're dancing in the clouds,
And I'm sitting on the ground, I want to fly!
You take me higher with your crystal love.
While you're dancing across the sky,
And I'm sitting in my tears,
I want to fly! You take me higher with your love.

Crystal love, that's what they call it,
The pathways of love,
That's what they say.
We're on a pathway of love into ourselves,
And we'll all get there one day.
On the pathway of love,
We're on the pathway of LOVE,
The pathway of LOVE.

YOUR BODY

Adolescence is full of changes: physically, emotionally, mentally, socially and spiritually.

Physical changes are the most obvious as your body grows quickly from a child into an adult. Your body becomes unfamiliar. You may have a feeling of being out of control. That's because the changes that are happening are in the control of your hormones, your DNA intelligence and Nature.

So much is going on, it can be bewildering. Your developing body, growth spurts and hormonal changes, bring on mood swings and out-of-control behaviour. Life may seem a little chaotic at times. Your bodily changes can happen slowly or quickly. This can be embarrassing or exciting. Each one of you is unique – you are growing perfectly for you.

What happens to you between ten and twenty years of age changes you greatly. Enjoy your changes – dance, move, love and embrace your body, as it transforms itself.

Adolescence is the stage in between the child and adult.

You are metamorphosising.

"The body is made up of many parts and all parts are interdependent and inter reliant. The eyes cannot say to the feet, "I don't need you," any more than the body can say to the head, "I don't need you." The loss of one part will always cause the body to be less functional."
– THE BIBLE, Paul's Letter to the Ephesians.

Walking Miracles

These facts may impress you about the miracle of your body:

- You have over six hundred muscles, which make up half of your body weight. Involuntary muscles work without you reminding them. They suck air through your lungs, pump blood through your heart and push food through your digestive system, which is eight metres long.
- You have two hundred bones, with ligaments that hold them together. These protect your organs and your brain.
- Your heart beats over seventy times a minute, circulates blood throughout your body 1,000 times a day, through 96,000 kilometres of blood vessels. An adult has about 35,000,000,000,000 (35 trillion) red blood cells. Each second, two million of your blood cells die, to be replaced by two million more.
- Your skin has two million sweat glands. There are sense receptors in your skin, sending messages to your brain, which maintains body temperature, keeps you dry and lets you know when you've hurt yourself. Your skin constantly renews itself.
- Your lungs filter oxygen through six hundred million pockets of folded flesh.
- Your eyes have a hundred million receptors so that you can see in colour.
- Your ears have 24,000 fibres that vibrate so that you can hear.
- Your brain contains between ten and one hundred billion (A billion is a thousand million) neurons. It is like a computer that files away and records every perception and action you have experienced since birth.
- You have enough atomic energy in your body to destroy any of the world's great cities… and rebuild it.

Adapted from LOOKING AT THE BODY, David Suzuki and THE GREATEST MIRACLE IN THE WORLD, Og Mandino.

We are all incredible creations of a Wisdom that we are totally connected to. Let's remember to be thankful for our bodies and not take them for granted.

Your Body is a Sacred Site

A sacred site is a special place. A sacred place is where people usually go to pray, like a Church, Mosque, a Synagogue or in Nature. Your body can be your own place of worship. It is special. It is the temple of your Spirit. You could not be flesh and blood or living on this planet without your body. If you are an expression of God or a Great Intelligence, then your body is a sacred place. When you sit quietly and are still, you may feel Spirit, the Life Force, moving within you. You can take care of your body as a sacred site by doing some of the things suggested later on page 72.

Am I Normal?

This question is one that most teenagers worry about. Just about all the changes you are experiencing, everyone else around your age does too. IT'S ALL NATURAL!

It can be scary. Don't worry. It can also be FUN! Mood swings, confrontations with parents, thinking that you're not attractive enough, being sexually attracted to others, having crushes on people. It's all normal. Relax!

Each person develops differently and it happens in its own time. The thing is that most teenagers try to be cool about it, so when you look around everyone else seems fine. This can make you feel abnormal. A lot of people wear masks. Look closely and see if you can find out who are.

It is not useful to compare yourself to others. If you do, it can cause unnecessary insecurity and pain.

A lot of sleep is good at this age because your body is growing. There's a lot of hormonal stimulation and your system gets tired and exhausted. At times the changes you are going through are stressful, not only physically, but also emotionally and mentally as well. It can be too much. Sleep helps you integrate your new experiences.

If you sleep too much and don't use your excess energy, you may feel restless, heavy, lethargic and tired. It's good to notice when you're just being lazy.

Looking after yourself during adolescence can be an insurance policy for a healthy body as an adult. At this time your body benefits by special care as it is growing itself up. Many people become sick because they don't know how important it is to look after themselves.

How healthy would you like to be when you are old? If you take care now you may be glad that you did!

The Difference is the Same

"Every one is unique! Everyone is the same! I was destined to be different. I was born with Cerebral Palsy. The part of the brain which co-ordinates the body muscles was damaged. I was fortunate to have parents who believed in me. I spent twenty-two years in and out of institutions. As an adolescent male in an institution, girls were very wary of me and probably believed they would catch a disease. They didn't understand I wasn't sick or diseased. I was just like everyone else, different and trying to be the same. I wanted to be likeable. In high school everyone was trying to be the same, yet those who succeeded in any way were being different and knew it. We all have different bodies, different opinions and come in different shapes and sizes.

People used to stare at me (and still do) out of curiosity. I figured out quite early that people only stared at famous people, like rock stars, movie stars or politicians. So I felt at ease when people stared at me. One time I even stared at someone staring at me. It was quite funny. The guy was only trying to understand how different I was, I was trying to see how we were the same.

When I was eighteen I worked in a special workshop for people with Cerebral Palsy. A beautiful young woman wanted to go out on a date with me. She really liked me. I said, "Sure". The boss told her if she did, she'd get fired. Instead of hurting me, this gave me quite a boost. The boss had been trying to date her for six months and she chose to go out with me.

Even as an adolescent I liked the way I looked in a wheelchair and all my jerky movements. I didn't have to be cool! I've always owned my difference. It's part of me. Not everyone is going to like my difference or the way I look.

Being afraid of being different or of people judging you for the way you look is normal. All the differences in the world make you and I uniquely the same. How you feel about your body is a matter of how comfortable you are with yourself. If you know you are beautiful – YOU ARE. You are you! You have no need to be perfect. Perfection is only someone else's judgement. The secret to a happy and full life is to believe in yourself no matter what anyone tells you. These are some words of wisdom from my childhood that have made me feel good about being different."

Jacob, now fifty, was awarded the Australian Achievers award in 2000 for his work in the disability field. He has done things that most people would find difficult to do and lives life enjoying his differences and those of others.

Boys and Girls are Different

Boys and girls grow up and develop very differently. Look at a group of twelve year-olds and this is obvious. Girls generally mature physically and emotionally faster than boys do. Growth spurts can take place two years before boys, so twelve year-old girls are generally taller.

Growth spurts affect not only your height but also the size of your head, hands and feet. The muscles grow in size and strength, especially in boys. Boys usually catch up at about fourteen.

Early adolescence can be a stormy time. The activation of the hormone system can increase excitability and emotionality. Adolescent mood swings are caused by hormonal changes. Males can become more aggressive. Females may react aggressively and may become more depressed. Sexual feelings also increase for both males and females. Don't get too concerned if you feel out of control, when your hormone levels settle down later on, so can you.

Growth during adolescence can last between two to ten years. Teenagers are usually physically mature by the time they are eighteen – if all has gone according to Nature's plan.

It is helpful to understand about the differences between males and females. It allows us to be more compassionate towards each other as well as to get along better. If we truly understood about gender differences, there could be fewer fights and less divorces. See from page 129 on Gender – Female and Male Differences.

You may find it useful to read all of this section, whether you are male or female. There is a great deal of information for all of you. As a young male you can gain understanding by reading about females and their menstrual cycle. You may be more understanding of your mother, female friends and later your lover or life partner if she is female.

As a female you can be gentler with the boys around you. They may seem less mature simply because they develop differently.

What Changes in Males?

Male sex hormones are called Androgens. They stimulate muscle development, pubic, underarm and chest hair, as well as beard growth.

Testosterone increases by **800%** in the adolescent male. Whew! That's incredible! This can cause acne, pimples, strong sexual feelings and general restlessness. This hormone makes for leaner males who have a higher metabolic rate than females. It takes until the mid-twenties for the body to get used to this amount of testosterone, then things begin to settle down.

The male peak growth spurt is on average around fourteen years of age. He may develop breast buds but they disappear after about a year. Between approximately ten and fourteen the testes enlarge. About one year later, his penis begins to grow and about a year after that he may experience his first ejaculation. This is when sperm from his testes and fluid from his prostate gland are powerfully released through his penis. Hair may increase on different parts of his body. Pubic hair appears first, followed by body and facial hair a few years later. Because the larynx gets larger, his voice breaks, making it deeper. This is the last obvious physical sign of puberty.

Adolescent growth spurts in young males can affect the ear canals. They sometimes stretch, become thin and block up. This can lead to periods of hearing loss.

Note to males: You often get into trouble for not listening at home or at school. It's temporary. Make sure you can hear what others are saying, so you don't get hassled.

"Rapid brain growth can also make you disorganised and dopey for many months. Ask your parents to act as a substitute brain for you for awhile."
– RAISING BOYS, Steve Biddulph.

"When I turned seventeen it felt like I'd just been plugged in. My reception crystallised. I hadn't realised how blurry everything had been before. Suddenly, unexpectedly, everything became clear." – Duncan (18)

First Ejaculation

First ejaculation is a personal and private event. You may be feeling unsure or uncomfortable about this, here are some stories from men:

"I was about thirteen years old. I'd been having erections many times during the day for a couple of years. At least I knew THAT part of my body worked okay. It was a sunny summer's morning when I awoke to find my belly covered with dried semen. It was a yahoo moment! My question was answered. It worked! I vaguely remembered the sexual dream I'd had during the night. I smiled for the rest of the day. – Glen, an Employment Adviser.

"I found my mother's sex manual beside her bed and took it to my bedroom. I read the whole thing, including how to masturbate. I then successfully practised. It was quite a shock to realise my body could do that! It was such a strong feeling. I was excited by my discovery. I haven't looked back since!" – Andrew, a Massage Therapist.

"I grew up in an orphanage for boys. I remember one day during a play fight with about seven other boys they held me down, pulled down my pants and began to masturbate me. I don't remember much about how that happened. But I do remember how pleasurable my first ejaculation felt! I have a hazy sense of some shame. I became fascinated with the pleasure that my penis and masturbation could bring me. When looking back on this it may have caused me to be over sexual. This may be because I was sexually abused but didn't realise it until recently." – John, a Counsellor.

Ejaculation and also masturbation are a natural part of life. You don't have to hide it, or believe you have done something wrong. Make your first ejaculation, whether it happens without you doing anything, in a wet dream or because you choose to masturbate, special in some way. Find a way to celebrate it that feels good for you. See page 71 Activating Your Life's Purpose.

Your Journey into Manhood has begun. It is a long and complex one. It doesn't happen overnight. If things get tough find a man you trust and talk about what is going on for you. Ask him what growing up was like for him. This may help you understand and feel more comfortable about the changes, thoughts and feelings you are experiencing.

Journey to Manhood

In some cultures young men are sent out into the wilderness and given challenging tasks. This assists them to find their purpose in life. The story of Shining Sun and Running Water, at the beginning of the book explores this. Finding ways to support yourself on your Journey that are appropriate within your own community is important.

A Celebration Journey

If you have men around you who you trust, ask them if they can get together in a group to support you in your Coming into Manhood Journey.

- They could take you camping in the bush for a few days.
- They could organise challenges to stretch you beyond your current experience of yourself and your limits. This could be something like white water rafting, abseiling or climbing a mountain in the dark.
- They may ask you to build something out of materials they provide.
- They may also leave you alone in the forest, staying close by, for one night or more.
- They could decide that you go without food for a day or so.

After successfully completing your challenges the men could invite other men and boys to join the group. Form a circle where everyone can share with you their experiences of growing up and the challenges they faced. They may also tell you how they dealt with them. If you listen closely you may learn from them.

You may end your Journey by inviting the women of your community to come together for a celebratory feast. Everyone could speak of some quality they see in you that is admirable. At this point it is your gift to the whole group to share what you have learned about yourself through your Journey. Keep men's business as that. Don't tell females the details of what you did. It adds power and mystery to male and female rituals when they are not talked about publicly.

By doing all this you are supported on your Journey and your manhood is recognised and valued by your community.

What Changes in Females?

The first sign of puberty is breast budding. This can happen any time between nine and fourteen years of age. The breasts and nipples get larger and then pubic hair grows.

One female hormone is Oestrogen. The other hormone, progesterone prepares her body for pregnancy. There is an increase in breast size, hips widen and there is sometimes an increase in fat deposits. Yes! A female requires more fat to store hormones. Her sense of smell gets more sensitive. The vagina and womb mature and her external sex organs grow – the clitoris and labia. When her time comes she experiences Menarche – the first time her body bleeds. This is when the womb releases menstrual blood.

Menarche

Menarche is a milestone – it signifies a huge change. It is a special event in a girl's life. It is something that deserves recognition and celebration. The girl is becoming a woman.

Some girls are not ready to grow up. Others dread it and are confused about how their changes will affect them. Their first blood can come as a shock because they are unprepared. Some girls who do not know about menstruation think they are sick and in rare cases, even dying when they first bleed. Many feel excited and anticipate their changes.

Get support before your body starts to bleed. If you have not yet experienced Menarche, ask your mother and/or close women friends about it. Do this even if you are already bleeding – ask them to share their stories with you. It's great to talk about women's business together.

If there is no one for you to talk to, check out good books or look on the Internet. Educate yourself, even if you think you are too young. It helps if you are prepared.

Ask your mother to buy you pads. Make yourself a little bag or basket for the things that help you at this time – red panties, cotton pads and a little bag to carry pads to school in.

Knowing you are prepared when you bleed can add to your confidence.

Problems can arise around Menarche and Menstruation if you are:

- not told what to expect,
- not given practical support,
- not encouraged to be open about it in your family,
- not in a culture that honours womanhood and this very special aspect of it,
- not welcomed and celebrated.

FATHERS – As well as being supported by women, it is important to have some kind of acknowledgment from your father or a close male friend at this time. He could take you out to dinner, buy you flowers or a special piece of jewellery. This completes the circle of recognition. A man's involvement can affect your relationships with men in later life.

When you Menstruate...

Menstrual blood forms a lining in the womb. It is sometimes called the uterus. The blood leaves the womb through the cervix and then the vagina. First menstrual blood might appear brown.

There can be emotional upheaval as the body prepares to shed its blood – tiredness, cramps, a bloated, then heavy feeling. What happens in the body at this time is directly related to stress, hormones and lifestyle. There can be a greater sensitivity to sounds and smells. Some girls don't experience any of these things.

Imagine the womb as a guestroom. It prepares itself for a visitor. It cleans itself out every month when it does not have a visitor – the sperm from a male. When sperm joins with an ovum (or egg), it starts to make a baby. This is called conception.

Every menstrual cycle the womb prepares itself for possible pregnancy. It creates a warm and soft lining, which is shed once again if conception does not occur. And so it goes on for between thirty and forty years of the life of a fertile female.

It can take a couple of years before a regular cycle is established. The average menstrual cycle is once a month. This varies for each female. We are all different! Some females don't menstruate because they over-exercise, become undernourished, ill or highly stressed. During pregnancy and for some time while breast-feeding, females do not menstruate.

Pregnancy can occur when sperm is ejaculated from the penis into or around the vagina. To prevent pregnancy when sexually active with a male, use a condom to stop the sperm from entering the vagina. Condoms can also help prevent sexually transmitted infections (STIs). A healthy and clear attitude towards your sexuality can also help to keep you free of disease. Make sure you use some method of contraception, if you wish to avoid pregnancy.

Female Cycles

Menstruation has been made into a taboo rather than accepted as a sacred function of a female's body in our society. Menstrual blood is in fact the lifeblood that keeps the race going. It is powerful! It has the nutrients to create a human being. Without this blood there would be no human life on Earth.

Menstruation is also the source of a powerful and subtle connection to the rhythms in Nature. It cleanses and re-inspires you spiritually when you give it a place in your life. You cannot access its power and what it has to teach you if you attempt to ignore it.

When you menstruate you are:

- able to receive visions and inspiration for your next monthly cycle, for both yourself and others,
- more psychic and intuitive and full of power,
- open and emotionally sensitive and/or vulnerable,
- in an altered state – a dreamy, more lateral thinking/ feeling space, in non-focussed and non-linear time.

Connected to the Mystery of Life

Menstruation connects you to the cycles of the moon and to the rhythms in Nature. It has an impact on you.

Every month you have an opportunity for a mini-Initiation. You can go into the uncharted waters of your psyche and experience a deep cleansing on all levels of your being.

You may not know how your body or emotions are going to respond as you move into your next cycle. You can gain tremendous wisdom by listening to your body's knowing, doing as she bids you. Resting when you're weary, taking yourself away from others, turning inward if you feel like it. If you are able to let go and surrender into your body, your cycle can initiate you into a greater connection and depth within yourself. By listening you can experience your Wisdom.

Trust the process of your cycling nature as deeply as you can. Be curious about your body and what is happening. Talk to helpful women, your friends and your mum, step-mum or female guardian. Break the silence around your cycle. As a female you are moved by the cycles of the moon. Connect yourself to the Mystery of your Moon-time.

Moon-time Journal

Keep a special Journal by your bedside if you haven't yet bled. This is to record the dream you may have just before your first bleed. It may show you the purpose for being here.

It is useful to record the changes you experience during each monthly cycle. Make notes of changing emotions and keep accurate details of the dates and number of days you menstruate. In later years this can help you become conscious about when you are ovulating and can become pregnant. If you do this you can avoid unwanted pregnancy.

Look at www.amritahobbs.com or www.moondiary.com.au for moon-time journals.

Let's start listening, respecting and honouring ourselves as girls and women. Let's start to listen to the songs that our bodies sing. Let's encourage the messages they offer us.

Be Willing to Let Go

In some ways as a female you are not in control of your body. Nature has her way with you, not only through your monthly cycle but also when you are giving birth.

Your body invites you to rest, regenerate and retreat. Menstruation is a time to let go and cleanse on all levels of your being, preparing you for another new cycle.

You can attempt to override your body and the emotional upheaval your hormones may create during the premenstruam. You can ignore the changing tide of your body and be more like men. If you choose this, it may affect your physical and emotional experience. It also takes away your natural connection to your power and the great teachings your body offers you. It may remove you from your feminine spirituality. Another choice is to stay connected to your body. Accept and ride with it.

Menstruation has become something to be fixed up by a tablet or a drug rather than being seen as a natural process in a woman's life. When females take time off from school or work, these are sometimes considered sick days. **You are not sick! You are menstruating!**

What is going on in your body may feel beyond your control unless you take the Pill or use other medical intervention. Some doctors suggest young females use the Contraceptive Pill because they experience pain or have irregular periods. When you take the Pill your body does not ovulate. Drugs stop the normal functioning of your cycle. This is not recommended.

Menstruation can be a time to retreat and rest.

Staying Healthy?

The way you relate to your blood and are connected to your menstrual cycle deeply affects the way you experience yourself as a female. It's unhealthy for you to ignore or disrespect any aspect of your body.

Many females neglect themselves during their cycle through ignorance. Your menstrual cycle affects you for almost half your life. If you ignore cramps, headaches, feeling tired and the call from your body to rest you can seriously harm yourself. Some women may also ignore what is happening emotionally and are determined **to carry on as normal.** This is not natural behaviour. Your body is speaking and you may not be listening.

Women who ignore menstrual symptoms over time can become sick. This can result in having a hysterectomy – the removal of the womb and ovaries. This operation not only stops women from having children, it can also screw up their hormonal system for the rest of their lives. Some women no longer feel like women after this. In America one in four and in the UK and Australia one in five women have hysterectomies!

If you take care of yourself as a cycling woman, your body can reward you. You can do this by eating healthy food, reducing sugar intake, getting enough sleep and regular exercise **and** expressing your emotions appropriately. You can gain wisdom by paying attention to your cycle.

Most menstrual symptoms are not natural. If you are suffering – attend to it. The way you experience your cycle is your responsibility. There are many natural therapies that can help – Acupuncture, Naturopathy, Massage, Osteopathy or Yoga.

Note: Many commercial pads and tampons are made from plastics, bleached cottons and rayons and can do damage to the tenderest parts of your body. There is an increase in cervical cancers that may be connected to the use of some sanitary pads and tampons. You can buy or make cotton cloth pads that wash out. These last for years. They are a great alternative to mass-produced products that are full of harmful chemicals as well as damaging to the environment. You can buy natural fibres and unbleached products from health food stores. Check out: www.wemoon.com.au

Tampons can be dangerous to your health if not used properly. Toxic shock can result by leaving tampons inside your body for too long. Some females have died because of this. Make sure you know what you are doing! Sea sponges can be used as a tampon substitute.

I have not covered all of the physical/ biological facts about your body. You may have biology classes in school and there are many books available. What is offered here is the more magical and mysterious aspects of your fertility cycle.

Ritual Celebrations for Her

It adds meaning to life when we celebrate what are considered ordinary, every day events. Menstruation has been misplaced in this category. It is an extraordinary event that has been hidden in the past. It is time for that to change.

Girl-Becoming-Woman Ritual and Celebration

This ritual is best after a girl's first cycle and before her second. Or at the first opportunity if it's already happened.

Mothers: Gather a group of women friends together and maybe a special friend of your daughter. Ask them to bring flowers, candles and a gift that is in some way symbolic as an offering to the girl-becoming-woman. You could all wear white and red clothing if you like. This adds specialness to the occasion. Bring food to share for a celebration feast. It's special to end rituals by sharing food.

The Ritual

- The women sit in a circle in silence for a short while.
- The girl-becoming-woman moves and sits in the middle of the circle. She makes eye contact with each of the women present.
- The mother moves into the middle of the circle facing her daughter. They are tied together with red ribbon or wool.

Mother / Daughter Honouring

- Taking it in turns, the mother and daughter repeat each phrase a few times to each other:

  Something I appreciate about having you as my mother/daughter is..... add your own words.

  Something I let go of about being your mother/ daughter is.....

- The mother then says to her daughter:

  A gift I wish you to take into womanhood is.....

- The girl then says:

  Something I take from you into womanhood is.....

These statements could be repeated a few times.

- The cords joining mother and daughter are then cut, signifying their changing relationship.
- The mother returns to the circle of other women.
- The women honour the girl: Each woman, in turn, around the circle tells the girl – what qualities she sees in her, how she has watched her grow. She then gives her the gift she brought and tells her why she chose it.

You can vary this Ritual in any way you choose.

Reclaiming Menarche or Menstruation

The way you experience Menarche can affect the way you menstruate for the rest of your life. If you have already begun menstruating, what was your first experience like? If you enjoyed it – wonderful!

If you didn't, here is something you can do about it.

Write in your Journal about the first time you menstruated in as much detail as you can remember. Look particularly for the shaming or discouraging messages or feelings that you had at the time.

- Remember in vivid detail what happened.

  Which people were around you? What were their attitudes towards your first blood? What was said?

  What were the feelings you experienced?

  Allow yourself to fully feel those feelings again. What is that like for you?

- Spend some time imagining how it could have been.

  How could you celebrate? Who could you invite? In what ways could they celebrate you? What wonderful things could they say to you on this significant occasion? What gifts could they bring you?

- Close your eyes and imagine the celebration exactly as it could have been. Make sure you feel special.

  You can change the rest of your life, if you are able to feel this visualisation deeply.

  Use this process to honour yourself. Is celebrating your cycle now important to you? If so, invite friends around and make up a Ritual for yourself even now.

  It's never too late!

Activating Your Life's Purpose

When girls first menstruate or boys first ejaculate and this bodily fluid symbolically touches the Earth, some Aboriginal people believe their life plan is activated.

Maureen, a senior Aboriginal woman explained that the placenta, sometimes called the afterbirth, carries a map of the purpose of our lives. The placenta is an organ that connects us to the nourishment and oxygen supply from our mothers when we are in the womb. It usually leaves the womb shortly after we have been born.

Many of our mothers gave birth in hospital and the placenta was destroyed. In this case the placenta was not buried hence, our life plan is not set in motion. Maureen believes that's why so many young folk are confused and disconnected.

She offered a ritual you can do for yourself:

Go into Nature and find a stone. A fairly good sized one. Cut a small piece of your hair. Prick your finger with a sterilised needle. With the blood and hair placed on the stone, bury it face down into the Earth. This symbolically represents your placenta. Believe your life's plan has been activated the next time you bleed or ejaculate.

This Ritual can be used at any time you feel disconnected – when you move house, go to another country, feel ungrounded or that you don't belong in a place.

Rituals can be adapted to any number of Passages that have not been celebrated for both males and females.

Photo taken by Cheze

Taking Care of Your Body

Notice your growth spurts. Your muscles, organs, skeletal system and skin are changing structures and can use all the help you can give them. Caring for your body is one way of honouring and respecting yourself. By looking after yourself you are giving yourself the best possible life chances you can. Treat yourself gently. Allow time and space just for you. Quieten your mind, feed and cleanse your body and be at peace in yourself.

There are many ways to nourish yourself. Beautiful surroundings, comfortable and colourful clothing, spending time in Nature, doing the things you love to do with people who care about you.

Food is nourishment and it is important that you choose to eat healthy foods. Food is not the only way you can nourish yourself. If you do not feed your mind, body and soul in other ways, you may attempt to fill yourself up with food and create unhealthy eating habits.

Food

Eat a range of these foods daily for a balanced diet:

- fresh fruit and vegetables,
- whole grains (bread, rye, oats, rice, etc.),
- proteins (animals raised organically or grains and legumes). Fish is a valuable source of brain nutrients,
- use cold pressed oils in small quantities,
- include raw food in your diet (salads, grated vegetables such as carrot, beetroot, celery, etc.).

Use organically grown products if possible.

Junk Versus Whole

When you eat junk foods: potato crisps and greasy chips, fast food, donuts, too many lollies, etc., your body is not satisfied for long. They are not whole and healthy and your body knows it. If you eat only junk food over a long period of time, you are not feeding yourself well enough to grow and maintain a healthy body. If your body becomes deficient, it leaches (takes) nutrients from your bones, muscles and organs. They become weakened and can waste away. This may create cancer, ulcers, brittle bones that break easily, diabetes and mental disorders.

Soft drinks and cordials are full of sugar and chemicals that are damaging to your body. They are not a substitute for water. Drink at least two litres of water every day, filtered, rainwater or from a spring, if possible. This keeps your body hydrated and flushes toxins out of your system.

Because of depleted soils you don't always get the nutrients necessary from the food you eat. Some of you may require supplements. If you do not have enough vitality or feel unwell see a Naturopath. Your body is growing quickly and it is important to maintain its health.

If you love and respect yourself you can avoid patterns of unhealthy eating.

Pimples

Don't take pimples too personally. If you're not careful one pimple can wreck your whole day, for the time you are focussed on it! You may think it's the only thing about you that others see. Acne and pimples are a normal part of adolescence and are related to hormones and/or a poor diet. The skin is the largest elimination organ of the body. If you are eating food that is not eliminated through your bowel, your skin will do the job. If you suffer from pimples because of hormonal changes and imbalance, be easy on yourself.

Remedies: Tea-Tree oil works wonders and is a natural antiseptic. It dries up pimples and reduces inflammation. Put a few drops, into a 200 ml spray bottle and fill with water. Spray affected area regularly.

If your hormones are way out of balance or you have serious problems see a Herbalist or Naturopath. Some herbs cleanse the blood. Herbs can also help balance hormones and offer antiseptic properties.

To stay healthy eat healthy

Take Regular Exercise

Your body thrives on regular exercise – that keeps it healthy. Make a promise to yourself to do some form of exercise every day – stretching, dancing, aerobics, sport, walking, Tai Chi or martial arts. The lymph system is pumped by exercise and eliminates toxins from your system. The elimination system, which deals with urine and faecal materials from food and liquid we ingest and from the breakdown of our bodily tissues, is stimulated through regular exercise.

"Women who exercise regularly can look forward to on average, up to twenty more years of productive living than those who don't."
– WOMEN'S BODIES, WOMEN'S WISDOM, Dr Christiane Northrup.

Wow – that's a lot!

Get Enough Rest

Sleep for at least eight to ten hours every day. When you over extend your physical body make sure you take extra rest to balance that out. You may also benefit from extra sleep when you are experiencing stress.

Be Happy

- think happy thoughts,
- imagine happy scenes, places and faces,
- put pictures on your bedroom wall that make you feel good.

Does all of this, a healthy diet, exercise, enough rest, sound unappealing? Maybe, but doing these things gives you the potential to live a long and healthy life. It is worth the effort!

There are great resources around. Books, gymnasiums, classes and practitioners you could contact for professional health care and exercise plans. This could help.

For Both Him and Her

Things you can do to take care of your body:

- It is important to keep your body clean, showering **at least** once a day and sometimes pampering yourself in a relaxing bath. You can regularly oil your body to keep your skin soft and supple.
- Give yourself a skin scrub and a massage, followed by a hot, then cold shower. This increases circulation and keeps your skin clean.
- Take a shower or a bath and imagine that you are also cleansing your aura, which is the energy field surrounding your body. After a busy day, surrounded by people and experiencing many emotions, this is a healthy thing to do. This kind of cleansing is as important as washing your physical body.
- Walk without shoes on soft grass, sand or the ground as often as possible. This connects your body and head to the Earth.
- Massage helps to relax your muscles when they are stressed and is also pleasurable. Allow yourself to touch your skin and sensitise your body, that way giving yourself pleasure. Self-massage is a way that you can learn to appreciate your body and stay connected with it. You can do this when showering, bathing or resting on the floor or in bed. You can do a massage course to become more skilled.
- Share massages with a friend. Be gentle with each other.
- When you have tension around your head area, rub your head and scalp. Rosemary Oil improves your memory and Lavender Oil soothes and calms the nervous system.
- Beautify and enjoy yourself in your body. The more you appreciate it, rather than ignore it, the more attractive you become.
- Wear clothing that is not too tight because it restricts blood flow, oxygen intake, movement and the way your organs function.
- Wear clothes that allow your body to breathe and when ever you can, wear natural fibres. This may make you feel better about yourself and also helps the environment.

Do you appreciate your body?

If so, you may like to thank it. Is it serving you well? Your feet and legs help you to walk. Your hands allow you to write. Your arms, to hug. Your heart keeps you alive. What else is there to thank your body for?

Make a list if you feel like it.

Don't take the miracle of your body for granted. Otherwise it might go away!

Body Image

Magazines written for teenagers are full of skinny looking females that pout at cameras. They usually include information about dieting and weight. This simply serves to hook some young women into a lifetime of obsession with weight and food. It can also lead to males having a false image of female beauty.

The definition of looking good becomes the way models look. There are few images presented to us of real bodies, healthy pink-cheeked young people who look as if they are enjoying life. This can keep energy and power tied up until they finally find the courage to stop believing the media lie, accept their bodies as they are and also look after them in healthy ways. This can free up an enormous creative energy for those who have been judging themselves as not good enough as they are.

Is it wise to model yourself on the models? Don't believe the media lie.

By keeping yourself clean and getting enough sleep and exercise you shine your own radiant beauty. Have the confidence to love and listen to your own body. Be happy with yourself – just the way you are! Only you can do this – no one can do it as well as you.

Beauty is a State of Being

Many judge people to be beautiful merely from their appearance. If you look closely at people who seem beautiful you may observe that some of them wear cleverly crafted make up, or that they are handsome but hardened. Take care not to judge yourself or others by external appearances. When you look superficially you can be easily fooled. See beyond the surface and be careful not to become emotionally involved with people because of the way they look.

If you are not happy on the inside and follow fashion, buy clothes and wear make-up as a cover up, your true beauty is hidden. You appear superficial and may remain unseen if you adorn yourself on the outside without loving yourself inside first.

The media presents unreal images of unreal people. Are you buying into popular images of skinny, sulking, or cool looking people? They are not REAL! They are acting out a role and their bodies are paying a great price for this.

True beauty is something that is revealed from within.
Radiance on the outside reflects who the person really is.

"The difference between a flower and a weed is a judgement."

– TO LOVE IS TO BE HAPPY WITH,
Barry Kaufman.

Touching

Research has shown that babies placed in orphanages at an early age die if they are not given physical contact. Some people have been starved of physical affection. Touch deprivation affects everyone as they grow older.

Some things you can do with a partner:

- Sit facing each other. Focus your attention on breathing consciously together.
- Decide who is to receive touch first.
- Take one hand, gently stroke and caress it. Keep your eyes closed and do not speak.
- Do this for some time, then change hands.
- Change over so the other person gets a turn.

This exercise can also be done on the face.

Physical contact with another person is preferable. If that's not possible for you, the following suggestions may be first steps to enjoying physical pleasure alone.

- Hug yourself and give yourself a massage.
- Pat a dog, cat, horse, cow or any other animal.
- Take a long, deep bubble bath, with essential oils that you enjoy.
- Roll around in the sand, the grass or mud, and feel your body sensations. Stand in the rain or in the shower and feel the water on your body.

In some families and in many school playgrounds, touch takes the form of mock battles. This is not a substitute for close physical contact but is sometimes used as such. It is often safer to keep people at a distance, especially if you are not used to close contact.

Hugs are a way to receive touch

Hugging makes you feel better about your body because touch affirms that you are lovable. Touch increases your sense of well-being and improves the state of your health. It encourages closer, more intimate contact with other people and gives you a chance to relax and be supported.

Make an agreement with yourself to get at least three hugs every day. This may involve changing the way that you relate to your family and friends. The initial awkwardness is worth the effort when you feel the results in your body. If you can't find someone to hug you, give hugs to yourself. You may feel great benefit from this.

LET'S HUG

***There's a hug to say I love you,
And a hug to say goodbye.
There's a hug to say how are you?
And a hug to say we tried.
There's a hug to bond a friendship,
And a hug when the day is through;
But the hug I love in all the world,
Is the hug I get from you.***

Eating Disorders

Dr Christiane Northrop says that models weigh 25 percent less than the average weight of the normal female population. This image is not reachable for most of us. Having these popular images to live up to puts a lot of pressure on teenagers – young females in particular, to be too thin.

Eating disorders cause a great deal of despair for those suffering and also for their families. Both males and females suffer. The numbers are increasing, especially among young people. Anorexia and bulimia are ways to stave off hidden anxieties and can also be a slow road to suicide!

If you **think** you may be suffering from an eating disorder or **know** you are, seek help. Find a counsellor you are able to trust, a Naturopath or a holistic doctor who knows about these problems and their associated issues.

Alternatively, be prepared to educate yourself and **take ACTION – as soon as you can!**

You have an eating disorder when your eating habits are unhealthy and if you:

- have over-concerns about body shape and weight,
- generally feel bad about yourself,
- are disgusted by your body or with eating,
- become seriously depressed or suicidal because of food.

Anorexia

"An anorexic lives out a system in which needs, wants, desires and feelings have all been abolished. The logical end to this process is death, since it is impossible for any of us to go on living unless we are prepared to accept our needs. For her the needy part of herself is totally unacceptable. She only likes and approves of the needless self." – THE ELEMENT GUIDE, Anorexia and Bulimia, Julia Buckroyd.

Anorexia develops over a long period of time. It usually starts with going on a diet. Anorexic people come to enjoy the feeling of being hungry. Sometimes they start by cutting out food that is considered fattening such as fat, oil, sugar, cakes, etc. Over time the diet becomes so out of balance that the body's need for protein, carbohydrates or fat is not met. What they are eating is not enough to sustain their bodies or maintain normal body weight.

There are some young people who suffer mild forms of anorexia and don't know they have created a dis-ease from their eating habits. It can be a long time before people recognise their symptoms.

One way or another anorexic people become increasingly preoccupied with food, weight, shape and size. They are not interested in living ordinary lives.

Some points to help you recognise people who are suffering from Anorexia. They are:

- not able to eat a normal meal with the family,
- isolated from other people,
- deceitful about eating habits,
- anxious about food,
- eating alone,
- believing they are fat, when it is clear to all around they are thin,
- over exercising – even when in extreme cases the muscles have wasted away,
- extremely self-critical.

Anorexia slows growth and halts normal development in adolescents.

The long-term effects of anorexia on the skeletal system are not reversible. Eventually starvation brings exhaustion, weakness and can lead to an early death.

When an anorexic person starts to eat normally again, some bodily functions can be restored, but bones don't grow anymore.

Bulimia

Bulimia tends to be experienced in late teens. It can be the most secret eating disorder because it does not show on the outside.

How to recognise if you are a Bulimic person or a friend is?

Bulimic people binge eat – they consume a massive amount of food in short periods of time and either vomit or take laxatives to get rid of it. Usually the sufferer is alone and feels a lack of control while binge eating. A great deal of tension and excitement can be created in planning a binge.

Emotionally they may feel out of control, ashamed, weak-willed, ugly, guilty, anxious and self-hatred. Once the frenzy and excitement is over, they are likely to be over-taken by feelings of panic because their preoccupation is with losing weight.

Obesity

When people are overweight they are storing excessive fat or fluid in their bodies. This may be a layer of protection or armour against pain they have avoided experiencing.

Being overweight can be caused for many reasons.

Physical problems – such as a thyroid dysfunction when the thyroid gland in the neck does not allow the body to metabolise food properly. It gets stored as fat rather than eliminated. Other organs may not be functioning properly. If this is the case, it is advisable to have a thorough medical check up.

Emotional disturbance can cause people to use food as a way of stuffing down unwanted emotions.

Eating can become a way to avoid facing:

- anxiety,
- problems which seem too big to handle,
- unresolved issues with people. Either because they are not confident enough, or don't have the skills to deal with what's going on,
- traumatic experiences, because they are unable to resolve them in ways that free them of their effects,
- looking attractive and getting unwanted attention.

Dr Christiane Northrup says obesity is defined as being 20 percent over a person's desirable body weight.

By this definition, she says that 27.1 percent of American women between the ages of twenty and seventy-five are obese.

For **big** women with big energy, or who clearly love and respect themselves, being overweight is not a problem or even a health hazard, as some medical professionals would have them believe. In some cultures big women are honoured and are considered wealthy.

Comfort eating can cause obesity. This can be helpful in the short term, but if it happens over time, it can create long-term problems. For some comfort eaters, this may be the only pleasure they experience.

Overeating becomes a way to make people feel good because very little else in their lives does. The challenge is to find other ways of fulfilling themselves and take the emphasis off eating whenever possible.

Sexual abuse is a common cause of obesity. The body surrounds itself with a protective layer of fat. Being overweight may make people who have been or are being abused, feel safer in some ways. Also it makes them less sexually attractive. It can become a way to hide.

See page 163 about Sexual Abuse, if you think you have been abused in any way.

Unhealthy role models – if parents eat unhealthy food, then excessive weight can become the norm in the family.

A number of the above factors may be involved.

Being overweight is never simple.

If you have an Eating Disorder

- Be willing to admit you have a problem.
- Listen to your body and become aware of what you are eating, why, when and how much. Eat only when you are hungry. Be aware of false or addictive hunger. Learn to tell the difference.
- Nourish your body for you, not for others, or to fit into society's image of underfed and skinny beauty.
- Eat vital and whole foods, rather than over-processed, over-cooked and dead food.
- Concentrate on enjoying the food you are eating. Don't talk to others, watch TV or gobble your food down. Eat slowly and be conscious that what you are feeding your body nourishes and gives you vitality. Eat as a meditation.
- When you feel yourself craving food or avoiding eating for fear of gaining weight, tell yourself that you love and respect yourself and see what happens.
- If your eating habit is a serious problem, write down everything you eat for two weeks. Bring all your attention to it. What changes can you make?
- If your eating is out of control, get professional help to make a structured food plan for a number of weeks. This can break existing eating patterns and change the way your body metabolises the food you eat.
- If you are eating for emotional comfort can you find other ways to comfort yourself ?
- Educate yourself by reading and finding out about healthy lifestyles and habits.

As you recover, can you give yourself permission to eat what you enjoy? Can you do this moderately?

Use Your Journal

Write about the underlying issues you are facing which may be causing eating disorders. Re-read what you write and ask yourself questions to deeper explore what is going on. Can you learn to love and accept yourself as you are?

Helping Others

If you have friends who are suffering from an eating disorder, talk to them about what is happening. Let them know that you care about them. Tell them about the effects.

Let a caring adult and their parents know if they are not already aware. Your friends may ask you not to do this.

If their condition is serious it may be better to break confidence in order to protect them.

My Body Story

I remember my teenage years. I was tall and as thin as a pole. I mostly felt ungainly and uncomfortable. I had been given messages that I was ugly and believed them. Of course, I was not ugly, none of us are, even if at times we believe we are.

I related to the story of the Ugly Duckling. In the beginning of the story the duckling felt out of place. He was picked on in the farmyard. He was gangly and clumsy. When fully grown, this little Ugly Duckling was transformed into an elegant and graceful Swan.

During adolescence I felt awkward. I was disconnected from my body. I hated sport for many reasons. Afterwards we would all have to shower and everybody was checking every body else. My classmates had breasts before I did. I was a late developer. I felt like hiding. I'll never forget the joy of my first bra - a 32A. (That's very small.) I bought it from the two-and-sixpenny shop in Leeds. I thought I would die without one but Mum refused to buy me one. Desperate, I bought one myself. I had to be the same as everybody else, acceptable by others' standards.

Our family ate fish and chips, eggs or baked beans on toast and a Sunday roast dinner. This is an unhealthy diet.

That's a long time ago! I'm over my half century mark now. What is clear to me as my hair turns silver, my joints creak and my eyes don't see as well as they used to, is that if I don't care of myself, my body will fail me. I like to imagine myself at ninety, still walking in the bush, being strong, flexible and healthy. Whether I am like that or not is up to me.

Me at 12 years old

YOUR MIND

You may now be aware that everything going on around you impacts on your mind, body and soul. Every experience, sense, taste and touch is recorded at a cellular level in your body and in your brain. You are a huge sense organ. Most of you are walking around in a polluted world – the air, the noise, the hustle-bustle and pressure you are faced with daily from traffic, television, radio transmitters, people, at school, at home and on the street all impact on you in very powerful ways. You are indeed that sensitive! So much so, that many people dull their senses in order to survive, especially if they are living in unnatural environments. Some very sensitive people suffer from mental illness. Another extreme of this is autism. These people find their environment unbearable.

It has been scientifically proven that the vibration of heavy metal or rock music makes plants stop growing and even kills some. The words used are sometimes violent and full of hatred and often people listening are not conscious of what they are hearing. The words, in that case, go directly into the subconscious mind. This may cause disturbance and can be unhealthy, damaging and dangerous. The negative influence may bring people down rather than uplift them. If you listen to this kind of music, are you aware of what you are feeding your mind?

The thoughts you feed your mind are similar to the food you eat. They create a reaction in your body. Your mind is affected by every impression, judgement and assessment that you make. Be aware of what you are taking in from your surroundings and the thoughts you think. Become conscious and selective, remembering that you're like a computer that retains every single memory.

Reading inspirational books, uplifting poetry and stories, listening to classical music and meditating are all ways that can nourish your mind. These things may not seem cool or be appealing to you. Give it a go and see what happens.

This section offers an opportunity to look at changing beliefs that no longer work for you and to reprogram your mind.

Get Out of Your Head

Many people become head oriented and are often not in touch with what their bodies are telling them.

The following behaviours suggest you are living in your head. You:

- don't feel hungry,
- are unaware that you are overly hot or cold,
- are clumsy, stumble, trip over or drop things,
- cut your finger when chopping vegetables,
- injure or burn yourself and have accidents regularly,
- are generally unaware of your environment,
- are light on your feet. Your full body weight does not connect to the ground.

Some people are so disconnected from their bodies, that they hurt themselves. They don't get the messages they are being given, until they get sick. Then they have to listen. You can intervene earlier by paying attention to what is going on in your body and how it feels. It can also help to get into the habit of grounding yourself and your feelings, by getting back into your body, after mental strain, or a heady experience.

THINGS TO DO!

- Shake yourself, starting with your hands, then your arms, shoulders, torso and legs. It's good to make a sound while you're doing this. Shake everything loose. Then stop very still and feel the tingling sensations in your body.
- Breathe deeply and bring your attention to your feet. Out on the grass or soil, rather than concrete, jump up and down, landing flat on your feet, keeping your knees bent. Do this for several minutes – making an 'ooogh' sound. Allow that sound to come from your belly area, a bit like you would imagine a caveman doing. This brings awareness down into your body and grounds you.
- Lay down on the ground, focus on the energy moving in your body.
- Learn to meditate. This can slow down your thoughts and calm your whole system.

Link Between Mind and Body

It's possible to gain a whole new perspective on your mind/body relationship. Your body is like a garment, a dress, jeans or a jacket or like clay that can be moulded. The mind creates the body the way it is. You can take control of your conscious mind and experience its power and find out for yourself that this is true. When you acknowledge the creative power of your mind you may discover you are not a victim of the condition of your body. You can often change it by the thoughts you think and the actions you take.

You can decide to be consciously aware, both about what you feed your mind and also what you were fed as you grew up. Weeding out subconscious thoughts that run your life is quite a task.

Going to the doctor to fix up something that is wrong with your body when nothing changes in your mind often provides a temporary fix. Dis-ease crops up somewhere else if the true cause, which may lie in your belief systems, or your subconscious mind, is not dealt with thoroughly.

Metaphysicians, healers and therapists have known about this mind/body relationship for centuries. They have talked about the effects of damaging thought patterns on the body and how they create illness. You can choose to live from your Essential Nature and free yourself.

"What we are today comes from our thoughts of yesterday and our present thoughts build our life of tomorrow. Our life is a creation of our mind."

– The Buddha

Choosing Your Own Thoughts

Few people live their own truth. Their decisions are influenced by others – parents, teachers, friends or TV and movies. When you listen to others more than to yourself, you may overlay their thoughts onto your current experience. When you do this you miss the opportunity of being authentic.

The unhelpful influences from childhood role models can be overcome when you are aware of where your thoughts come from. The mind can be reprogrammed. It takes effort and a strong intention. When you listen to yourself, you can experience yourself in a new and different way. When you do this, you are GETTING REAL!

Listen carefully to your own inner voice – your Essential Nature. Hear this as opposed to hearing only the thoughts and opinions of others.

Take this time to reflect on what your beliefs are and attempt to separate them out from those around you. What thoughts that belong to other people have you taken on?

The biggest changes begin with just one thought. Keep that thought going. It's like a journey that begins with one small step – you get there in the end if you keep going.

THINGS TO DO!

Have your notebook and coloured pencils ready.

- Write down a list of your thoughts and beliefs about – life, parents, God, friends, money or anything else you'd like to explore.
- Read it through and circle in one colour those that belong to you.
- For each person who has strongly influenced you choose a different colour and circle what has come from them.
- Examine your responses carefully so that you can be clear about which ones are yours.

Choose to create new thought patterns for yourself at any time. You can be the master of your own mind.

Observe your thoughts carefully... they have the power to create your World

What You Think About… GROWS!

The following is an example where thoughts, being powerful, work against you. If you are about to do an exam or going for a job interview, thinking that you won't do well can make it really tough. You get all worked up, creating stress and even though you may not get the result you like, you make it much harder for yourself.

When self-defeating thoughts arise, you can decide to consciously change them. You could find studying getting easier and easier… and may sail through the exam and get great results. You may get the job! By thinking it, it can be so.

Things are never bad; it's the way you think about them." – INITIATION, Elizabeth Haich.

Your mind may rebel at first as you offer it new ideas because it is used to your old ways of thinking. But over time it becomes more flexible.

Self-Talk

The messages you get from your parents while you are growing up have so much influence that even as an adult they stay with you. Internalising your parents voices can be a bit scary if they are unsupportive.

Watch your self-talk for a while. Notice the kinds of things you say to yourself. Are you telling yourself the things that your parents told you? All limiting messages you get from your parents are not necessarily the truth. Often they are simply being repeated from generations before. Start becoming aware of things that have been, or are being, said to you.

Writing them down is useful. For example, if you are told you are a lazy good-for-nothing, consciously change that around and remind yourself that you often work hard and achieve, if you do. If you are told you are dumb, tell yourself the ways in which you are intelligent. If you are doing something, say at school and a voice in your head says you are stupid, ask yourself who is saying that to you… your mum, or your dad, someone else or yourself? Whoever it is, remind yourself, this is not a **true** thought about **you** and change the thought. When you are aware of these other voices in your head why would you continue to pull yourself down in this way?

If you're told you're ugly – stand up for yourself! Say out loud immediately, "The truth is, I am beautiful/attractive/lovely." Only people who think of themselves as ugly accuse others of this.

Speaking Up

Speaking your mind involves listening to your inner voice, your body and your own wisdom. When faced with a situation that makes you feel uncomfortable, because someone is not being honest, be willing to communicate what feels true for you. At times, you may give your Essential Nature away by not listening closely to yourself and then not speaking honestly to others or taking action.

Being true to yourself takes courage and also practise. Opportunities are often missed in the moment.

An example: A friend said he would come to visit you. He rang at the last minute to cancel and it was too late for you to make other arrangements. You were disappointed, but didn't tell him. You made it easy on him. You may be left with what you felt like saying running through your mind.

It's never too late to finish something off, or say something you didn't say. You can ring your friend later and tell him how it was for you. You can then experience peace of mind.

You may feel misused by friends and are afraid to speak up for fear of losing their friendship. It can be scary! There seems a lot to lose. But sometimes it is important to speak about how you feel. Think it over. Don't act hastily. Then speak from your heart. You may feel better about yourself and closer to them. All you can do is trust that they understand, respect your courage and respond, thereby creating more intimacy.

They may move away. You can't lose true friends by being honest with them. What you can gain is a stronger sense of yourself and your own integrity. Don't shy away from being honest with others. You develop strength of character and experience yourself being more of who you really are.

Don't forget to offer praise, encouragement and gratitude when that is appropriate.

"Our thoughts have exceptional power to draw on the negative or positive energies around us. When they draw at length on the negative, the result can be a weakening of the body's defences. This is especially true when our negative thoughts are centred on ourselves… we are at our most self-centred state when we are depressed. Nothing can sap our natural strength and health as much as prolonged depression. But when we make the effort to move ourselves away from self and begin to concentrate on the needs of others and how to serve them, we begin to heal. Service is a balm to both the spirit and body."

– EMBRACED BY THE LIGHT, Betty J. Eadie.

Many Selves

We may think of ourselves as one big lump of personality. That I am who I am and it's as simple as that. Not so! When you examine yourself more closely you can find lots of aspects of yourself inside that you are not always conscious of.

You are being constantly bombarded with messages from these different parts of yourself. An example of this is if you see a really big ice cream, your first reaction may be "Yum… I'll have that." But a voice comes in saying "You'll get fat." That's the bit of you that is health conscious. Then another voice may say "You're too greedy." That could be your critic. Yet another voice may whisper "It's not good for you." That could be your internalised parent. Then you may go ahead and buy the ice cream, joyously licking it from the child aspect of your personality. You are a complex creature with a lot going on inside of you.

See if you can discover the personalities in your internal play. Give each aspect an identity and a name. Write a little bit about him or her.

Here are some examples:

1. Your so-called friend abandons you and goes off with your group. You find someone to listen to your story and gossip about her behind her back.

   Calling that aspect of your personality Bitchy Beth you might write:

   I am feeling low, not so good about myself. So talking about my ex-friend behind her back allows me to feel in control and gives me some sense of power.

   I'm really hurt underneath so I protect myself with Beth. She shows up when I feel insecure. I use her to protect myself and make others wrong. I believe this helps me feel better about myself but it doesn't really. I'm left with feeling more separate from my friend and negative about myself.

2. You see someone you would like to get to know. You are keen to go and talk with her/him but are afraid of rejection.

   So... Fearful Phil shows up.

   You might write:

   I felt like talking to her/him. Summoning all my courage I walked over. Just at the last minute I lost my nerve and walked right on by. I told myself she/he wouldn't like me and my fear got the better of me.

   Fearful Phil keeps me limited to the people I already know and feeling bad about myself. Then I don't have the confidence to meet new people. When Fearful Phil shows up he sabotages any chance of even having a friendship with someone I would like to get to know.

3. Someone you know has stolen your date. She invited him to a school disco and he's going with her. You are really pissed off.

   So… Nice Natalie shows up:

   I really felt like telling her to get lost and leave him alone. When she came up all smiles and said she hoped I didn't mind, I felt sick inside and felt like screaming. Instead I smiled ever so nicely at her and said I was just about to ditch him anyway. Nice Natalie allows me not to face up to myself or other people. She keeps me superficial and safe. But also stuck in my fakeness.

Spend time identifying as many of the internal aspects of your personalities as you can. You might be amazed at who you find lurking in there. With this kind of perspective you learn how complex your inner workings are. You can understand yourself better. With this knowledge it may become easier for you to live more of your true self – your Essential Nature, rather than all the other defensive, negative, controlling aspects of yourself.

Right and Left Brain Hemispheres

Research has been conducted on the relationship between our right and left brain. Each side of the brain performs unique functions, processes information differently and deals with various kinds of problems.

If you are left-brain dominant you are:

- logical, analytical and linear, arriving at solutions by working them out,
- word-focussed and hear thoughts when problem solving,
- interested in specifics, details, analysis and in breaking things into parts,
- bound by time, space, distance, the three dimensions of length, breadth, depth,
- a sequential thinker, thinking a string of thoughts.

If you are right-brain dominant you are:

- intuitive, creative and lateral, arriving at solutions without working them out,
- picture-focussed in problem solving or Clairvoyant, Clairaudient (intuitive hearing) or Clairsentient (intuitive feeling),
- interested in the whole and the relationship between the parts,
- concerned with synthesis, putting things together,
- free of time constraints and other limits,
- using simultaneous and holistic thinking.

Left-brain dominance is where logic, words and measurement are highly valued in a materially orientated world. The more creative, intuitive, sensing aspect is undervalued and at times suppressed. This creates severe imbalance. When both aspects work together we can be whole.

This gives you some idea about the different brain hemispheres. Although you use the two sides of your brain, one side is generally dominant. The ideal is to have both aspects available in different situations. As humans we can get caught in the comfort zone of our dominant hemisphere and process every situation according to either right or left-brain preferences.

Can you imagine a man rowing a boat with only one oar? What happens to the boat? Yes! It goes around in circles. This is fine if this is his goal. Usually he is aiming to get somewhere and requires both oars and therefore both sides of his brain.

It is similar between male and female. With equal balance between the masculine and feminine we can get somewhere.

Most people only use a small amount of their brain capacity. Can you learn to access more of your innate capacity for Brilliance? You have the potential. Are you willing to use it?

BRILLIANCE
is your birthright!!!

Great Intelligence

There is a Great Intelligence within you, which gives you inspiration and new ideas. Sometimes though, the mind is so busy with its chatter that there is no chance for these new ideas to get through to you. **You are moving too fast.**

There is great value in spending some time every day alone in a peaceful place, even if it's your bedroom, where you can allow your mind and whole system to slow down. One way to do this is by focussing on your breathing. Do it now and see how long you can concentrate – just on your breathing! Probably not for long before your thoughts come rushing in again. The benefits of quietening your mind are great – new ideas, understanding, guidance, inspiration, increased creativity and a sense of well-being and peace. Sitting quietly allows you to connect to your Essential Nature as well as to the Great Intelligence, God or Great Spirit.

Anything is possible. Acting on new inspiration makes it real!

Einstein did this. The story goes that he struggled in vain trying to work out answers to his theories – staying up for days he totally exhausted himself. Then, when he collapsed and slept, the answers came in a dream or popped into his mind when he woke up. Giving up his personal struggle allowed space for the answers to come.

When you are able to let go of what you **think** you can do, you get ideas that are beyond your mind's usual capacity. A person with a closed mind, with rigid thinking, is inviting that rigidity to snap. This can cause broken bones and dislocations in the body and mental illness in the mind. Be as flexible and as open as you can.

Mind-expanding experiences are available in many different ways – through meditation, surfing, mountain climbing, uplifting movies and alternative therapies such as acupuncture, hypnotherapy and group processing. You can also expand your mind through intense experiences in Nature, through drama, dance, playing music and bush walking.

"Once you have an experience of this invisible dimension – and you know this higher place you can go to within your mind and receive guidance and, yes, even the help in creating real magic for yourself – you will have shifted from being an exclusively physical person, a human being having a spiritual experience, to a spiritual being having a human experience."

– REAL MAGIC, Dr Wayne Dyer.

Expect the unexpected and miracles can happen!

Being Here Now

Thoughts usually take you away from your experience NOW! When you make yourself busy all the time you may be avoiding issues that are calling for attention. For example – you've had a fight with your best friend. Instead of sorting it out you may call your other friends for a chat, watch movies or you might clean out your room. By keeping yourself busy you may be avoiding taking responsibility for the conflict.

Another way you may avoid **being here now** is by getting involved in mind chatter – such as worry thoughts, constantly attempting to solve problems in your head. You may go over conversations, imagining how you could have made it better. You may be **over-concerned** about schoolwork, relationships, what may happen next week.

Your thoughts can often take you away from your present experience into fantasies about the future. You may spend hours exploring exciting possibilities and fantasising about romance and new experiences in your mind. You may waste hours doing this. Your mind may take you back into the past. Reliving experiences that you can no longer do anything about. You may complain about past events and regret missed opportunities. You may spend hours planning future events and activities. Sometimes this is necessary in order for your life to function and again you may be wasting time.

As John Lennon said, "Life is what happens when you're busy making other plans."

Real power lies in the present moment.

Affirmations... What Are They?

Affirmations are positive statements you make about yourself or aspects of your life. They can be useful for a specific purpose.

Use them when they can benefit you in a challenging situation you are facing. Some people use them constantly and this can defeat their purpose. Be careful not to get addicted to them.

Affirmations can assist you in reprogramming your mind. They:

- allow limiting thoughts and beliefs to transform into ones that enhance your life,
- help you process your thoughts,
- are a means of accessing what is going on in your subconscious mind,
- allow you to dig out thoughts and beliefs that are no longer useful.

After some time of processing your mind and redefining your beliefs, you may only choose to use affirmations occasionally.

A good affirmation has five basic ingredients.
It's personal, positive, present tense, can be visualised and has feeling content.

Some guidelines:

- Use 'I' statements whenever possible.
- Use present tense only. For example: I am... It is now... Do not use: I will... Or Tomorrow... because that's future tense.
- Use short powerful and uplifting statements.
- Write in the positive: 'I am strong and powerful', rather than 'I will not be weak'.
- Write affirmations down and say them out loud.
- If you hear your mind making statements and judgements that bring you down, catch them and change them around to positives.

If you think you can or you think you can't – you're ***RIGHT!***

THINGS TO DO!

Affirmations can be made in different ways. Here are some examples:

- Think of issues or thoughts that are limiting you in your life. These could be –

  No one likes me.
  There is never enough money, love, food (or whatever) for me.
  Everything I do goes wrong.

- Write down your own issues in your notebook.

  You can change these thought patterns by making them into positive statements and using them as affirmations. Like –

  I am lovable just the way I am.
  People appreciate me for ME.
  Life supports me. I am healthy.
  Everything I touch succeeds and works out perfectly.

Affirmations are most effective if repeated in writing and also verbally (out loud) until the situation begins to improve. For them to be effective and to go more deeply than just on the surface level of your mind, allow them to penetrate into your subconscious mind to create lasting change inside.

Going deeper

To work on deeper levels you can write affirmations in a way that digs up unconscious negative thoughts. This is an unravelling process that helps to get to thought patterns that are below the level of your conscious mind.

- Find a double page in your notebook.
- Use an affirmation from the work that you've done before.
  Write it down on the left-hand side of your book.
- On the right-hand side write down your immediate response.

For example:	Affirmation:	Response:
	I am doing well at school.	Liar, look at your exam results.
	I am doing well at school.	Don't kid yourself, the teachers say you're dumb.
	I am doing well at school.	Well, maybe I'm not doing as bad as everyone says.

- Write the same affirmation over and over again. It could take two or three pages until the negative responses become positive.

You can do this process as many times as you like, but don't change your original affirmation. What may happen is that another thought may pop into your mind and you may be tempted to stray from the affirmation you're working on – don't. Stay with it until it is complete for you. Then, go back to the new thought and work on that.

It's worth the time and you can do this on any number of subjects:

I am loved by all of my friends!
My parents think I'm great! I love myself!
I am enjoying a wonderful relationship!

The more you work with this kind of processing the more you release from your subconscious mind. It takes some time and perseverance to reprogram your mind, so be patient.

A Warning – Your first responsibility is to yourself. You are who you are. If the people around you don't like that, then it's up to them to deal with their reactions. Mind games are not useful. Don't use thoughts to influence another person. Affirmations are a tool to clear out your conscious and subconscious mind and feed it with new and positive thoughts. Only use affirmations for that.

You cannot change another person's thoughts or behaviour. They are responsible for themselves. If you understand this you do not exhaust yourself trying to make it better for others. There are things you can do that support others.

My Story – how my mind sabotaged my life

Many of the thoughts I had recorded on the old tapes of my mind were from my parents. They didn't know about positive thinking or that thoughts create our reality. I internalised messages that said I couldn't get it right. Even using the same words and calling myself 'a silly clot' when I made a mistake.

Before I took charge of my mind a lot of my thoughts were put-downs. They weren't helping me to like myself or get the most out of my life. On and on these thoughts went, stopping me from being spontaneous and having fun. I was a slave to my mind and gave it power over me. Thoughts such as, "You can't do that, you might get hurt," stopped me rock climbing, even though I might have enjoyed it. "Don't go and talk to her, she won't like you anyway," destroyed chances of new friendships.

I realised that my mind was actually out to get me. It was sabotaging my life.

I once went to listen to an inspirational teacher. During his talk he constantly said, "Everything is all right now, isn't it?" Even if you've got no money, no food, even if you are ill – everything is all right now! Isn't it?

I heard that repeated many times and began to see the truth of it.

When I surrender to that thought, everything around me magically sorts itself out.

> *"If you have a past that dissatisfies you, forget it now. Imagine a new story of your life and believe in it. Concentrate only on those moments in which you achieved what you desired, and this strength will help you to accomplish what you want."*
>
> – THE FIFTH MOUNTAIN, Paulo Coelho.

ABOUT SCHOOL

In schools which provide a harmonious and fertile environment for learning, the aims, values and atmosphere encourage individuals to reach their goals. Uniqueness is valued and the potential of each student is realised. Teachers, parents and the wider community work together for the benefit of the young people who attend. Everyone who is involved in this school community is enriched. The genius of every student unfolds, is discovered and nurtured. Not all schools achieve these ideals and some fall short by a long way.

"Every child is born a genius... It is my conviction, from having watched a great many babies grow up, that all of humanity is born a genius and then becomes de-geniused very rapidly by unfavourable circumstances and by the frustration of all their extra-ordinary built in capabilities."
Buckminster Fuller.

Until one hundred years ago only the wealthy had access to any kind of education and most people would not have been able to read or write. In the early 1900's if parents were factory workers children probably were the same. By the time they were ten, they may have been working fourteen hours a day in a mine or as cheap labour in a factory. How does that appeal to you?

When attending a Centenary Celebration at a small country school some time ago, I listened to the stories of the oldies. I was amazed by their attitude about school. In the early days of free education people were desperate to learn. Parents who missed the chance for schooling themselves were keen that their children didn't. The desire to get to school was so strong that children rode bare back on horses for miles in the pouring rain to get there. Sitting in wet clothes all day was worth it. The only equipment was hard benches to sit on, chalk, a blackboard and a cane. The curriculum was the three R's – reading, 'riting and 'rithmetic.

The education system has come a long way since then. Now we have access to a wide range of options – we can learn manual skills, music, graphic arts and languages and we have computers. Most of us in our society have an opportunity to attain basic literacy and numeracy skills. This can allow most of us some kind of economic freedom.

The long-term effects of technological, intellectual and social changes and our adjustment to them, remain to be seen. In the last hundred years, life as it had been known for centuries has radically changed. This is phenomenal and it has opened up a whole new life expectancy.

Why School?

"If as a culture we want to make the most of it, our education system is generous. It can be incredibly stimulating for the mind that wishes to be stimulated," says Barry, a Head Teacher of English/History. "Those people who really go for it at school have everything to gain in a system that has much to offer – skills, equipment, instructors who can share their knowledge and craft. There is information to be gained and shared."

Schools can teach you the skills to learn. If you apply these skills you can have access to an almost infinite amount of information and learning experience. Schooling doesn't end when you leave. Life is your school. It's your teacher for the rest of your life.

"Learning is finding out what you already know. Doing is demonstrating that you know it. Teaching is reminding others that they know just as well as you.
You are all learners, doers and teachers."

– ILLUSIONS, Richard Bach.

A discussion group with students suggested that while there could be alternatives for students who are not academically orientated, school can offer everything to the person who is. For those who fit in, school works.

Motivated students see the value in their education and benefit from it. Those who are able to discipline themselves see school as a means of achieving their goals. They succeed in getting their educational requirements met. You may see these students hard at work. They get results and generally enjoy their experience. School supports their growth.

School can:

- be enjoyable and fun,
- teach you social skills,
- give you a love of learning,
- show you that there is competition in society,
- offer valuable learning and survival skills for later in life,
- give you basic knowledge of how to work within society,
- be a means to find employment that gives you economic stability,
- give you an understanding of the world.

Taking School for Granted

It is easy to take the opportunity that education offers for granted. Some students resent having to go to school. Is it because school is compulsory and you don't have legal choice about attendance? Is it that the curriculum is not appropriate for you? Is it because knowledge and information based learning is not as useful for some students as life and relationships skills could be?

Society is changing so rapidly that the education system has not been able to keep up. Young people today have totally different lifestyles and therefore challenges, from those of only twenty years ago.

We live in a complex culture. We have computers, video games, movies and TV and these things have changed the way we see life and the way our minds function. Many of us have become very sophisticated. The way we perceive reality and the world has been expanded.

In the next two decades we may see major advances in our education and social systems, which could blow our minds. There is a spiritual wave coming through. How that affects the structures that exist in our current system are as yet unknown.

Issues about School

Spending some time considering your issues about school may help you get to know what your own thoughts and feelings are.

Here are questions you can think about.

You could write your thoughts down if you'd like to:

Why am I at school?

What are my attitudes about school?

Can I improve the quality of my life at school by changing my attitude?

How does the behaviour of others affect me?

How can I affect my school environment to make it a better place for everyone?

Can I get more out of and put more into my school life?

How can I assist myself and others, to be creative, happy and empowered?

How can I add value to the lives of the people around me?

What social skills can I develop at school?

How can I enhance my genius at school?

TEENSPEAK

"During your school education you gain social skills, you have the opportunity to participate in sports, creative and academic activities. School gives you an opportunity to extend yourself, to learn basic skills." – Carlie (14)

"By attending school you gain knowledge, you develop a group sense, rather than being just an individual. You begin to understand social structures. Indirectly you learn how to relate to people, to understand them. This happens through your own experience at school rather than by what you are taught." – Jessie (15)

"School can provide a key to life – to change. It pushes you forward and demands discipline. Participating in life at school can result in achievement – mental, physical and emotional. These things can only be gained if you as the student are prepared to participate in what it offers. Some people gain tremendously." – Tom (14)

"In any situation you can give of your best, you can be prepared to participate, co-operate and to enter the competition. You can offer support to others, your peers and your teachers. You can respect others. You can also give of yourself by communicating. You can share your ideas and the information you have." – Simon (14)

"I would like to say to the education authorities: We are human beings. Help us find ourselves and don't ignore us as individuals." – Debbie (15)

"I enjoy going to school. It gets me out of the house. Sometimes I am picked on but some of the teachers really like me. When they do, my grades improve. Being a prefect has been good for my self-esteem. I am learning about being responsible and about options that give me a greater choice of career. Being in schools plays is fun and I make new friends." – Ros (16)

A story about Animals

Once upon a time, the animals decided to do something heroic to meet the problems of the world, so they organized a school. They adopted an activity curriculum consisting of running, climbing, swimming and flying. To make it easier to administer, all animals took all subjects.

The duck was excellent in swimming, better in fact than her instructor and made excellent grades in flying but she was very poor in running. Since she was low in running she had to stay after school and also drop swimming to practise running. This was kept up until her webbed feet were badly worn and she was only average in swimming. But average was acceptable in school, so nobody worried about that, except the duck.

The rabbit started at the top of the class in running, but had a nervous breakdown because of so much to make up in swimming.

The eagle was a problem child and had to be disciplined severely. In climbing class she beat all the others to the top of the tree, but insisted on using her own way of getting there.

At the end of the year an abnormal eel that could swim exceedingly well and also could run, climb and fly a little had the highest average.

Adapted from THE ANIMAL SCHOOL, Dr R. Reavis.

We are Different

You are beautiful, unique, special and precious just the way you are. These things do not depend on your achievement at school OR how high your level of intelligence is. The fact is, you are valuable without doing anything. You are good enough! Accept your own uniqueness. Do not compare yourself to others or stress-out trying to meet others' expectations of you. Appreciate yourself, knowing there is a place for you even if it's not within the school system.

School is not easy for some students. For those of you who are not academically orientated, the quality of your educational opportunity could be improved. When young people don't get supported at school they are often unable to cope. If they are not able to learn in an academic situation, there can be a tendency to switch off, become disruptive or isolated.

I have a young friend who gets home from school unhappy and depressed. He has sagging shoulders and a sad look on his face. He's not participating because he can't see the relevance of the information he is being taught. He is like other students who are not achieving and complain about boredom. They are unable to reach their potential because the system does not work for, but against them. Others are alienated in a system that sometimes doesn't seem to care.

Let people know what you are feeling and ask for support within your school environment. Challenge the system if it is not working for you. Do that in a respectful way. Your voice counts and you can bring about change. If you keep quiet you may not be noticed and the system may remain the same.

Find the courage and get real. It only takes one.

The education system may not provide all students with an ideal tomorrow, but with each step forward, with input from students and caring adults, it can provide appropriately for more of today's youth.

Creating Change

Every person at school has got feelings. Some are not happy. Others are. Everyone benefits from support. Check people out at your school. Observe and discover how many people are really happy. How many people are wearing a mask to hide what's really going on for them? You may get quite a surprise at what you see when you look closely.

It could be different if you pay attention. If you see someone who is isolated or vulnerable, approach him or her.

Have you heard the story of the shellfish on the beach?

One day an old man and his grandson were walking on a beach. To their horror it was covered in stranded shellfish. The boy immediately began picking them up and throwing them into the water. The Grandfather looked at him in disbelief. "Why are you doing that, it won't make any difference?" The boy said, "It does to this one!" He kept on going. His Grandfather helped!

Can you remain sensitive and bring about change in your school environment? This could be your challenge.

You may find some of these suggestions work for you:

- Talk to others about how violence affects you. You may find that many people don't like what's happening either.
- You can make a difference to the atmosphere in your school by ceasing to be the victim or being silent.
- Start **getting real** with others. Communicate and find people who feel as you do.
- Take action against people who are breeding aggression in your school.
- You can embrace each new day with an attitude of discovery and excitement.

Find others to support you and create a Change Agent Club.

Change Agent Club

Gather a few people together who are interested in making your school a better place. If you feel confident enough, you could look out for troubled kids. Offering support could help. Doing this as a group may make it easier.

- Decide on the aims of your Change Agent Club.
- Hold group meetings to share your feelings and support each other. Decide how often to meet.
- Make decisions about how you would like your school to be.
- Let those who can use some help know that as a group you are there for them –

  help people in the playground who are being bullied,
  befriend students who look sad, or are left out,
  support students going through change or stress.
  For example – divorce, death of a parent, addictive parents or illness.
- Create exam support groups to reduce stress and tension.
- Organise nurturing times together and perhaps after school events – talk with teachers and those in authority to bring about curriculum/social/political changes into your school.
- Invite your favourite teachers to occasionally attend your meetings to talk about their personal lives and share their wisdom.

Look out beyond your own position and help to take care of the wellbeing of others. You may find your group getting bigger and bigger.

Life can take on a different meaning for you if you do take care of yourself and others.

What can YOU do to make a difference?

A story about Animals

Once upon a time, the animals decided to do something heroic to meet the problems of the world, so they organized a school. They adopted an activity curriculum consisting of running, climbing, swimming and flying. To make it easier to administer, all animals took all subjects.

The duck was excellent in swimming, better in fact than her instructor and made excellent grades in flying but she was very poor in running. Since she was low in running she had to stay after school and also drop swimming to practise running. This was kept up until her webbed feet were badly worn and she was only average in swimming. But average was acceptable in school, so nobody worried about that, except the duck.

The rabbit started at the top of the class in running, but had a nervous breakdown because of so much to make up in swimming.

The eagle was a problem child and had to be disciplined severely. In climbing class she beat all the others to the top of the tree, but insisted on using her own way of getting there.

At the end of the year an abnormal eel that could swim exceedingly well and also could run, climb and fly a little had the highest average.

Adapted from THE ANIMAL SCHOOL, Dr R. Reavis.

We are Different

You are beautiful, unique, special and precious just the way you are. These things do not depend on your achievement at school OR how high your level of intelligence is. The fact is, you are valuable without doing anything. You are good enough! Accept your own uniqueness. Do not compare yourself to others or stress-out trying to meet others' expectations of you. Appreciate yourself, knowing there is a place for you even if it's not within the school system.

School is not easy for some students. For those of you who are not academically orientated, the quality of your educational opportunity could be improved. When young people don't get supported at school they are often unable to cope. If they are not able to learn in an academic situation, there can be a tendency to switch off, become disruptive or isolated.

I have a young friend who gets home from school unhappy and depressed. He has sagging shoulders and a sad look on his face. He's not participating because he can't see the relevance of the information he is being taught. He is like other students who are not achieving and complain about boredom. They are unable to reach their potential because the system does not work for, but against them. Others are alienated in a system that sometimes doesn't seem to care.

Let people know what you are feeling and ask for support within your school environment. Challenge the system if it is not working for you. Do that in a respectful way. Your voice counts and you can bring about change. If you keep quiet you may not be noticed and the system may remain the same.

Find the courage and get real. It only takes one.

The education system may not provide all students with an ideal tomorrow, but with each step forward, with input from students and caring adults, it can provide appropriately for more of today's youth.

Ideals for Learning

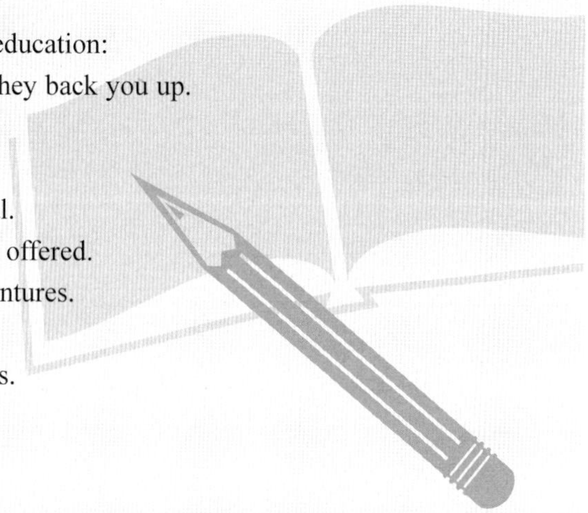

The following conditions assist you to get the most out of your education:

- You have people around you who care for and listen to you. They back you up.
- You have help when things get tough.
- Everyone celebrates the opportunity you have to learn.
- The atmosphere at your school is caring, respectful and helpful.
- Everyone sees the best in you, each other and in what is being offered.
- Your life is full of enriching experiences and challenging adventures.
- You are encouraged to fulfil your potential.
- Your uniqueness is placed above social and economic demands.
- You enjoy a happy, nurturing home life.

Unsupportive Environments

Without support at home it can be difficult to reach your potential at school. School can be challenging for you if you are dealing with emotional insecurity, upheaval or trauma in the home.

It's easy to see the vicious cycle – if you are someone who is mistreated or abused at home – parents fighting, drunkenness, violence, abuse, death or divorce. You go to school and the teacher may blame you for not concentrating. You are then in trouble and may be punished. You may sometimes respond by getting angry at the teacher, because of the hurt you feel. More trouble! Perhaps you cannot easily express your anger at the person who is mistreating you... and so it goes on!

In order to learn, it is helpful to have basic needs taken care of. If you are hungry, over-tired, stressed or traumatised your brain does not have the capacity to concentrate, take in information or learn. Don't blame, judge or put yourself down. If you are living in an environment that does not support your education do your best. If you are not living with ideal conditions and you don't achieve the results you would like, you can catch up with your education if you choose later in life. I did!

**Whatever your circumstances,
be gentle with yourself.**

If you are having difficulties, your school counsellor, may be able to help. Speak to your Head Teacher or Department of School Education official if it's really tough.

Alternatives in Education

Maria Montessori was an educationalist in the 1900's. She presented a different orientation for learning. Her aim was to place the responsibility for learning as much as possible in the child's hands. The teacher was to be an observer more than anything else. Students could work as if the teacher had ceased to exist.

Rudolf Steiner's vision encompassed the spiritual as well as the emotional and creative gifts of the child. Children were viewed as spiritual beings and were accepted as whole entities in their own right rather than as unformed adults in need of shaping.

There are many other educational alternatives: Community Schools, Higher Education Colleges and home schooling. You are, by law, required to attend school (or be home schooled).

How can you do it differently?

Some parents and even teachers have unhelpful attitudes about school. Don't take these on. Most adults have had their chance at education. Some of them blew it. Now it's your opportunity. Be careful not to allow another person's opinion about the education system, or of your abilities in it, stop you making the most of your education.

Do you waste your time at school? Your school experience can be the seeding ground for your adult life. You can develop communication, inter-relationship and teamwork skills. You can excel academically, artistically or wherever your interests lie. School is not just about achieving good exam results.

Make choices for yourself.

This is your life!

Respect Others

Create a two-way relationship, which is based on mutual respect with your teacher and with other students. Practise a new way of relating at school.

- Give compliments and reassurance to others.
- Develop an awareness of yourself and others.
- Be there for others less able than you.
- Tell others how you feel.
- Encourage and care about your friends at school.
- Allow yourself to create mutual bonds with teachers you like.

Imagination

Allow your imagination a place to express itself. Your imagination connects you to the Mystery of Life and can be a constant source of new ideas and inspiration. Avoid becoming stilted and over-intellectual. Imagine school being the way you would like it to be and yourself doing really well in it. Allow your feelings to flow.

"Now scholars can be very useful and necessary in their own dull and unamusing way. They provide a lot of information. It's just that there is Something More, and the Something More is what life is really about."

– THE TAO OF POOH, Benjamin Hoff.

That Something More is what GETTING REAL... about growing up! offers.

Don't Play Victim

There is a danger in blaming a system that you see as faulty, then placing yourself as a victim in it. Are YOU relating to the school system like this?

Some students complain about the system and do nothing, either about the way it operates or their attitudes towards it. If you do that you stay stuck – feeling powerless – a victim. Another aspect is being dependent on someone else, a parent or teacher, to make it better for you. If you deal with your school experience by only complaining about it, this does not change anything. Your actions can!

It's not helpful if you get disinterested or bored and you switch off, shut down and lose your life force. Then we lose your creative potential and your unique gifts. These are essential for our World to evolve.

Put Downs

In lots of schools there are put downs amongst students. This is unnecessary and cruel. How many people do you know who enjoy being put down? No one does! You probably don't either. You can look at what you value and your attitudes so that you no longer accept put downs or put others down.

Take responsibility for what you are creating.

Express your Essential Nature!

Creating Change

Every person at school has got feelings. Some are not happy. Others are. Everyone benefits from support. Check people out at your school. Observe and discover how many people are really happy. How many people are wearing a mask to hide what's really going on for them? You may get quite a surprise at what you see when you look closely.

It could be different if you pay attention. If you see someone who is isolated or vulnerable, approach him or her.

Have you heard the story of the shellfish on the beach?

One day an old man and his grandson were walking on a beach. To their horror it was covered in stranded shellfish. The boy immediately began picking them up and throwing them into the water. The Grandfather looked at him in disbelief. "Why are you doing that, it won't make any difference?" The boy said, "It does to this one!" He kept on going. His Grandfather helped!

Can you remain sensitive and bring about change in your school environment? This could be your challenge.

You may find some of these suggestions work for you:

- Talk to others about how violence affects you. You may find that many people don't like what's happening either.
- You can make a difference to the atmosphere in your school by ceasing to be the victim or being silent.
- Start **getting real** with others. Communicate and find people who feel as you do.
- Take action against people who are breeding aggression in your school.
- You can embrace each new day with an attitude of discovery and excitement.

Find others to support you and create a Change Agent Club.

Change Agent Club

Gather a few people together who are interested in making your school a better place. If you feel confident enough, you could look out for troubled kids. Offering support could help. Doing this as a group may make it easier.

- Decide on the aims of your Change Agent Club.
- Hold group meetings to share your feelings and support each other. Decide how often to meet.
- Make decisions about how you would like your school to be.
- Let those who can use some help know that as a group you are there for them –

  help people in the playground who are being bullied,
  befriend students who look sad, or are left out,
  support students going through change or stress.
  For example – divorce, death of a parent, addictive parents or illness.
- Create exam support groups to reduce stress and tension.
- Organise nurturing times together and perhaps after school events – talk with teachers and those in authority to bring about curriculum/social/political changes into your school.
- Invite your favourite teachers to occasionally attend your meetings to talk about their personal lives and share their wisdom.

Look out beyond your own position and help to take care of the wellbeing of others. You may find your group getting bigger and bigger.

Life can take on a different meaning for you if you do take care of yourself and others.

What can YOU do to make a difference?

TEENSPEAK

"Change the system! The system is uncaring, puts people down and scares some of us. It needs reworking. Don't just concentrate on academics." – Jenny (15)

"When I see people fighting I feel frustrated, powerless, annoyed and downright mad. Frustrated and powerless because there's not a lot I can do. That annoys me no end. Trying to talk to these people is usually pointless and using violence is lowering myself to their levels." – David (15)

"I get mad because when I see violence in the playground it is usually the result of somebody invading somebody else's space, mentally or physically." – Suzie (15)

"It makes me really mad and angry when I see other people fighting physically or verbally. When it happens there's not much I find I can do. I try! But usually they just attack me. I've tried different approaches but they don't usually want to know" – Paul (14)

"I have learned that an awareness of yourself and others opens the doors to many more opportunities. When you understand yourself you can understand others. Everyone needs support and friendship, no matter how strong they may seem." – Sam (15)

"I get really nervy about exams, get all shaky. Afraid I'm not going to pass." – Jason (14)

"We're not encouraged to cheat, but it seems like the only alternative. Sometimes I study really hard and I think, "I'm not going to pass anyway", so I write on my hands and cheat. Don't worry we're going to wash it off." – Trish (13)

"The only thing that exams do is show the authorities and employers that you can learn. Exams are pretty stressful. A lot of the time I feel overwhelmed." – Susan (14)

Dealing with STRESS

Don't sweat the small stuff. It's all small stuff!

There are many things about school life that create stress – put downs, relationships between students and teachers, assignments, exams, the big clock, unnatural structures and competition.

"We cannot deny that we live in a competitive world and each nation has the responsibility to provide its young with a high quality education which leaves them well equipped to confront the challenges of not only their individual lives but of the world at large. For we desperately need responsible, caring citizens whose vision extends beyond the confines of their individual and national concerns."
– THE EDUCATION OF THE CHILD, Rudolf Steiner.

Healthy competition is to compete against yourself. Can you strive to raise your own standards of achievement and not be concerned about being better than others?

Exams are stressful. Being fearful of failure creates stress. Don't take exams too seriously. Be aware to get regular exercise, eat healthy food and get enough sleep. Do things that are fun to balance yourself out. You don't have to succumb to the pressure. Relax as much as you can. There are activities throughout the book that offer ways to reduce stress. You can make choices that make it easier for you.

Chris did a two-week camp just before his High School Certificate exam. He learned how to relax, to be centred and to meditate. Less stress, relaxation, self-confidence are better ways and proved more successful. He went through his exams easily and surprised everyone by the high grades he got.

Sophia Mundi Steiner School, Year 11 Students.

About Teachers

Next to parenting, teaching is one of the most significant roles on the planet. Teachers are assisting young people to realise their potential.

Teachers are often dealing with pressure and enormous expectations from Head Teachers, educational authorities and from government directives. In some situations they have little respect from students, parents and sometimes from other teachers. Most teenagers have not considered that teachers are often as powerless as they are in the system. This can make it difficult for teachers to relate to students in ways they would like to. Because the environment in some schools is de-sensitising, some teachers and also students, at times become hardened in order to survive.

Some students and some teachers play control games to feel powerful. Students often rebel against the role a teacher takes, thereby missing the person behind the role. Sometimes there is no sensitivity for each other as human beings.

Speak up when others are abusive to teachers. This wastes their time and yours. The abuser gets attention and slows down the learning progress of the class. There is a cost to you in this. If this behaviour affects you, talk to the students who are being disruptive or the teacher involved. Speak up for yourself. The chances are that many of your classmates feel the same as you do.

"Getting at the teacher is the only way we have of getting back at the system." – Dustin (15)

By getting back at the teachers so that you can buck the system you miss the opportunity of gaining from their experience, knowledge and wisdom. Futile, no-win situations are not constructive. It's easy to criticise rather than appreciate the magnificent job many teachers do.

With the focus on learning, the 'them and us' battles in schools cease and rather than create separation all can come together for a common purpose where everyone wins.

When teachers are able to show that they care it makes a lot of difference in the lives of students. This interview with Shannon (14) expresses this:

"I'm getting a lot of recognition for my environmental achievement and a lot of support from one of the teachers, to do this. This makes it easier. I know what's happening. I've got support behind me. That gives me more confidence. I did the milk bottle thing – the blue plastic milk bottle tops were getting around bower birds' necks and strangling them. Lots were dying. With Barry's help we got the colour changed. He has helped me to excel."

My Story

I was told I was dumb and believed it. So I became an average student. When I realised I was intelligent I attended night school and did very well. I did teacher training as a mature-age student in England before moving to Australia. Learning to be a drama teacher was exciting and fun! It was different from working in offices from nine to five which I had been doing for the nine years before.

My teaching qualification has been invaluable to me. There have been times in the past when I could have been in dire straits without it. It has allowed me to assure parents that as a qualified teacher I am worthy of the care of their teenagers in the camps I offer. With a formal qualification I can almost always make a living.

It was the experience of Teacher Training College that led me on my Journey of personal growth.

While at College I discovered my love of teenagers.

I went to Silver Royd Secondary Modern High School for Girls. That's me second last on the right.

Seize the day!
Use your precious
time wisely!

YOUR PARENTS AND THE FAMILY

We all have parents; without them we wouldn't be here!

We are born helpless into this world. We depend on parents or carers to provide for our basic needs. To feed, bathe, change our nappies, hold, comfort and shelter us. Later on we need someone to wipe our noses, send us to school, make our packed lunches and teach us how to cross the road. Parents usually do the cooking, cleaning, shopping and washing.

They also nurture, care for and love us. There is plenty for parents to do even before thinking about what our emotional, mental and spiritual needs may be.

It is also parents' responsibility to provide their children with experiences that are educational and fun. They show and teach us ways to live. Parents can offer authority and wisdom. This makes us feel safe. They may bring other supportive adults and children into the life of the family to expand our sense of the world and our place in it. If they offer stability, we have a solid foundation on which to base our lives.

Parents provide us with an environment in which to grow, for better or worse. It is not the easiest job in the world.

Not everybody is cared for by biological parents. Grandparents, adoptive or foster parents, brothers or sisters may be major caregivers. Some children sit in front of television and that provides their main influence and source of comfort.

When you read this section change the word parents into carers if that is appropriate for you. Adapt what is said to fit your situation.

The ideal family situation is one in which children are fully nurtured and lovingly cared for. It is a place from which a young adult could leave having been affirmed, taken care of and loved in a way that enhanced her or his Essential Nature. That makes moving out to the world a natural and easy adventure.

About Parents

If your parents are loving and kind people who are helping you to grow into healthy adults, be grateful. They gave you life and helped you to grow into the person you are. Good parenting is one of the greatest contributions people can make to the World. It provides a good quality of life for children.

With such parents, children are likely to grow into mature adults who know how to communicate, love and live peaceful and fulfilling lives.

With loving parents, children experience and learn:

- a gentle authority,
- moral values,
- mutual respect and compassion,
- feeling loved and understood,
- positive attitudes towards themselves and life,
- how to be contributing members of a working unit,
- that they have something to offer their community and the World.

Ideally parents:

- provide positive role models,
- know how to take care of themselves,
- do their best to communicate openly and honestly with their children,
- are generally balanced and contented people,
- deal with the challenges of life in a mature way,
- are at peace with themselves.

Some people do not understand what their parental role and responsibilities are. They may not have been well parented themselves and so did not have appropriate role models to learn from. They make mistakes! Some are neglectful and others may be cold, cruel, hard, unavailable, disrespectful, abusive, violent, uncaring, distant, aggressive, hurtful, arrogant, hateful, unloving, demanding, unreasonable and unhelpful.

Some parents may not have the means or ability right now to show that they love you in loving and nurturing ways. More often than not, they do love you. But, sometimes parents do not love their children!

People don't have to be qualified to become parents. There is a lot of learning by trial and error going on. We are all here to learn.

A Message from Me

I have not had children myself. In the camps I run, I have been a replacement mother to other people's children for short periods of time. I am not an expert in parenting. My own relationship with my parents and working with teenagers for over twenty years is the experience I draw upon for writing this section.

Changes in Parenting

As you grow from a child into an adolescent the role and responsibility of your parents changes. Looking back to past generations, their role was immensely different. Our great-grandparents raised children to be seen and not heard – to speak only when spoken to. Children were whipped or beaten into place. This way of parenting was probably the way your grand-parents and perhaps some of your parents were raised. This is not what mostly happens today.

These days parents are generally more educated. Some are aware about choice, personal responsibility, being assertive and the power of positive thinking. Many parents know about different options in childrearing and can offer a broad experience to their children. Parents are out there on the edge, juggling careers, mortgages, hobbies and social lives. They are also dealing with issues that arise when their children become teenagers, like the dangers of drugs, alcohol, fast cars and over exposure to television and computers. It's especially challenging when teenagers resist their guidance. It's challenging for parents who wish to protect their children to see them exposed to people who don't care and could harm them. Some parents may be concerned about the effects of wars and terrorism on the emerging psyche of young people.

Our world is not always a safe place to grow up in.
But for many, it is!

Where there is righteousness in the heart, there is beauty in the character.
When there is beauty in the character, there is Harmony in the home,
Where there is Harmony in the home, there is order in the nation.
*When there is order in the nation, **there is PEACE in the World.***

– Sai Baba, an Indian Teacher.

The Gift of Life

Some of you have great parents. Others don't. Some parents may not be coping very well. Some may be sick and unable to take care of you. Others may have parents who have died and some of you may be adopted.

Whoever your parents are, from whatever country and in whatever circumstances, it is useful to understand that usually your parents are doing the best they can with what they know. Their education, upbringing, life situation and experiences all add or take away from the quality of parenting they offer you.

If your parents did not get their basic needs met as children and have not healed their own wounds, they may not give you the love and support necessary for you to grow. They may also be unable to provide you with positive role models. It is helpful to realise that parents are the products of all their experiences. Many children don't get their emotions or their Essential Nature acknowledged when parents have not experienced this themselves.

If you are willing to consider that you chose your parents on some level, you may no longer be a victim of circumstances that seem beyond your control. If your parents are cruel, hurtful and uncaring people, it is possible for you to move beyond external influences and find another way to live for yourself. It may be challenging and also take time, but it is worth it.

If you remain a victim of your family circumstances, it is unlikely that you can reach your own potential. You can take responsibility, learn your lessons and be on your way to a successful life.

Without adequate parenting you may feel isolated and be left wounded. You may relate to the world by manipulating, fighting, pleasing, competing, complaining or feeling like a victim. You may have difficulty embracing the whole of yourself. The pain of the wound, if unattended, leaves you unable to live life fully. If you are wounded, it is essential to take responsibility for your healing as soon as you can.

If you have been or are being abused by your parents, you can explore how your upbringing has affected you by working with the suggestions in this section and also see page 79 in Your Mind. You can also find people and organisations to support you so that you grow into an adult in your own right.

Whatever your present circumstances, the one thing you have in common with everyone else is that your parents gave you the gift of your life.

The question is... WHAT CAN YOU MAKE OF IT?

My sister Jan, Terry and their sons, Dylan, Ali and Brinley

The Importance of Mothers

Mothers are vitally important to their children. Nurturing children is essential for the wellbeing of everyone. There are many ways we can contribute to make this a better World – mothering is one of the most significant. It is hugely undervalued in our society.

The bond you have with your mother, if it is a healthy one, is one of the strongest you have in your whole life. Invisible strings connecting you to your mother are real and she can be the most powerful influence in early life.

Until recently it has been expected that women who can, should have babies. However, not every female is naturally a child rearer. To some women it comes easily and it is their greatest joy and fulfilment. Natural mothers are amazing to be around. It seems like they can handle anything and have boundless love and patience. Others may find the mothering role difficult and it does not suit their nature.

Having given birth, the commitment to that child's life lasts up to and beyond twenty years. If a woman chooses not to give birth then she is free to follow her own inclinations. It is wise to seriously consider the responsibility of bringing children into the world before becoming pregnant. For some females parenting is not their true calling.

In most species of the animal kingdom, females naturally do everything for their young. Interestingly enough many males disappear after fertilising the female. There are only a few who stick around. The Australian Emu is one example – he hatches the eggs. It's natural in the animal kingdom for females to nurture, nourish and protect their young.

There are many options for parents that take them away from what's natural these days. Careers, social events and the glamour of the world can lure some away from the home. This works for some families. For others it doesn't. If children are coming home from school to an empty house or are having to take care of themselves, this can be considered neglectful.

In the past, extended families with grandparents, aunts and uncles took care of children when parents were away from the home. So far a suitable parent substitute has not been found. Computers and television are not. Nannies, kindergartens and nursery schools are a poor substitute for a mother's love and nurturing in the first few years of life. The long-term effect of absent parents on their children is not yet fully known.

Mother love is the fuel that enables a normal human being to do the impossible

– Marion Garrety in CHICKEN SOUP FOR THE PARENT'S SOUL

Your Mother's Gift

The greatest gift your mother can give is the example of how to mother and nurture yourself. If she succeeds in teaching you how to take care of yourself, she no longer has to over mother you as you get older. She can then become your friend and guide during adolescence and beyond. This is only possible if you have been taught how to look after yourself. A mother can only pass these skills on to you if she is able to mother and nurture herself.

If your mother did not love and nurture you as a child, you may yearn for the mother love she didn't give you as you grew up. This may stop you flying free. Your challenge now is to re-establish trust in your own innate wisdom. What was not learned instinctively from your mother, you can learn for yourself.

When you were little if your mother did not:

- recognise your timing and rhythms, above her own at times,
- support your ability to trust yourself and your own instincts,
- help you make your own choices,
- teach you to mother yourself,

then she may be taking responsibility for you well past her use-by-date. This can stifle you if you are seeking freedom and independence. Smothering love when you are ready to become independent is damaging to you.

If your mother did:

- let you safely express your emotions and your interests,
- feed you when you were hungry, not when she thought you should be fed,
- listen to what you had to say,
- respect you as an individual,
- allow you to play freely and be spontaneous,

then she gave you a sense of wellbeing and confidence in yourself. This can provide you with a solid foundation for the rest of your life.

Imagine a mother bird clutching her offspring's wing in her beak, trying to stop it flying. The baby bird's flight from the nest enables it to feed itself. This marks the end of the mothering role. This kind of holding on does not happen in the natural kingdom but it happens for teenagers within our culture.

The greatest gift a mother can give her teenager is independence and freedom when the right time comes.

Letting Go!

Adolescence is a pulling away time. You have been little and your parents big. Now it's changing. Over the next few years you are becoming bigger and making your own decisions. Going your own way. This is natural. There may be a tug-of-war to begin with, especially with your mother or the person who has held that role. For much of your life until now, she has been protecting you and thinking for and about you. For some mothers, children have been their reason for living. This is not true in all cases. Some have maintained a sense of themselves as separate from their children during the child rearing years.

When you reach teenage years and are preparing to leave home some mothers tend to resist. What she feels for you makes her unwilling or afraid to let go. If you are not allowed to develop independence or make your own choices at the appropriate stage of development, you may stay dependent and immature. If your mother is fearful and lacks confidence or is out of balance in any way, perhaps you may be also.

Even if your mother's intentions are good, don't let her smother you or keep you in a child's role. This can be crippling and stop you from becoming responsible for yourself. Being responsible may mean you do your own washing, prepare meals for the family and help with household chores – **even when you don't feel like it.** When you are preparing to leave home, your parents could allow you to practise flying from the nest and to leave it at the right time.

Dear mommy,

I love you. Thank you for taking care of me. I'll always be your friend and daughter. – cajun

A MOTHER FOR MY POEM

Somehow
in Earthy becoming
i misrealised
the how was of it
and fighting gravity
strayed above ground

my earth Mother
safe and beckoning
could entice only
momently and then I made flight

Somehow we missed each other
oppositely headed
crossing in inconnected spirals
we lost each other

Time is an unnecessary happening
not a part of my reality
but nineteen starts and new
beginnings
have brought us full circle
both wiser and more knowledgeable
the last is the first step in rebecoming.

I worked with cajun (19) and her mother in South Africa. Their challenge was to find love for one another in spite of the difficulties they had always faced in their relationship. It had not been easy for cajun's mother to nurture her.

The Importance of Fathers

In the womb you have a connection with your mother. Your father is outside of you. A different kind of bonding and relationship is developed.

Gabrielle Roth in MAPS TO ECSTASY, suggests that your relationship with your father determines your relationship to the rest of the world.

If you are curious to see how true this is, look closely at your relationship with your father and see if that affects how you relate to others. You may be amazed at how powerful his influence has been.

A good father:

- offers protection, guidance and support,
- stays closely connected to you as you move through your changes,
- listens, is open, is willing to share and gives you his attention,
- assures you that your changing body and emotions are okay,
- teaches you how to relate to others and the world,
- encourages you to achieve, compete and perform,
- gives genuine praise for your achievements and celebrates them,
- shows you how to be in your heart with yourself and others,
- teaches you about and assists you around issues to do with money,
- lets you know that your emerging sexuality is natural and healthy.

Your relationship with your father determines whether you can be yourself and express your heart or whether you strive to achieve, perform, charm, seduce, compete, please, demand, negate or destroy – to feel recognised. Whatever you do to get daddy's attention and approval you may do in your relationships with others.

Parenting can be challenging for fathers. If they have been providing for the family, they have the daily stress of creating income. They may also be removed from the emotional environment of the home for most of the time. This can leave some children wondering where dad is and why they feel abandoned. More and more fathers are absent, either because they are at work or because they've left the family altogether. The long-term effect of this has a big impact on society.

To young males: It's particularly important that you spend time with your father and other men. Not only being spectators in something but also doing things together. To have physical contact, to be challenged and to test your strength allows you to find your limits and go beyond them. In this way your father feeds you in a vital and energetic way. Doing things together provides nourishment for you as you are growing up. This is as important as the milk of your mother was when you were a baby.

If your father is not around ask a close family friend or relative to step in for him in ways that support you.

A message to Dads: Never doubt how important you are in your child's/teenager's life. Even if you have been unavailable or unloving up until this point, it's never too late to offer your hand to your son or daughter. As young adults your children may understand what you have been going through more easily than when they were younger. You can talk together and repair broken bridges. As the adult you can help the healing. Are you willing to?

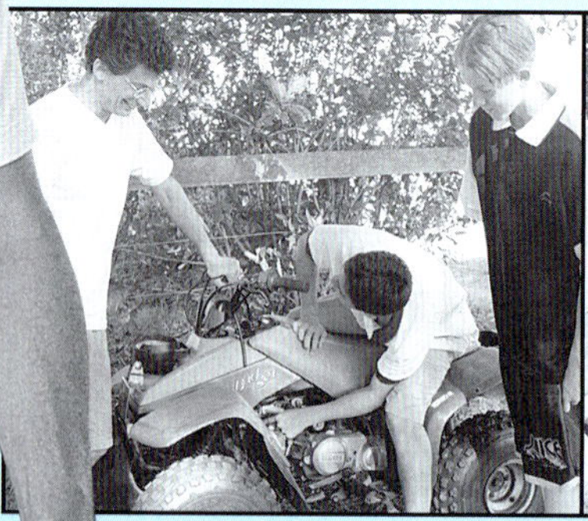

Do things together!

To young females: Your relationship to your father supports you to create healthy relationships with other men in your life. If treasured by your father you feel valued as a female.

"One theme I see is that I don't have a father who has been a part of my life. I've only recently been willing to have pain about that. Because of his absence, there was no father who could say, "I see you, you are my daughter." I am seeing that in my relationships with guys I have a feeling of not being recognised.

I am not standing as a victim because of this. It brings me to the questions that I need to be asking about men and women. So I am thankful for that as part of my biography and I know that's a big part of the questions and the work that I bring." – Rachel (16) USA.

It's never too late to change your relationship to your father. Adolescence gives you an opportunity to do that.

FATHER
Clare (14)

Father don't pretend to be so strong,
You've always been the one to rely on.
If you don't feel confident,
I'm willing to lend a hand.
If you can't do it, I promise I'll understand.
Don't hide your emotions,
Or suppress your fears.
Don't hold back laughter,
Especially don't hide tears.
I won't be the one to judge you,
Or make you feel ashamed.
We are all equal, our emotions feel the same.
If something is not right,
Please go ahead and speak,
I'll do the best that I can,
To help you find your feet.
Please tell me that you love me,
More often than not,
It will be weird at first, it will come as a shock.
But as the two of us get closer,
I know we'll be ok.
'Cos I really need a daddy,
Just like yesterday.

"I'd never had a strong relationship with my dad but I really, really yearned for one. This poem to my dad expresses how I was feeling. When he heard me reading my poem I knew he felt the way I did. Since then we've done heaps of stuff, sung a duet, we have long conversations in the car on the way home from piano lessons. I feel more relaxed around him now. He's not as angry. He's nice to me and I'm happier."

Fathers Leaving

It is hard for children and teenagers to accept that fathers have left them either physically or emotionally. Some teenagers have never known what their dad looks like. They look into the faces of men… wondering is this my dad? Everyone is affected differently when dads leave. It is vital that their dads stay in some kind of relationship with them.

Some Dads:

- become overwhelmed,
- don't realise what parenting is about before their children arrive,
- don't stick around long enough to take responsibility for their family,
- leave the family without a word and never contact their children again,
- muddle through, not quite knowing what to do or what's expected and do the best they can,
- take care of the physical requirements of their kids but not the emotional or spiritual,
- commit themselves fully to their family and give everything they can to ensure the wellbeing of their children.

A father, who has not grown up emotionally and is still behaving like a boy, can be a burden in a family. It can be like another dependent child to the mother who may be struggling to keep her head above the water.

It can be heartbreaking for men, when for many reasons, their wives kick them out. They can lose everything – care of their children, their home, the emotional support a relationship gives them. Men in this situation can easily feel displaced, abandoned and alone. Sometimes they can become depressed. If your father is in this situation and does not make contact, it may be because he is not dealing with his pain very well and may not be able to reach out and support you. Maybe, if you are ready, you could reach out to him. This could mean a lot to his sore heart.

In the current legal system, women almost automatically get custody of children when parents separate. This is painful for the men who have been loving and caring fathers.

"At school I was getting a lot of stuff from people who didn't understand that I wasn't the same as them. It was making me really sad and angry all the time. Then I started feeling the effects of my parents' divorce. I was missing the fun of having a dad for the first time in my life. It took a while but we talked about it. Now he knows what I've been going through. I also found out a lot about my father that I had not known before. Now I will do the same thing with my mother. Actually I was also annoyed at my father because I thought he had left me and mum out in the cold, but after talking to him I found that he really cared and tried. Talking is a great way to making you feel better about things." – Malcolm (14)

Everyone is Learning

Most parents are learning as they go, especially if you are their eldest child. You are also learning. Real, open and honest communication, whenever possible, can be a key to supporting your process of growing up and moving on. Often, people don't have the skills for dealing with the conflicts that may arise at this time. You are part of a family in which everything is changing because you are changing.

It's not useful to compare yourself to others or your parents to those of your friends. Everyone is different! Accept those changes and create as much flexibility as possible. You can only do the best you can and so can they!

The role of your parents is changing and there is adjusting to do on both sides. Whatever the relationship you have with them, the time comes for a gradual separation. As you become more of an individual this process accelerates, you then negotiate new ground rules. This usually ends in your complete independence from parents in your late teens or early twenties.

Sometimes parents don't feel ready to give you this independence. Letting you go brings major change into their lives. This can create difficulties for them.

Some people think that it's the teenager who is the problem when teenage/parent relationships break down during adolescence. This is not always the case. It may become impossible for you to communicate with your parents or they with you.

Many of you sail through this time and develop even stronger bonds. For others, the push for independence becomes a battle you **must** win.

In some cases, even as you rebel, you are holding onto the apron strings for safety. There is the pull to let go and the fear of doing so. This changes over time and the natural process ensures that you become independent at the right time for you.

Note: Be careful not to rebel for the sake of it. Going against parents' wishes or the boundaries they set, in order to assert your independence, can be self-defeating and at times destructive. Especially if you are also going against your own true Nature. If you don't connect to your own knowing, you can do things just to spite your parents. Watch this – it is reactive behaviour. It can harm your relationship not only with your parents but also with yourself. Rebelling for the sake of it helps no-one.

Most relationships between young people and their parents present challenges to both. Parents who unconditionally love and accept you, give you a foundation within yourself and somewhere safe to return to.

As you grow up, it helps if you:

- have opportunities to learn your own lessons,
- know when your behaviour is unacceptable to other people,
- feel cared for and loved even though your behaviour may not be approved of,
- have parental support and encouragement so that you can explore who you are and find your own limits,
- are given limits and boundaries to contain you, but which are flexible and give you a sense of your own power,
- allow your relationship with your parents to change. They are no longer the authority/expert, but could become more like a friend and consultant,
- have a safe place to recover from the hustle and bustle of adolescent experiences,
- learn about taking responsibility and being accountable for actions when your behaviour causes damage.

It helps to be constructive when there is change in your life. Do your best to understand your parents. Be as honest with them as you can and give them the benefit of the doubt whenever possible. No one is perfect. They are not, neither are you. Can you accept that?

Your Changing Body

When your body develops and your sexuality begins to emerge, your relationship with affectionate parents of the other gender may also change. It is possible that they are concerned about having a sexual response to your body. They may not know how to deal with sexual feelings towards their teenager. It can cause discomfort and is often not easily talked about in this culture.

Your parents may not readily make the transition from parent-of-child to parent-of-sexually attractive and gorgeous teenager very easily. This is not rejection. This is their way of honouring your changes and also showing you about boundaries, both theirs and yours.

If you are noticing awkwardness between you and your parents, talking about what is happening may save unnecessary discomfort and distance. Be courageous! Ask them to talk with you if they don't raise the issue. Let them know you are aware of this. Ask them to support you by talking about how it is for them and then listening to how it is for you. For some of your parents this may be challenging. It may be worth it and you may feel more connected to each other afterwards.

TEENSPEAK to parents

"There are some mistakes that you made when you were young, we won't always make them. It's important that you warn your kids about what's out there, then let them learn for themselves. They learn better that way." – Cassie (13)

"Try to understand where your kids are coming from. Don't overlook all the possibilities of what they are trying to say. Most parents speak harshly to their kids when they've done something wrong. If you speak softly to a kid, it gets through to them more than if you yell. They just rebel if you yell." – Kevin (13)

"Parents should treat this child/adult as a person unto him or herself. They shouldn't try to make them live like they do or think like they think. They should respect their ideas and values. If these seem unhealthy they shouldn't brow beat them to try and change them. You should be a loving parent who they can get along with and talk openly to. Parents could help them to learn and love themselves." – Jessica (19)

"Parents shouldn't feel that just because they are older and have children that they know everything. They shouldn't stop learning, because everyone has to keep on learning all their lives. They should just accept their mistakes and keep learning from them." – Leonie (16)

"Parents can let them work it out for themselves – even if it means learning the hard way. Give them independence. My parents are great. I think about how lucky I am. They talk to me if I need it but they let me work things out for myself. They are pretty laid back. They walk a bit on the wild side. If I need them I know they're there for me." – Alexander (16)

"Adolescence is a time of breaking boundaries and rules, of finding out what is possible, finding yourself. It is the end of childhood, the end of your most impressionable time. It is perhaps the most difficult time for parents. I know it was for mine. We gave them hell. I remember the constant push for my freedom but, unlike my friends, we were given almost complete freedom. 'Oh I wish I had your parents. They let you do anything. They're so-o-o-o cool.' But the funny thing was that I relished the very rare moments when mum would put her foot down. I wanted guidelines, rules and regulations, if not for anything else, but to disagree and break them." – Mia (18)

Note to parents: Boundaries and limits help make young people feel safe and loved. They rely on your stability and strength.

If Parents are Not There for You

There are many reasons why parents may be unavailable to you. Can you relate to any of the following examples? Is it possible that:

- your parents are insecure, unhappy people who have been hurt and have not resolved this? They may not have been able to grow up either as a child or a teenager.
- your parents are not mature adults? If they have low self-esteem, are poor communicators, are cut off emotionally or don't offer you affection or warmth. They may not be able to be there for you, physically, emotionally or in any other way.
- they are not educated about child rearing and don't understand what helps you to grow up because they may have missed out themselves?
- your parents have too many children and are too busy to give each of you enough attention?
- one or both or your parents are sick and therefore preoccupied with their own problems or illnesses? They may not have anything left to give, even though they love you.
- your parents are abusing you, are alcoholics or drug addicts?
- you have no parents? They may have abandoned you in some way. They may be in prison, in hospital, in a mental institution or have given up parenting you.
- you have been adopted? You may feel like you don't fit in or that your natural parents abandoned or rejected you. Most children who have been adopted feel loved. Some don't and some are abused. Note: By law you can now contact biological parents.
- your mother gave you up at birth? If she was a young mother she may have felt powerless to keep you, unsupported by her family and had nowhere to live. She may have believed she had no other choice.
- one or both of your parents have died? Not only do you have the loss of your parents to deal with, but also a lack of parent role models, support and love.

The above examples create challenges for you to grow yourself up. If you are unable to look after yourself you may be able to get outside help. You may find kind people who can become substitute parents for a time. You can seek support from grandparents, friends, teachers or neighbours. Look for caring people who can love you and give you guidance and support. If you are unable to get that kind of support do the best you can for yourself. You may find help from books, support groups or a school counsellor.

Don't give up! By doing the exercises in this book you can make a start. See if you can imagine yourself and situation in a bigger picture.

There really is no substitute for the love you can experience from a caring and kind adult who loves you.

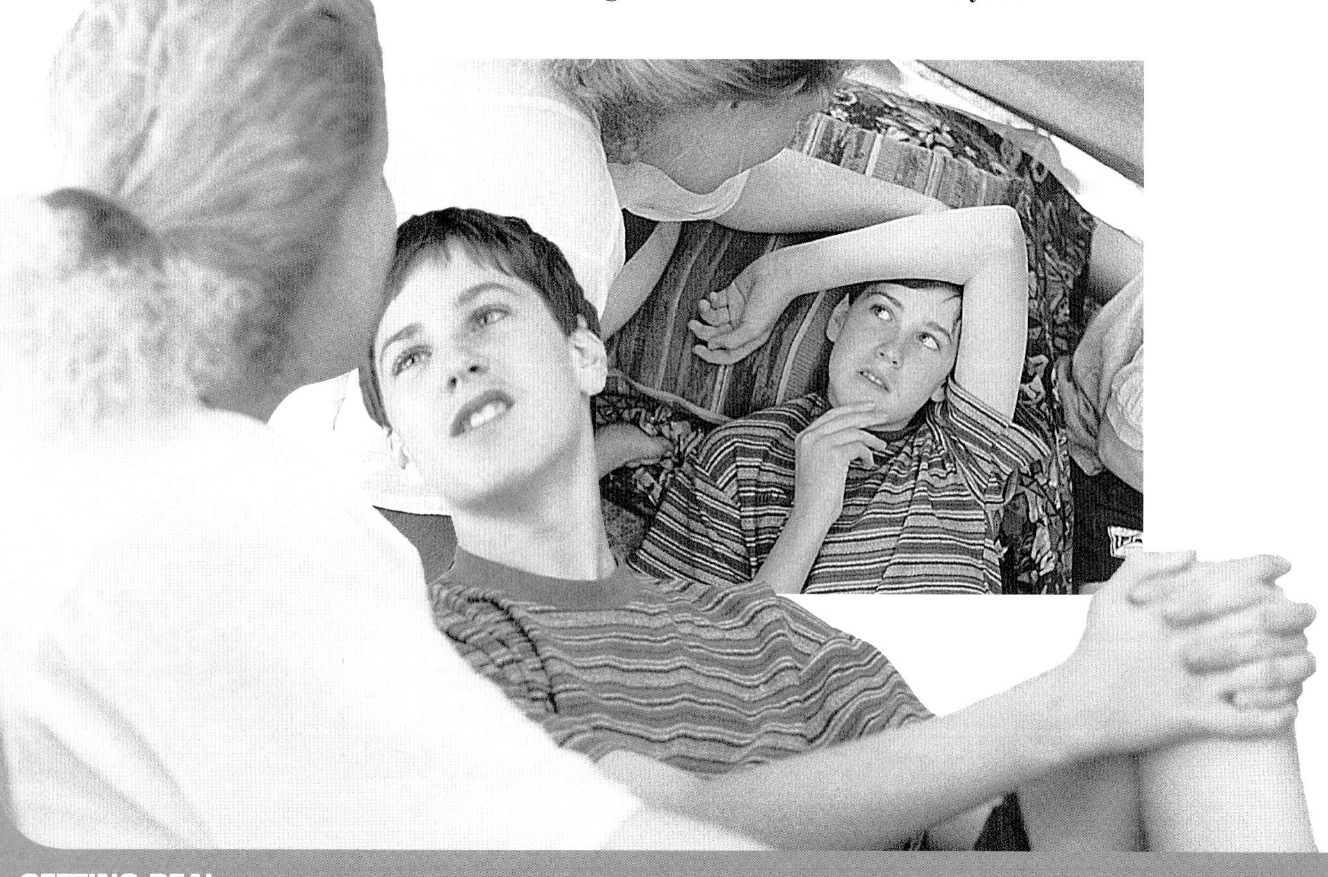

Shutting Down, Running Away or Being Kicked Out

One way some teenagers claim independence when parents do not freely give it, is to cut themselves off. They do this by either totally blocking emotional feelings or running away from home. Both can be dangerous. If there is absolutely nothing else you can do to improve the situation, see if you can find somewhere else to go BEFORE leaving home. Make running away, if you don't have a safe place to go, your last option. Try everything else first.

As you get a little older it may seem tempting to be out on your own. In the usual course of growing up, you leave home when you can take care of yourself financially and otherwise. It is not safe for young adolescents living on the streets. Not everyone in the world has good intentions. If you are alone on the streets you are vulnerable to the possibility of being misused. You may be tempted into situations that you don't have the skills to deal with.

Some street kids have left because of abusive and violent homes. Sometimes their behaviour became impossible for parents to deal with, so they were kicked out. Some young people are doing okay. Life on the streets suits them. Others become distressed, turn to drugs and become sexually promiscuous or hardened.

Home Atmosphere

The atmosphere in the home determines the wellbeing of the children who are raised there. Sensitive children may pick up what is going on for their parents psychically. Even when parents are not conscious that they have unresolved childhood hurts and issues, some children can sense it. When parents do not recognise their anxieties consciously or speak about their fears some children may take these on. Sometimes parents project their unconscious fears onto their children, as this example demonstrates: A woman visited me and I noticed she kept a night light on. She told me her child was afraid of the dark. I sensed that it was her fear about something that happened in her childhood. She was not conscious of this and projected her fear onto her child.

Parents often do this without being aware of it. They set out to protect their children or teenagers from their own unconscious fears. If they become aware of these projections, their children may no longer experience unexplainable fears.

A Reminder: When reading GETTING REAL... about growing up! if the language is difficult to understand with your mind, try getting the sense of it with your heart. If you don't know or understand the meaning of some words, look them up in a dictionary or ask someone who does.

OUR WHOLE LIVES

Amrita

What have we to base our lives on?
Nothing in the past we can Trust, it's gone.
No one around to understand our hurting.
We can't see adults with lives that are working.

Kicked out, on the streets, all alone.
Where's the foundation without a home?
Parents gone, no back-up or support.
What can I do? What have I got?
No one here to see the Truth.
No one around to give me a roof.
Confusion of heart, mind and soul.
HOW AM I GOING TO MAKE MYSELF WHOLE.

This poem was my way of sorting out feelings of despair after working with street kids.

Inherited Beliefs

You may by now understand that the way your family functions, has an effect, not only on the way you feel about yourself, but also on your beliefs about yourself and the world and how you live in it. You can look at some of these and change them around.

Many of the belief systems that have been handed down by your parents and your parents' parents may no longer work for you. However, you may keep them going because you remain unconscious of them. For many people it seems easier to go along with or not question their background. This maintains life as it has been because it is familiar and comfortable.

It is useful to take the time to look at the things you do and say. If you do this you can choose whether to continue living out your inherited behaviours or not. By encouraging your parents to talk about their childhood memories and finding out about their experiences and beliefs you gain further insight. Getting this information may require patience.

Taking Out the Weeds

Your parents and all the generations before them are the cultivating soil of your life. It's from them that you learn. If you are ready for life to be different, take a good look at the beliefs and behaviours that are no longer helpful. It's time to pull limiting beliefs out by the roots (sometimes painful) and to decide what to replace them with.

Do this weeding now. It's worth the effort. Instead of a big impenetrable mass of weeds in your mind you could be cultivating things that nurture or feed you, like fruit trees, vegetables, roses, lavender – a delight to your senses and herbs that heal you. It's a wonderful process – just like replanting your garden.

"My understanding of the way in which a child grows is that you create the garden, you don't grow the flower. You can merely fertilize the earth and keep it soft and moist and then the flower grows the best it can."

– Ram Dass.

THINGS TO DO!

Doing this process with the whole family can make real change possible. You can also do this exercise alone or with a friend.

Turn to a double page in your notebook.

- Think about the behaviours of your parents. You can also do this about your siblings, grandparents or others who brought you up, if they are a big influence in your life. Imagine that you can see them in front of you now. See them in different situations. Take a few minutes to do this.
- Write down on the left page of your book all the behaviour that you think is not helpful to inherit. If they eat or drink too much, smoke, worry and talk too much or are very angry. If they nag, complain all the time or are violent. Write it all down.
- Go about being a detective and keep observing them until you've got a long list.
- Ask yourself: Is this how I choose to behave? Yes or No! Write your answer against each point that you have made.
- Next, write down your preferred behaviour or attitude on the right-hand page of your book. Can you improve your own behaviour when you see more clearly what you are inheriting?

You can do the same exercise with verbal messages.

Verbal Messages

- Write down on the left page all the things your parents or significant others say about you that are not helpful to your health and sense of self. As you do this feel your feelings. Get as long a list as you can.

  For example:

  You're a silly thing.
  You can't do anything right.
  You'll send me to my grave.
  When will you ever learn?

- Write down what happens in your body when people say things like these to you. Do you feel hurt, angry or anything else?
- Allow yourself to feel them now.
- Write about or draw pictures or express these feelings. Blocked feelings can keep you stuck. When you express them, you are putting them outside of yourself rather than keeping them inside.
- Check out your self-talk. Go through your list and ask yourself, do I say these things to myself? Give yourself a score: 0-never, 5-sometimes, 10-always.
- Become aware of how much you have picked up from your parents.
- On the right-hand page change unhelpful messages into ones that support you.
- At this point look at what you have learned about yourself and your parents (or others).

To complete this process:
You can then choose to discuss it with the members of your family who are participating or your friend.

Become aware during the day when you give negative messages to yourself.
Watch for the things you have picked up from others.

Watch Out for What's Worth Keeping

Be careful in this process of clearing out. There might be a very valuable plant amongst all those weeds. Now is the time to look at your parents (or others) and discover what is really great about them.

They may be generous and giving people. They may laugh a lot and have fun. It could be any number of things. Your parents may have qualities that you are pleased to inherit. These are worth acknowledging and developing in yourself.

THINGS TO DO!

In your notebook

- Write down all the good qualities you like about your parents, siblings and grandparents.
- When you have done this check out:
  What would you like to keep as part of yourself?
  Is there anything to change?
- Write down these changes and focus on how it can be.
- What do you choose for yourself? Write a poem, a story or just a sentence or draw a picture about the person you intend to be as an adult.

What you focus on GROWS!

The different aspects of your life's experience, if tackled while you are moving through adolescence, can be like fast-forwarding tapes. You can erase what no longer helps you and re-record yourself and your story. Play some great music, dance along with the tune and **enjoy the ride.**

"This is my older brother"

Dealing with separation and divorce

Separation and divorce is usually difficult for everyone to deal with. For some children and teenagers it may seem like the worst thing that can happen.

When:

- a marriage relationship has totally broken down,
- parents have been fighting and arguing,
- there is violence and abuse,
- parents no longer have love for each other and there is no intimacy,
- the children are not safe,

then separation and divorce may be the best thing for everyone. It can make the home environment safer and calmer for those remaining in it.

TEENSPEAK

"My parents divorced when I was 14. Being in a family that was genuinely unhappy for three years was tense. My brother and me had to put up a front. It was hard. Dad had another woman. When he left it was easier. I see dad every three weeks for lunch and on special occasions.

Financially we were pretty stuffed. Mum hadn't worked in 20 years. She had to retrain and go back to nursing but didn't earn much. Mum has no one to talk to and is very lonely sometimes. She wants a partner badly. It's really hard on us. She's got menopause. Helping mum out with major issues gets pretty heavy at times. When we can, we do. I've got my own problems." – Luke (17)

If your parents separated when you were little you may have been powerless to do anything to change what was going on. It's possible to resolve the feelings now that you had then. If your parents' divorce is more recent, the hurt is closer to the surface. If dealt with immediately it can be healed more quickly.

What can you do when parents split up?

- Talk about it. Find people you trust who can help you deal with your feelings and thoughts about it if it's happening right now. Even if in the past, unresolved feelings can still be released.
- It was normal for you as a child or now as a teenager, to feel pain. You may also feel anger, frustration, loneliness, isolation or confusion. These are all appropriate responses to a situation that is out of your control.
- Sometimes children or teenagers blame themselves, believing that it's their fault. This is usually untrue. The separation is a decision that the adults have made. You are not responsible for their decisions. **Do not blame yourself.**
- When you feel ready and mature enough, talk with both of your parents separately about what has happened. Listen to both sides of the story. Let them know how you feel about what is going on or went on in the past. Be fair, don't blame, judge or take sides. If you look at the situation without making either of them wrong, it can help you to understand and accept.
- Explore both sides of the story, your mum's and dad's, either with a friend or by writing in your Journal. That may help you to be more objective about what happened.
- To gain clarity about what you wish to say, write in your Journal before approaching your parents. It may help.
- If it's difficult to communicate directly with your parents, talk it through with a friend or kind relative. Get support and feedback. If no one is around, talk to a pillow or a teddy bear. Imagine that it can talk back to you. It's amazing what you can get out of this – freed up emotions and clear thinking.
- Write, kick and scream about it. Role-play, dance and sing it – anything, so that it does not eat away at you or remain unfinished. A way to resolve it may be through forgiveness or by writing letters to your parents. Get it out of your system.
- As soon as you can, make peace in your heart about the situation.

The Past Influences the Future

The way you deal with your parents breaking up and in fact, your relationship with your mother and father generally, influences the way you relate with others, especially an intimate partner in later life.

This note from a young woman whose parents had recently split up demonstrates this:

"I read an article in a magazine about the work you do and how you help teenagers my age with the problems of losing a parent. I know that the situation with my mum and dad affects relationships that I have with other people because I've been noticing since I read the article how much I take out my anger or depression or confusion or whatever it is on my boyfriend."

When you have conflict and unresolved feelings about your parents, not just as a child but at any age, it can get in the way of your intimate relationships. Why is this? By leaving a situation unresolved you have unfinished business with it. Thoughts can remain in your subconscious mind and cause difficulties in your life. If you don't recognise their influence you may go through life living out your unresolved problems.

It could be different:

- by bringing awareness to emotionally difficult situations and issues,
- by having an intention to resolve them. Take appropriate measures to do that and you can have clearer intimate relationships.

Find a safe way to express your feelings and release the pain of your experience. Talk to others about how it is for them. Sharing with friends and having Heart Talks is great. See page 59 in Who Are You?

Many people are faced with unhappy relationships between parents or have parents who separate and divorce.

YOU ARE NOT ALONE!

Single Parent Families

When one parent leaves, either through separation or death and the other becomes the major caregiver to the children, it may at times be overwhelming for him or her. What used to be shared responsibilities now rest on one set of shoulders.

It may be that if you have younger brothers and sisters you take on the role of parent yourself. It is a way to support your remaining parent and to cope with the changes in your life. Be aware that if you are still a child you deserve a childhood. Your parent may be able to manage better than you believe.

If parents fight over custody of you, it may be because they are acting from the pain they feel inside. Don't take this battle personally. Don't blame yourself for what the adults in your life are doing. Disruptive living arrangements require flexibility. It may be that you spend some of the time living with each of your parents or they take it in turns living with you in the family home. That way YOU can be more stable.

Step Families

When a parent marries someone else, the family dynamic changes. It can become competitive. Children or teenagers, if insecure may reject the newcomer and hold on tightly to their biological parents. This might work for a time but it ultimately creates pain and tension for everyone. In this situation be aware that melding into a new family unit has its challenges. Going to war does not make it easier. Are you willing to be open to the good in the new partner your parent chooses? Can you help create a harmonious home for everyone?

These family situations affect many lives. There are books available covering this subject more completely.

A fun loving single mum and foster parent.

Death of a Parent

The death of a parent can be a shattering experience. As children you are naturally dependent on your relationships with your parents and sometimes grandparents. When people who are very close die, they disappear physically from your life. The love you have for them does not leave. They live on in your heart and memories.

"My mother got sick when I was twelve. She thought she had mumps. When she told us she had cancer, I said, Mum you could die of that. She told me she had leukaemia in the spinal chord and would become paralysed from her feet to her brain – then she'd die. She got better and then sick again. The worst time was in year nine. I was away at boarding school. I didn't know how bad she was – she was too weak to write. When I came home she was paralysed. That shocked me. I didn't go to school. I stayed up all night and looked after her. She asked for permission to die. The family said she could. Me and my sister were talking to mum and massaging her feet. Her eyes rolled back. We watched her die in bed. It was a big relief.

I'm scared that I am forgetting her. We were so young and she didn't get to see any of us grow up properly. Especially lately there are things I'd like to talk to her about, but I can't. I've been having a lot of dreams of her. I saw her and said, You're alive again. She said, Yes. It kind of sux!

She's there – I know she is. One day I drove past this cemetery and this song that she loved came on the radio. I turned it up and sat in the cemetery and listened to it. I talked to her then as if she was there and she talked back.

Everything seems to go my way and I think it's because she's there. My mum was very spiritual. I was taught to think that way and that's why I believe in it. A lot of people believe that once they die they are gone. That's unlucky for them I guess.

I pray to God every day…" – Dax (18)

Because we are spiritual beings we can communicate with each other on different levels, not just the physical. It is possible to have contact with a parent or anyone close who has died. Many people have spoken about the presence they feel around them, guiding and protecting them. When someone dies, imagine talking to him or her. By speaking from your heart you can heal the hurt and anything that is unfinished. This can be helpful.

Told to be Strong

Grieving is not something that is generally encouraged, even though it's a healthy thing to do. In some cultures there are rituals that send the souls of the dead off on their Journey. Some people believe if they smile when they remember their loved ones rather than feel sad, it helps their spirit to move on from the Earth more easily.

Some children and teenagers are not given the chance to grieve. Their worlds may be turned upside down. They are told by relatives to be strong and to look after the remaining parent. If this parent is emotionally unstable and not coping with the loss, he or she may develop a thick layer of protection or put a tight lid on everything to hold it in.

Your parent may pretend to be strong and hide his or her true feelings, thinking that it's better for you. He or she may believe you can't handle these feelings and may try to protect you. Teenagers who feel isolated from the remaining parent have no parent left at all. When you stay out of the way of the parent who is left, everyone is silently suffering confusion, isolation and pain – alone. No one reaches out.

Relatives and friends sometimes withdraw when someone dies. This may be because they feel uncomfortable and don't know how to relate to those who are left. It's a time when you could do with their help most. But it can be challenging for people to be there for you. When you can, reach out by allowing them to see how you feel. It may give those who love you the best chance to comfort you. If you are able to do this it may help them connect to how they are feeling. Grieving is something that can be shared. Healing happens when feelings are expressed and released.

Healthy grieving is important!

Healing the Hurt

If you have lost a parent, a sister, brother or someone you dearly love, give yourself the time it takes to grieve. Do as much as you can to keep your communication open with the parent who is left. If that's not possible or you lose both parents, find people you trust. Ask them to be there for you, to hold you and let your feelings bubble up. Allow yourself to feel and express them as much as you can.

You may feel:

- sad that you can no longer share your life with the person who has gone,
- guilty if you treated him or her badly,
- sorry if you did not tell him or her of your love,
- regret not saying goodbye and wish you had said the things you left unsaid,
- lonely, guilty, helpless or self pity.

The more crying, sobbing, breathing, screaming or anger release you can achieve the better. Yes, anger too. Many of you may be angry that this person has died leaving you alone. It's normal. It's better to get it out of your system than to let it eat away at you. Be careful not to get caught up in your emotions beyond releasing the pain. If you find it difficult to do this alone, talk to a caring adult or see a counsellor. Don't be desperately unhappy. Ask for and allow people to support you.

If you cannot find anyone who can be with you when your feelings come up, you can write them down in your Journal. You can do this as a poem. Give yourself plenty of time and have tissues handy.

My Story

My father died at 47 just after my 21st birthday. He died of hypertension (high blood pressure) and a brain tumour. His life had been unhappy and lonely. My sister and I sat with him in hospital as he fought to keep his body alive. Breathing heavily he used all his energy, until all that was left was a thin layer of skin and bones.

Grieving for my father was short-lived. I squashed it down. It took me years before I dealt with the grief. Mourning at the time could have made it easier – before the feelings became so deeply buried. Just before my father died he couldn't speak. There were many things left unspoken.

Years later in a workshop I had a sense of communicating with him. We talked. He told me that he had always loved me even though he didn't show it. Also that he was really proud of what I was doing with my life. That was great for me to know.

MISSING YOU
Lisa (13)

I think about you all the time,
I miss you so much.
Years have passed but I'll never
be able to forget about you.

You'll always be in my memories.
I hurt so bad when you left me.
I didn't have anything to hold on to,
I just kept thinking of you.
At least you know I'll never forget you,
I'll try to remember the good times
And not the bad ones.
All you have to do is remember

I LOVE YOU FOREVER.

Dedicated to my mother.
She passed away when I was little.

THE FAMILY

You may be aware by now of the great benefits of belonging to a happy and healthy family. If you have mature parents as your guides, you have had a good start! Your life has been blessed. As you read on you may discover that others have not been as fortunate as you have. Knowing about the dynamics in families broadens your outlook about what life is like for others. This may help you to be more supportive of your friends and those less fortunate than you.

Dysfunctional Families

There are families that are not working very well. There are varying degrees of dysfunction – emotional, mental, physical, economic and/or spiritual. Here, basic needs of love, protection, nurturing and respect may not be met. In extremely dysfunctional families it is unlikely that people are connected to their Essential Nature.

For some children and teenagers life is a nightmare. If your family is not providing you with a safe or loving place to live, it may be left up to you to take care of yourself. You can learn to do this. You can discover ways to make it different.

It is possible to thrive in later life no matter what kind of childhood you had.

A lot happens in families that outsiders do not get to find out about. A lot of attention goes into making everything appear normal. This can be distressing for a child or a teenager who is aware of the lie that is being presented to the outside world. The kids know what goes on behind closed doors, but perhaps have no way to reveal it. Sometimes neighbours don't even know that anything is wrong, even when they suspect someone is being mis-treated, they may be reluctant to interfere.

The legal system offers some protection and more adults are taking responsibility and protecting children and teenagers these days so they can live in a safer World.

As a teenager you are the foundation of tomorrow's World.

No matter what your situation is, you can make things better for yourself and for all children and their children's children.

You can help break the cycle of dysfunction in the family.

My Story

My family did not function very well in some ways. Except for a short time after my father left when I was four, I was taken care of materially. There was so much going on that I closed down. Emotionally, it felt like I'd died. I didn't know how else to deal with life. My mother was in major distress and poverty.

After that time we always had enough food to eat and Mum made our clothes. But there were six children and she worked at night to bring in extra cash. My mother was often emotionally upset. As much as she loved all of us, she didn't express her love in ways that made me feel loved. Baking cakes and keeping the house clean and tidy did not give me the kind of reassurance, affection and emotional stability that allowed me to feel her love. The emphasis seemed to be that everything looked good to her and the outside world.

I lived in fear of anger and abuse in my family. As a consequence I made myself small – becoming as invisible as possible. I was afraid to stand up for myself. No one knew what was happening in the home. When my dad visited, he did not consciously recognise my distress or that of my sister and did nothing to protect us.

As it was, I didn't feel support for my emotional self. Intellectually I was not stimulated. There were no basic religious beliefs that I can remember and no spiritual awareness. This resulted in a severe sense of isolation for me. If there had been someone to explain how my upbringing affected me or there had been a book like this one when I was a teenager, I could have taken care of myself better and grown up more quickly.

In order to heal my childhood wounds I have attended personal development courses, meditation retreats, workshops, therapy groups and rebirthing residentials. I have read hundreds of books about personal growth and spirituality. I am whole to a greater degree than ever before.

A Special Family

James, Bronte and daughters Cassie (14) and Morgan (10).

James and Bronte have attended personal development courses for fifteen years and are caring parents. I am amazed at how much of what they have learned they pass on to their daughters. I admire the way James treats them. He is the best father I have ever seen.

James speaks, "My role as a father has changed over the life cycles of my daughters. In the first six months it felt like I didn't do anything. I used to say to my wife, "When is 'it' going to do something?" She used to make up a bottle so that I could feed my daughter and feel like I was doing something. As they grew, I coached my daughters in the physical education sense. By throwing, catching ball and if they had running or swimming events at school, I supported them to do well.

With Cassie, I've noticed myself pulling back, so that I don't smother her. As a young woman, there are some things we don't do now. Like her sitting on my lap. We don't have the same degree of physical contact. It doesn't feel right to snuggle up in bed, telling her a bedtime story, like I do with her ten year-old sister. She can't have the same relationship with me that she could have with a boyfriend. As a young woman I respect her space. When she is dressed we hug and kiss. When she isn't, we don't. It's not that I'm rejecting her. It's just that I acknowledge that she is growing into a woman and the boundaries between us are different. It's a privacy issue. I don't go into her room now without knocking.

Another role I play with Cassie is that I give her information. I'm in the world of work and I bring the outside world back into her life. I also offer early career guidance and talk to her about her options, like helping her to decide on her school subjects. Rather than disciplining and punishing her for not doing homework, I sit and help her do it. It's hard for me to do this. It takes time and a lot of patience. I'm there for her as a teacher and to help her figure things out. She couldn't work something out once and said she was stupid. I came down on this hard. I fiercely defend her sense of self-esteem and protect her against her own negative self-talk. I stick up for her.

I let my daughters know that not all people are going to make sure their lives work out perfectly. As their parents we do all that we can to make sure that everything works well for them. Other people probably won't do that. Especially boys, they are going for it and making their own lives okay. Other people won't have the same priorities that we do as parents. That is one of the ways I attempt to give my daughters a sense of reality. Another is I instill in both my children that their feelings and responses in their relationships and to the world are their responsibility. Their feelings and happiness are their choice."

Cassie and Morgan's mum, Bronte says, "My role is different. I'm the health manager. I take care of diet and other basic needs. I make sure they are getting enough exercise and sleep. I look after their social requirements – taking them to friends' houses or to the classes they take outside of school. I place and control the boundaries around the amount of time they watch television and are on the Internet. My role is to educate and prepare my oldest daughter, who is fourteen, for anything she is facing in her life. When she has difficulties in her relationships with friends, I encourage her to step into their shoes and see from their perspective. My job is to love her as much as I can even when I'm pissed off with her. I support her to be trustworthy."

Cassie speaks, "Mum is a role model for me. I watch her make mistakes and try not to make the mistakes she does. Mum gets very angry and she has the same temper as I do. I see her lose her cool and try not to do it myself. From my mum I want support and for her to understand me. I like mum to do things with me, like horse riding and shopping. I want dad to help me make decisions, protect me and keep me safe."

Identify your Family Type

Here are some examples of families that are not healthy for those living in them. It may be that they are at war with each other or that they are denying emotions that are under the surface. Some families are extremely violent. Others are cold and emotionless. By reading about different family environments you may recognise where yours is or is not working for you. With awareness you can take better care of yourself.

Happy Face Families

This is where everyone pretends that all is well, but it's not. There are smiling faces. People may call you dear and love, but there is no warmth or feeling of real love in the atmosphere. Sometimes in this situation children feel confused because they recognise the lie. There is no basis for getting real.

People in happy-face families are often too afraid to speak about what is really going on, to make waves or stand up for what they believe in. They are often afraid to face up to the falseness of their lives. They have lost connection with themselves.

What can you do?

- You can practise with your friends by being honest about your feeling and thoughts. Then try it with your family. As much as you can, GET REAL!
- You can challenge the status quo by not going along with false smiles and behaviour. When you feel confident enough you can speak up about the situation and tell family members how it feels for you. Tread warily. Only if you can be honest and vulnerable and express your real feelings can you touch another.
- If you try but fail to communicate with a family member, make sure you have a friend you can turn to for support. In this way you may not be left with unresolved feelings inside.

Battlefield Families

This is where everyone lets fly at everyone most of the time. The atmosphere is always charged with bombs going off or heavy artillery firing. There is anger, aggression and violence. The children either join in the fighting or make themselves invisible to avoid being hit. No one wins. The aggressor is usually not happy but doesn't know any other way to behave. It's hard to stay sensitive. Feelings are numbed in order to survive.

If you live in this family you may become a tough little fighter. If you lose against the adults, you may wage war with others your own age or younger to express your frustration. You still don't win – you don't make friends doing this. You may become disheartened. Maybe you can no longer love and so don't get the love, caring and acceptance that you deserve.

What can you do?

- Whenever there are arguments, ask yourself, "Does it help the situation when I get involved in fights or does it make it worse?"
- If you disappear yourself, could you stand up for yourself more? Can you feel big enough to show how hurt you feel? This might show the violent person what he or she is doing to you. You may have good reasons to feel too scared to do anything. And that's okay.
- Find someone to talk to about what is happening. See if there is an adult who can talk to your parents or protect you in some way. Find friends who can help you gain confidence in yourself.
- It may be useful to get professional help. Sometimes a school counsellor is the first step.
- Find a safe place where you can soften your heart. Talk to an animal, a flower or tree. Hug yourself lots.

Sexually Abusive Families

Sexual abuse within families is common. If you have been or are being sexually abused, read all of the section on Sexual Abuse from page 163 later in the book.

The Put Down Family

No one can do anything right. Everything that everyone does in this family is not good enough for the person who is putting others down. The atmosphere is uncomfortable. Everyone's energy droops and they walk on eggshells, afraid to do anything for fear of being punished or ridiculed for it.

When you live with people who put others down it's probably that they don't like or feel good about themselves. This could be true of the put down people in your home too. Check it out for yourself. Do they like themselves?

If you have been put down at home you might not feel good about yourself. You may be putting others down so you can falsely put yourself up. This does not allow healthy relationships and ultimately you keep hurting yourself.

What can you do in this situation?

- Talk to other family members about how they are dealing with what's going on. Discuss ways together to handle whoever is bringing your family down.
- Find out how your parents were treated by their parents. This may give you some clues.
- Give praise to members of your family and friends.
- Be aware when you do get it right. Write lists of things that you do well. Fill yourself up with the good that you are. Reprogram your mind with positive thoughts.
- Avoid comparing, measuring or judging yourself around others. If you notice yourself doing this, balance it by complimenting yourself.

Power Struggling Families

Power struggles in families can create an unhealthy atmosphere where no one can really grow. Usually one person dominates and has to prove he or she is right. Individual thoughts and ideas are not valued. By living in a competitive family you are brought up to believe there have to be winners and losers. Family members can become self-centred and uncaring, not showing affection and love to others. It doesn't have to be this way. You are who you are, doing the best you can. If you accept that and appreciate others, you create more harmony in your life.

What can you do in this situation?

- Refuse to play the power games.
- Become an observer and don't get too involved in the drama.
- Learn new communication skills. When you have enough confidence in yourself, express yourself and your feelings clearly to the power seeker.
- Stand up for yourself and others when you or they are being badly treated.
- Name their game! Expose what they are doing.

When you change on the inside, your world reflects that back to you.

Alcohol and Drug Addicted Families

Being raised in a family where parents are taking drugs or drinking excessively can leave the children in turbulence. Addicted parents are usually unstable. One minute they may be happy and loving and the next – violent and abusive. As a child in this situation you never know what's going to happen next. You may not be able to relax, especially if either parent is aggressive or violent towards you or your brothers and sisters. Living in this kind of environment could cause deep-seated insecurity. You may never be sure where you stand with people or accurately judge them or situations.

What can you do?

- Find a grandparent, neighbour or school counsellor – someone you trust and let him or her know what's going on. If it gets violent at home and there is somewhere you feel safe, go there if you can.
- If you are in any danger and you may be just by being there, if you are threatened or harmed, get help immediately. If the situation is extreme, see if there's anywhere else you can live.You don't have to follow in your parents' footsteps. You can make your life work for you.
- Find out about Alcoholics Anonymous – an organisation that offers support groups. AlaTeens is for teenagers with alcoholic or drug addicted parents. This is a worldwide organisation. Look in your local telephone directory or ask your school counsellor. Check on the web: www.alcoholics-anonymous.org

Violence in Families

Any violence in families makes children and teenagers insecure. The long-term effects of abuse, when not attended to, can be severely damaging. Sometimes if you are abused as a young child the memories go into your subconscious mind. This is a way your mind protects you so that you survive the trauma at the time. The memories may resurface into your conscious mind when you are ready and more able to deal with them.

Some people never remember traumatic events but their behaviour patterns reveal they have been abused as a child. These develop as a means of dealing with the stress or as a protection against similar events later in life. If you have experienced violence as a child, it may be difficult for you to feel safe anywhere.

There are often **reasons** for things to be the way they are. But there are **no excuses** for any abuse.

Important: If a family is physically, emotionally or sexually abusive, then removing children or teenagers may be appropriate. This is not always an easy choice. It is wrong to hurt anyone. It is time to stop ignoring family abuse. But until society changes, abuse is a fact of life. See your local telephone directory under: Kids Help Lines, Child Abuse Prevention Services, Child and Family Services, Lifeline or the Police to find the best agency. Check the web.

One day soon you will be leaving home. Do what you can to take care of yourself now! Trust your Essential Nature or God to get you through.

You are lovable. It's not your fault if your parents don't love you in the ways that make you feel loved. Most parents do love their children but some don't know how to show it. They haven't learnt how! It's hard for them too.

Check out your friends' homes and people in your neighbourhood. If there are stable families, see if you can spend time with them. That way you can experience how people live together in a healthy way.

Describe your Family

If none of the family types describes your family, write about how it is for you so that you can understand the influences in your life. Through observation you can become clear about your family dynamics. Look for repeating patterns. What are you learning? Check it out! Write about ways you can take care of yourself.

The miracle of Love can heal everything!

Forgiveness, a Key for Releasing

We live in a world where some adults are not doing a very good job. Some of their actions, which are damaging to children or teenagers, seem unforgivable. Mature adults are the guides, guardians, providers for and protectors of children.

If the adults around you haven't taken care of you and you feel hurt, resentment, hate, anger or other painful feelings, do something about how you feel. If you don't, you may be further hurting yourself. It is possible to heal the hurt, damage or wounds you have received in the past. With the help of others and through your own process of healing, you can learn to put past hurts behind you. One way is by forgiving those who have hurt you. Forgiveness does not mean that it is okay that they hurt you or that you are opening yourself up to more hurt.

It's possible to live in an atmosphere that is unsupportive and still be okay. By forgiving, you may be able to release the past and let it go. Forgiveness frees you from its harmful influences. It may take time and assistance. But holding on to hatred, anger and resentment creates illness and disease. It is often the person who holds on to these emotions who gets sick. Harmful thought patterns act against the thinker and don't always hurt the person they are directed towards.

Focus on helping yourself first. If you attempt to help the whole family you may fail. Looking at your own attitude and behaviour can maintain your balance and keep you healthy inside. Forgiveness is something that is helpful in all aspects of your life. It is not only restricted to your family.

THINGS TO DO!

How to Forgive

Work on a double page in your notebook.

- Write down who and what you forgive. This can be about parents, a girl or boyfriend, a teacher or anyone else. It could be something like this:

  Mum I forgive you for telling me I'm useless.

  Dad I forgive you for leaving when I was little.

  Dad I forgive you for expecting too much of me.

  Mum I forgive you for not loving me enough.

- Work on one statement at a time. Write that statement over and over again with a response and watch how it changes. For example: Dad...

Statement:	**Response:**
I forgive you for leaving.	Why did you have to go?
I forgive you for leaving.	I missed you.
I forgive you for leaving.	It was selfish of you.
I forgive you for leaving.	I hate you for going.
I forgive you for leaving.	Why didn't you love me?
I forgive you for leaving.	I love you

- Keep writing until you feel no more emotional charge and your responses become positive or you feel a sense of relief.

To take this process further:

- Write a letter expressing how you feel. If you feel angry or hurt, write about it. If you don't find love in your heart, let them know what is going on for you. Keep working on it until you feel lighter and at peace. Don't send the letter unless it feels right or until you are ready to face the response you get.
- Make a list of what you appreciate about them. In some situations there may be little to appreciate.
- When you are ready, write a letter and let them know how much you love them, if this is true for you. It's your choice if you give them the letter.

By staying with the process of forgiveness you may come to a place in your heart where you can face them. You may be confident enough to speak about what has been happening and what is now true for you. You may also be able to tell them you love them. Working like this frees you up and clears your mind.

Helping your Family Reconnect

If you have been living in a fragmented family it takes time to repair the damage. It certainly takes courage. It requires you or another member of the family to be willing to do it differently and change the whole dynamic. It only takes one person – that person could be you! By following the suggestions in GETTING REAL… about growing up! you begin that process.

If possible, make friends with your family. It is one of the best things you can do. Your family can provide ongoing learning and long-term connections.

Here are a few other ways that may help bridge the gap and re-knit your family in a loving way.

- Eat a meal together at least three times a week – without TV. During your meal, share the best things about your day. Then tell each family member something you appreciate about him or her.
- Find ways to talk to one another and listen to each other. It may be uncomfortable at first.
- Plan outings together. Allow everyone in the family an equal opportunity to choose and plan the activity – take it in turns. Make it fun!
- Learn to be more intimate with each other. Touching smiling and being understanding.
- If the family finds it too difficult to make changes without help, see a family counsellor.

Make peace with your parents.

If it's difficult to do this together, work on yourself and your part in it.

If you do, it can support all of your other intimate relationships.

Write your Story

The best outcome from any family situation is that you learn what you are there to learn! With awareness you may be able to free yourself from the patterns and behaviours you have taken on. When you recognise them and take steps to change habitual responses you are on track to connecting to your Essential Nature and your life's destiny.

Find out about significant events that have happened in your family. Go back in time and become a detective.

THINGS TO DO!

In your notebook:

- Write about what happened when you were conceived and about your own birth if your parents are open to talking about it.
- Record important events in your family.

  When brothers and sisters were born, how did their arrival affect you and the family?
  Major house or geographical moves.
  Career changes for either of your parents.
  Close family members dying.
  Any major events – traumas, accidents, sickness or inheritances.
- Record any personal successes like becoming a school captain, winning a swimming competition or meeting a new friend. Include anything really great that has happened so far in your life.

You can take a look at what you have learned while growing up and reassess it. Discover what value there is in the lessons and appreciate what is worthwhile. If this is painful for you, talk to a friend or find professional help.

Now, you could:

- draw or paint a picture,
- make a collage. Include photographs and items like awards, certificates or cloth from a favourite item of clothing,
- look at your creation to appreciate the Journey of your life so far. Be forgiving about the dramas.

Be gentle with yourself and others.

Your story so far has made you into who you are. Can you be thankful for that?

Celebrate your unique gifts!

Your Ideal Family

It can be useful to dream up new pictures of the way you would like it to be. You can do this for the family you may have one day.

- Do you have fun together?
- Is everyone allowed to safely express emotion?
- Are each individual's opinions accepted?
- Are you able to communicate clearly, honestly and in depth with each other?
- Can the family be open and caring with each other, clearing the air often?
- Are the children a priority in your ideal family?
- Do you have an intimate and mature relationship with your partner?
- Are family members respected as individuals?
- Does your family have balanced contact between other caring adults and relatives – an extended family?
- Are values and morals talked about and re-evaluated?
- Do your children feel independent and yet supported, guided and appreciated?
- Do people enjoy spending time with your family?
- Is there an atmosphere of peace and harmony pervading your home?
- Have you created an ordered and beautiful home?

Your list could go on. Dream up your ideal family. **Write about it or draw pictures.**

There is a lot to explore in this section. Unravelling the influences of the past and freeing yourself allows you to be more of who you really are. GETTING REAL…about growing up! offers life-giving alternatives. It's time to walk a different road and use new maps. **Live your dream!**

Miracles happen!

A PART OF LIFE

Tina (14)

The breeze through the trees,
And the rustle of the leaves.
The rivers overflowing,
And is it really snowing?
Learning to love.
We learn to sing,
We learn to open our hearts so
gradually
And our love to bring.

Like a thread through a needle,
That you sew broken hearts.
And the music that surrounds us,
It's a part of life.
Like the love that comes between a
husband and a wife,
The children crying in the background.
It's a part, yeh! A part of life.
It's a part of life. It's a part of life.

Some people live in extended family groups.

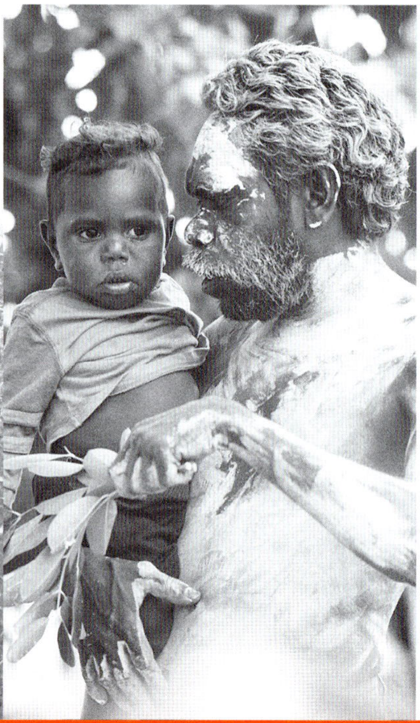

GENDER
Male and Female Differences

The issues surrounding gender – maleness and femaleness are complex. Only a part of the whole can be glimpsed here. With awareness of gender differences you can appreciate and get to know each other anew. If you are interested in gender, you can explore it further through reading and in discussion groups. There is much to be gained by understanding the issues. With awareness, there is a possibility of living in a harmonious World.

What is Gender?

Sociologists convinced me in the 70's that gender differences are a result of conditioning – the way we are brought up. That boys and girls are treated differently. If we weren't, the theory states, we would behave the same and have similar characteristics. Since working with hundreds of young people, I disagree! This perspective seems way off the mark. Males and females are **undoubtedly** different!

Young males are naturally competitive. When they arrive in a new social situation there is often immediate manoeuvring, sometimes subtle, sometimes not. They establish who is the top dog. This is done quickly. Later, the dynamic may change but it is a ritual for them on arrival. They also tumble play and are sometimes rough with each other. In fact, this is an easy way to relate for teenage males – more so than verbally. There is a lot of acting out, being cool. This behaviour could very well be self-protective. Sometimes bullying occurs and for many, this is painful. Sensitive teenagers often don't dare to be themselves. This can cause identity confusion. Those who are the toughest on the outside are often the softest on the inside, so they may create protective masks.

Young females enter new environments differently. They hang back – checking the place out and everyone in it. Some may exhibit nervousness and uncertainty to begin with but they are alert. They assess who may be a potential friend and somehow contact is made. They giggle and chat about this and that and before long are the best of friends. Friendship groups are formed quickly and members become inseparable.

Young males are often excluded and are sometimes frustrated by this. Most can't compete with the verbal and relational skills that many females have.

These are obviously stereotypical behaviours of males and females. There are many more – and then our unique differences to be taken into account. There are individuals who dare to defy stereotypes. They are just who they are and don't follow the usual patterns of behaviour.

Going Back in Time

Activate your imagination for a Journey back in time:

Once upon a time, a long, long time ago in a land of wildness where natural forces determined much about life, animals roamed freely and people lived together as a tribe.

Imagine yourself there now and see the cave where you sleep. There is a central fireplace and the people lying on the ground around you are covered in skins. Babies nestle at their mother's breasts. Men snore after a hard day's hunting.

In your dreaming you sense big beasts, wolves, leopards and lions prowling outside. They have their dens and usually leave your cave alone.

As a boy you awaken with the trickling light of dawn as it gently touches your face. You stir sleepily. You become aware of the men as they move quietly towards the opening of the cave. They are preparing for the day's hunt.

It is their job to roam the wilderness, seeking out prey on which the tribe survives. Winter is coming and the people gather food to see them through. They store dried meats, seeds and roots wrapped in skins.

Without speaking to each other, through silent action the men move as one. Some days they walk for miles before coming across game. Today they are lucky. After only a couple of hours they come across a herd of deer close to a water hole. They take positions for the kill. As a young one you know to stay near your father. Watching closely you sense him one-pointedly focussed, spear in hand, ready. Finding positions encircling the animals, the men move forward. You stay where you are. The deer, alert, know there is something wrong. The men now make a noise to frighten them. Spooked, they bolt, leaving one animal trapped. Not knowing which way to run it suddenly scampers in your direction. Your father lifts his spear and with full force hurls it through the air, aiming for the heart. It lands on target and the animal falls.

The men gather around the catch, watching its life's blood soak into the Earth. They give thanks to all of creation for the food it provides. After dismembering the carcass they leave some of the meat as an offering to other animals. You, your father and a couple of men take the rest back to the cave. The others go for another kill, so that extra meat can be stored. On your return the cave is empty except for the woman who is with child.

There is danger in the hunt. The men provide meat for everyone and have developed skills to do this. With one-pointed focus they have the ability to travel over great distances and to return home safely. A few men lose their lives hunting. The women know the risks and appreciate that the men are willing to give up their lives for the tribe. The men also protect the tribe from harm.

As a girl, you rise with the dawn, gather and prepare food for the people. Your role is clear. You offer a warm hearth for the tribe. You look after the younger children and talking, laughing, joking you wash by the river. You go into the forest but not too far away to collect herbs, seeds and roots.

In the afternoon, returning to the cave, you prepare the kill for that night's meal and dry the herbs you have found. You take care of the wellbeing of the tribe and sense the changing moods within the cave. You are a natural peacemaker. Your job is to defend the nest while the men are away. You are valued because you make the home and sustain the family. The men think that because you bear children, you are a magical creature. As a woman, you are the giver of life.

On returning the men eat and sit around the fire, telling stories of the hunt. They appreciate the part each one plays.

Survival is not easy in these times. Everything else takes second place. The relationships between men and women are not a focus. Survival is! But they value each other and the unique contribution that each one makes to the whole.

Bring your mind back to today.

Some cultures still live like this – some aboriginal people of Australia, the Inuit of Canada and Greenland and tribes people in Africa.

The chances are, if you are reading this book, the people of your culture don't live like this anymore.

Because of the centuries where our ancestors lived these well-defined roles, males and females are wired up differently. Their brains developed appropriate functions for the jobs they had to do.

We still have brains that are programmed for these tasks. If we can understand this and work together, we can achieve a whole new way of relating across the genders. Because our roles are no longer so clearly defined, many of us are struggling to find ways to relate that are workable. This generation may be the one that swings the pendulum back into balance and harmony for the good of us all.

"For men and women who live in modern civilised countries, these old rules have been thrown out – and sometimes chaos, confusion and unhappiness have been left in their place. For the first time ever we are looking to our partners for love, passion and personal fulfilment because basic survival is no longer critical."

– Adapted from WHY MEN DON'T LISTEN & WOMEN CAN'T READ MAPS, Alan and Barbara Pease.

The rules have changed in the last thirty years. We are seeking ways to redefine and reinvent ourselves – to find new ways of relating, so that we reach our potential and share our love and gifts with each other. Take some time to think about the other gender and the differences you recognise.

My Story

I was born female! I acted like a tomboy. I was unconsciously trying to be the boy my mother and father had hoped for. I didn't understand that until I was in my mid-thirties. I identified myself with boys and hated my sister who was the pretty girl my father favoured. I had confused my gender identity.

I didn't understand why men were not attracted to me. Because of my gender confusion, I put out an off-beat vibe. As well as behaving and looking like a tomboy, I was sending out fear signals because of childhood abuse. The world was receiving messages about who I thought I was, rather than who I truly was. People didn't know how to relate to me. I had a feminine body but had abandoned my feminine expression. I had shut her off.

I am getting clearer and more confident about myself as a female. I have realised more about what femininity means for me. In my heart I am and always was essentially female.

TEENSPEAK

"Guys can't cry is really stupid. If boys show emotion it's wossey, but with girls it's normal. I feel sorry for guys 'cos its a lot harder on them. She can cry but if a guy does he would be called all sorts of things. They say things about a guy being gay if he shows feeling. Girls can wear boys' clothes but guys can't wear girls' clothes. Girls don't get the same treatment as the guys. We're still looked down on." – Chelsea (13)

"If boys hang out with only girls in primary school they are considered gay but if they don't hang out with girls in high school they are also considered gay." – Kintasha (14)

"It's good being a male 'cos I don't have to deal with pregnancy or the menstrual cycle. I am physically stronger and more capable of defence. Jeez – there wouldn't be much more than that." – David (18)

"It's about 16 that girls and guys change a lot and you start to notice how the genders differ. Females are very different, in lots of ways. I see girls my age as a lot more emotionally unstable than guys are – it's a hard time for girls 16 to 18. They don't seem normal. A lot of them are so confused. I believe in the effects of hormones. We are dealing with the same level of problems but we seem emotionally stronger." – Liam (17)

"I can relate to my close girlfriends really well. I talk to girls a lot deeper than I do with my friends – guys don't talk that much. Sometimes I like talking to girls 'cos they are much more sensitive." – Ben (17)

"Sometimes I am extremely uncomfortable talking to girls, at other times I can flirt with all my heart." – Sam (15)

"I'd like girls to be more understanding to what I am really like. I wish girls would be more honest with me. Sometimes I'm scared of them because I don't know how they think/feel/react to things and because they are so different to me." – Paul (15)

"I like girls for their intelligence, beauty and personality. Basically these three and a good strong friendship." – Larry (16)

"I'm attracted to the juices in them, personality and appearance." – Simon (15)

"I'm attracted to girls who are nice with similar ideas and values to me. I have the idea that all girls are nice. Wrong, of course! But innocent until proven guilty." – Peter (14)

"If I am not really attracted to a guy, I can talk easily. But if I like them and don't know them I find it hard to talk to the male species. I'd like guys to really say what they are feeling. Communicate more easily. Not to be so embarrassed about what other people think." – Nancy (16)

"Sometimes, I'm scared that they aren't going to like me for what I am when I really like them." – Sheila (13)

"I wish guys could be more expressive with their feelings and emotions and not act so macho and try to show off. Just be themselves." – Robyn (13)

"These days it's a bit more even. It's getting there; girls are being a bit more equally treated as guys are. Girls should have a bit more say in things." – Angie (13)

"As a male I'm expected to go for the chase. I reckon there's a social imbalance like I'm a girl and I'm going to wait until he comes up to me. It shouldn't be like that. It would be nice to know that she's interested in you. It would make it a lot easier." – Dylan (18)

"I like sensitivity, honesty, good looks, nice personality and caring when they are with their friends. I'd like boys to talk more casually to girls and not have such a strong fixation on the physical aspect of a relationship." – Lisa (15)

Note: At some point as you mature you may choose to not think of yourself as a girl or a boy anymore. You can consider that you are becoming a young adult – either a young man or a young woman. If you become aware of the language you use to describe yourself, it may change the way you see yourself as you grow up. A friend of mine is eighty-six years old. She calls herself a girl and in some ways she still behaves like one.

GENDER CONFUSION

Many girls wish to be like boys because some don't see their mothers as positive role models and some believe that boys have more fun. Males seemingly have more power in society, they are not as emotional and have no menstrual cycles. Males have more permission to be adventurous, to be loud and playful.

Some males strongly identify with the feminine. They may express this by being soft and gentle, some may wear dresses and make-up or by being gay. Some abandon their masculinity if they are over-mothered or if they find the men in their lives harsh or violent. There are different reasons for becoming confused about gender. It's not a simple issue. It can be confusing for everyone if they are not clearly identifying with their gender.

The media, school, friends and parents may play a part in causing you to abandon your essential female/maleness. Portraying females as objects to be ogled at or males who are football playing, beer-drinking macho men, can place pressure on you to act out something other than what is true of your Essential Nature.

Recognising the Differences

There has been a great deal of research in recent years about how males and females are different. The following is adapted from MEN ARE FROM MARS AND WOMEN ARE FROM VENUS by John Gray. It was the first of many popular books written about gender like this. As the title suggests, it's as if we're from different planets.

Check this out for yourself:

MALES define themselves by achieving results – working out the details. Problem solving fulfils them.

Trying to fix things he offers solutions and invalidates her feelings. It is difficult for him to listen to her when she is unhappy or disappointed because he feels like a failure.

His deepest fear is that he is not good enough. The secret of empowering him is never to try to change or improve him. He is motivated and empowered when he feels valued. Not to be valued is a slow death for him.

It puts too much pressure on him if she makes him the only source of love and support.

To feel better a man goes to his cave. He cannot give her the attention she deserves when there (never go into a man's cave or you'll be burned by the dragon). Males should not be judged for withdrawing. He alternates between intimacy and independence. When he loves her he periodically pulls away so that he can get closer again. To a certain extent he loses himself through connection with her.

He thrives when he receives encouragement, trust, acceptance, appreciation, approval and reassurance.

FEMALES. Her sense of self is defined through her feelings and the quality of her relationships. To feel better females get together and openly talk about problems.

She is fulfilled through talking about details.

She offers unsolicited advice and direction, presuming he doesn't know what to do or that he can't do it on his own. She forgets he doesn't talk as much as she does. She often feels unheard. When he is silent, it's easy for her to imagine the worst. Her biggest challenge is to interpret and support him when he isn't talking. She argues for the right to be upset and asks for understanding. He misunderstands even this complaint. She should not be judged for seeking reassurance.

She is motivated and empowered when she feels cherished. She relaxes as she remembers she is worthy of love. She doesn't have to earn it – she deserves it. She rises and falls in her ability to love herself and others.

She gives as much as she can – only noticing she has received less when she is empty and exhausted.

She thrives when she receives caring, understanding, respect, devotion, admiration and approval.

FOR BOTH: When each takes the time to listen to their feelings, they are in effect saying: I matter, I deserve to be heard and I care enough to listen.

He typically gives in relationship what he expects, while she gives what she expects. When negative feelings are suppressed, positive feelings become suppressed as well and love dies.

Finding Balance

Believing that males and females are the same, can cause confusion and misunderstanding. Be compassionate about the differences and work together. Learn about the differences and enjoy each other.

Get real, get along and fly!

For the feminine:

The Feminine Spirit has been undervalued for centuries. The patriarchal world crushed the Goddess worshipping cultures. Since then HER beauty has not been allowed to radiate and HER love has not been appreciated. HER gifts have not been acknowledged – her healing, seeing, knowing, connectedness, intuition and wisdom. Many females, preferring not to identify with a disempowered feminine role hide their light under their cloaks! The disguise has fooled almost everyone around her, even herself.

As much as the feminist movement set out to liberate women, it may also have neglected empowering the Feminine Spirit. The hard work of feminists has done a great deal to change the work-place and legal and welfare structures in our industrialised world. Women are able to vote, attend school and are employed with more or less equal rights. Women can have a career that in the early 20th century was almost unheard of. BUT the pendulum swung the other way. Feminists literally and symbolically burned their bras! Many feminists took on a masculine identity, wore clothes like men and in some ways became like them as well. Some women have become more identified with the masculine and perhaps have injured themselves in the process. Patriarchy pushed them into masculinity as a means of surviving. Women's liberation emphasised that even further for many women.

If women had been able to stay connected with and express their Feminine Spirit, their beauty, wisdom, power and strength, a different battle could have been won. SHE, the bringer of Life and carrier of Light, could have been welcomed back into the World. SHE is rising now to create balance.

For the masculine:

"Any move to change the order of things which does not address the fact that men are equally lost, trapped and miserable, will only create its own resistance – the much talked about 'backlash'. Because some men are and always have been, deeply frightened of feminine mystery and power, they create a 'backlash' against women. When feminism is one sided, it fuels just such a reaction. Violent men, for instance, are rarely angry below the surface bluster. Scared, yes, lonely, yes. Anger is only a cover."
– MANHOOD, Steve Biddulph.

Many males are aware on some level of feminine power but don't meet her there. So they put her down in order to feel powerful themselves. Only a few men are violent towards women. Some are embarrassed and ashamed that men do these things.

Many recognise and celebrate woman in her power and consciously live in equal relationship with her. Many males are feminists.

It is true to say that some males are confused about their roles. This is not necessarily a bad thing. Having gone from the macho, patriarchal kings ruling the world, many men have chosen to become SNAGS (Sensitive New Age Guys). This does not work for them either. They lose their power and their connection to what is essentially male as they struggle to find a new sense of their identity.

Let's change the way we share the world.

Out of this current gender confusion there can be greater understanding, more equality, celebration of differences and the joy of coming together.

Conditions for Growth

Males and females think, feel and behave in very different ways. Because of these differences they thrive under different conditions. Here are examples for you to get a sense of this.

Females blossom from:

- their father's praise and admiration,
- being appreciated for who they really are,
- feeling beautiful from the inside and not being judged by appearances,
- being heard and being in relationship with others.

Males benefit from:

- spending time doing things with their dads,
- finding direction and purpose as they mature,
- encouragement and being supported to achieve their goals,
- being protected from the violent, macho stuff, not being hurt,
- good role models for positive manhood.

David Deida teaches seminars all around the World and offers a major paradigm shift (a change in the pattern) for relationships. He says that masculine sexual essence men have direction and move into the world seeking to fulfil their purpose and achieve goals. To find out if you have a male sexual essence ask yourself if you enjoyed playing war games or doing things that offered you a challenge as you were growing up.

David Deida's message to females is:

"If you... were born with a more feminine sexual essence… as a child you enjoyed playing house… playing with puppies and colours and make-up and flavours. You enjoyed getting clothing and jewellery… You may have dreamt of masculine saviours: horses, pop stars, white knights… that could take you somewhere new, somewhere magic. Deep in your heart, you felt that some day a man would see your true beauty, your true light, your boundless ocean of love and take you to the place you always wanted to be: surrendered open like the sky, filled with moonlight…

For one reason or another, you probably became convinced that it is better, stronger…" to hide your feminine radiance because of your fear of masculine force. So to protect yourself, you create a shell of superficial feminine expression. Rather than trust the love that you are: "You buy the jeans that all the popular girls at school are wearing, checking out your butt in the mirror, wondering if this will get the boys to want you. You spend hours purchasing and trying on not only clothing but also jewellery, fragrances and make-up – not as loving adornments of your abundant radiance, but because you feel love lacking. You feel unseen and unworthy, because the masculine shell you acquired as a child is hiding the full love and true shine of your heart." – Adapted from DEAR LOVER, David Deida.

Explore the Differences

There is a great deal of interest and enthusiasm from teenagers when they start to explore gender differences. It doesn't take long for the conversations to become intense.

THINGS TO DO!

- You can do this alone or it can be great fun with a friend or in a mixed group. If you are working in a mixed group it's helpful for the males and females to work separately. Spend time exploring the masculine and feminine but don't work together. That way the differences become even more obvious.
- Find 2 large pieces of paper. Also 2 huge pieces of paper to draw an outline about the size of a body and coloured pencils, crayons, pens, etc.
- On one large piece of paper write:
  Females Women Girls Her She.
  On the other:
  Males Men Boys Him He.
- Working on one at a time, either male or female, write down all the characteristics, behaviours, attitudes that you don't like that describe that gender. Here are some of the easier examples: Females can be bitchy, manipulative, over-protective, image conscious. Males can be violent, loud, insensitive and competitive.

Your lists can be as long as you like. The more the better! Get it out on paper so you can look at it.

- On the huge pieces of paper draw a female body on one sheet and a male body on the other.
- Write or draw pictures, using colour, about all the likeable, great, exciting things you can think of for each gender. Get a really good idea of the advantages of being that gender. Include as much detail as you like.
- Consider your work and see what you have discovered for yourself about gender differences.

As you move into living your Essential Nature, embrace the differences, live and be yourself while accepting the other.

Are You Comfortable with Yourself?

To discover where you are at around sexuality and the other gender answer these questions honestly and see what you come up with. You can write about this in your notebook or discuss it with a friend.

How do I feel about my body?

Am I comfortable talking to the other gender?

Am I sexually attractive to others? Why/Why not?

What attracts me to another person?

How do I feel when someone is attracted to me?

Am I frightened by the other gender? Why?

Complete these sentences:

I sometimes feel self-conscious when…..

I sometimes wish that boys/girls, men/women would…..

I would like to be more self-confident when.....

I feel most attractive when.....

You could repeat these over and over again. You may be surprised at what you uncover.

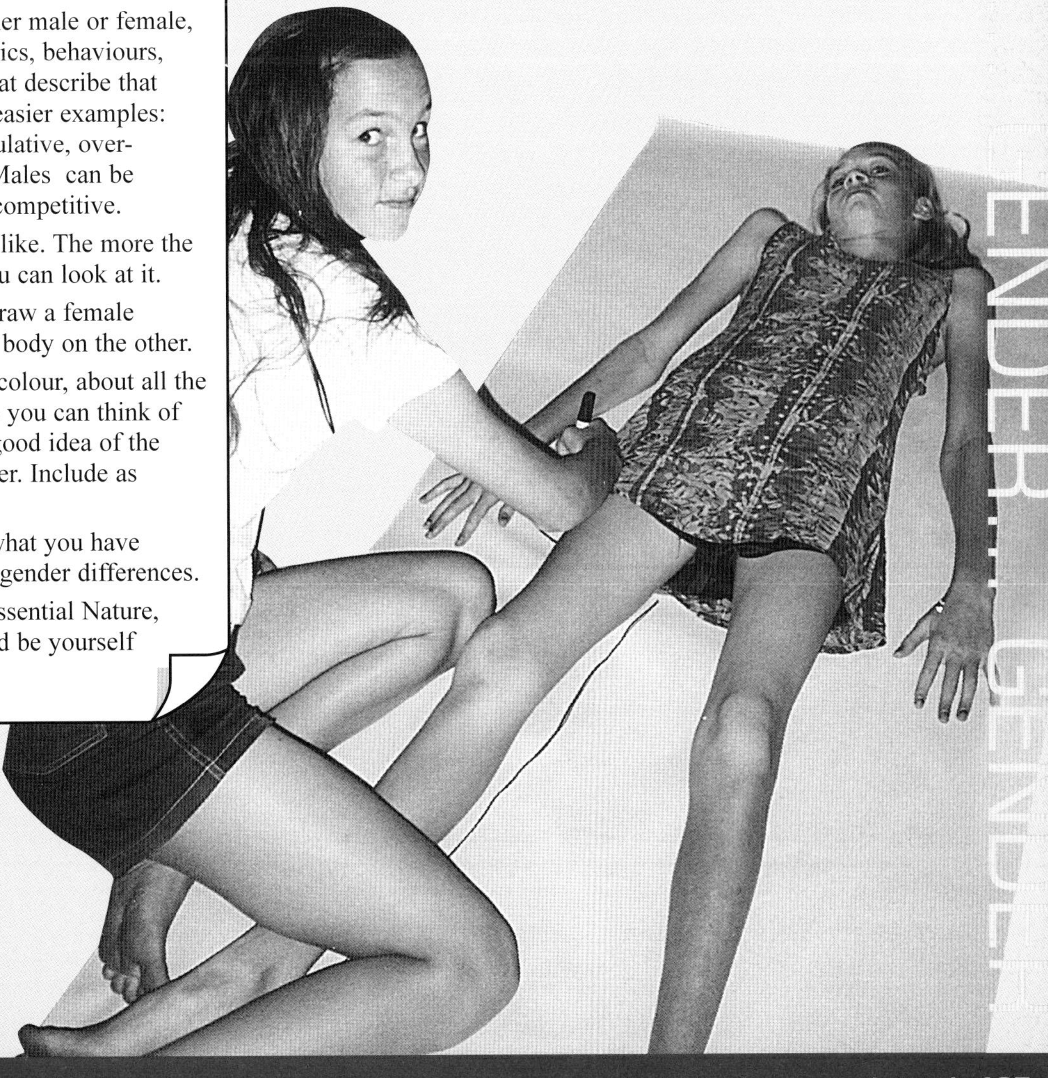

What are Your Questions?

When young people are able to ask questions about what it is like growing up as a female/male they are amazed to find that some of their beliefs about the other gender are not true. What has been discovered is –

That adolescent males:

- are not just concerned about a female's appearance,
- find too much make-up unattractive,
- are interested in personality,
- generally do not like females to be too skinny,
- tumble and play rough to release some of their energy.

That adolescent females:

- don't like male's who act macho and cool,
- prefer them to be true to themselves,
- are frustrated when they don't express their feelings well,
- don't like them acting noisy and rough,
- don't think looks are that important but personality is.

Teenage males raised the question, "Do teenage girls think of sex two hundred times a day?" There was absolute amazement when this group of fifteen-year-old females said they didn't think about sex at all!

Now that's a BIG difference!

THINGS TO DO!

If you have a mixed group of friends you could do the following exercise together. Taken seriously it can create safety, intimacy and a new understanding about yourself and the other gender.

- Cut up sheets of paper into small squares, big enough to write down questions.
- Males and females sit facing each other.
- Everyone spends time thinking about what they wish to ask the other gender – about growing up, physical development, thoughts and feelings about things. Anything!
- Write your questions anonymously.
- Fold them and put them into two bowls in the middle of the room. Males' questions in one and females' in the other.
- Take it in turns. Take a question out of the other gender's bowl. As a group take time to answer the question as honestly as you can.
- If a question is too hard or you would like to come back to it later, put it on one side.

Do this until you have answered all the questions or until you've had enough.

Two fun things to do for close contact with each other or a group:

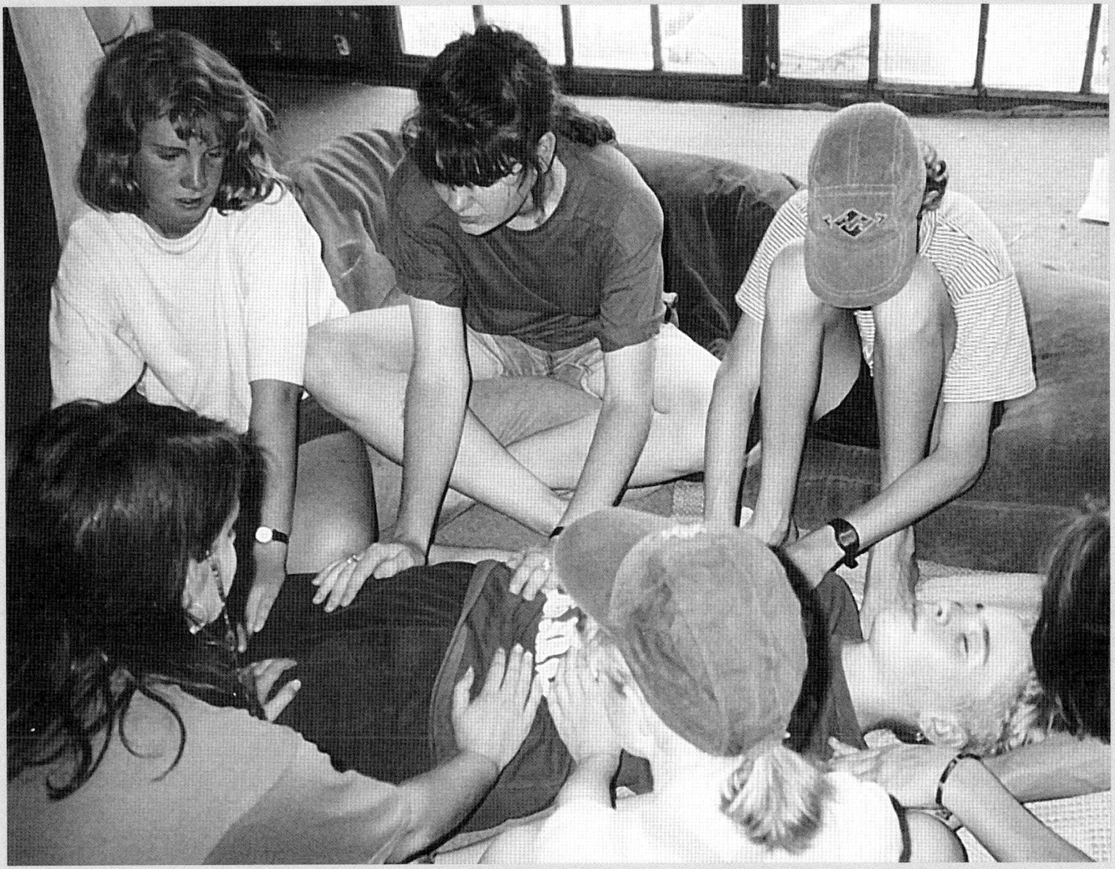

Love Wash

With a partner, find a quiet, comfortable and warm place. Play some soft or gentle music. Take turns – one of you being passive and the other active. One person lies in a comfortable position while the other gently strokes and touches. Use the whole of both hands. Do this for at least fifteen minutes. The one lying down stays as present with the sensations in his or her body as possible, keeping eyes closed. If you are the giver, focus your attention on the person you are giving to and at times on your own hands. Be aware of both giving to the other and receiving at the same time. After some time, swap.

A small group love wash. Be sensitive, gentle and caring with each other. One person stands or lies down in the middle with the others all around. Make agreements that there will be no touching of breasts, bums or genitals. Each person receives five to ten minutes of soft stroking and then change over.

Trust Walking

You might like to gather a blindfold, fruit, chocolate, feathers, fragrant oils, bells or anything else that stimulates the senses.

This exercise develops a sense of trust in each other. It is a way to stimulate your senses. Find a partner. One of you is blindfolded and the other gently guides him or her around. You can do this outdoors or inside. Offer the blindfolded partner objects or things that feel good to the senses. For example, touch the face or hand with a feather or a leaf. You could put a hand under running water, offer a sweet smelling flower or give a piece chocolate or a strawberry to taste. You can walk your partner gently into leaves, etc. Be inventive, gentle and caring. Move slowly to make sure that the blindfolded person does not bump into anything or hurt him or her self. This can be fun and pleasurable. After ten or fifteen minutes swap over.

New Gender Ground

The social and political changes brought about through the feminist movement are vital to move us away from a male-dominated world. Change is in the air. This offers fertile ground for new relationships. It is time once again for a major shift.

Imagine a bird attempting to fly with only one wing. It cannot. Let's allow male and female wings to work together. It is the only way we can establish balance. We can now do more than ever before to create an equal sharing of our power, recognising and bringing out the best in each other.

GETTING REAL... about growing up! asks you to become conscious in your relationships with each other. This generation can witness equality and live it in this lifetime.

Make New Choices

Can you imagine living in a World that is a paradise?

A balanced World where men and women, boys and girls understand each other?

Where males and females are equally valued for their gifts and get along harmoniously?

What does that World look like and feel like to you?

What are you surrounded by?

How do you relate to the people in your World?

What kind of intimacy do you share with others?

Close your eyes. Dream! Give yourself a few moments to create for yourself a special place, where you live and love to your full potential.

After some time, open your eyes and stretch your body. Allow yourself to feel that this is a new reality. When enough people focus their thoughts on co-creating paradise on Earth – because thoughts are creative, the World can be a better place.

Keep your dreaming alive!

LOVE, RELATIONSHIPS AND SEXUALITY

Throughout our lives we love many people. We usually love our parents, brothers, sisters, relatives and our close friends. If we live our lives with open hearts we may find ourselves loving more and more people. Sometimes, someone we meet for only a moment can open our hearts to wonderful feelings of love – if we are available to it.

In this section intimate and sexual relationships are explored. In these relationships we reveal more of ourselves. We become connected more deeply than we do with people we love but who are not so close. When we experience sexual feelings with someone we love, that person can become special in our lives.

Relationships with other people you are attracted to, offer opportunities to explore your sexuality. You learn about communication, intimacy and about what loving someone means. You can find out about creating boundaries, when to allow someone in close, how close to get and when to spend time alone. Your thoughts, feelings and emotions are stirred. You discover what it feels like to make close physical contact with another person: to kiss, stroke, fondle and ultimately to make love with him or her. You learn about taking risks.

As a young person you may move in and out of many relationships as you explore, have fun, get hurt and learn from your successes and failures.

In the beginning it's useful to create close friendships with people you feel sexually attracted to. Then you can explore your sensuality as you come to understand your body and its responses and those of your partner. If you do this before you become sexually active, you allow your body, mind and spirit time to adjust to the sexual feelings you may be experiencing. Take your time. Try not to rush! You may be learning about intimacy and sexuality for much of your adult life.

There is the thrill and excitement of your first date and kiss. Then as you move into more intimate relationships you may find yourself facing feelings of confusion, unfulfilled expectations, fear or disappointment. You may experience pain or have your heart broken open to love where the protection around your heart is softened for the next time you love another.

You may find someone to build a solid and long-term intimate friendship with at an early age. You may not! It's different for everyone. Every new experience in a relationship is another opportunity for growth, opening, freeing yourself up and intimacy. Every new situation presents you with something to gain, learn or share.

Many of us are given no guidelines. Our learning is by trial and error. By reading about teenage relationships here, you can begin your Journey of exploration and learning with greater understanding.

GO FOR IT!

TEENSPEAK

"Teenage relationships sometimes happen out of curiosity. What is it like going out with a
guy or how do people react when you do? If you come from a broken home or have a bad family life
you can feel cared for and supported." – Catherine (14)

"Teenage relationships are to experience, learn and grow stronger. Also to explore your own
sexuality and your boyfriend's. They are not always as serious as adult relationships.
It's just kind of getting ready." – Julie (14)

"Having fun, experimenting, getting to know your body and learning from
your mistakes."– Mandy (14)

"I suppose teenage relationships are to prepare you for true love." – Ben (14)

"My motivation for meeting girls is for everything that goes with
having girlfriends. Being able to talk to them about things that you can't talk about with
your mates. It changes everything to have girls around the place. Sex would be nice!!! It's one of the
main reasons. I don't want to know girls just 'cos I can have sex with them. I would be happy to be with a
down to earth girl that I really liked and we felt comfortable with each other. I'll probably be happy to go
into a year-long relationship. Not much longer than a year. It's a bit of a weird thing to say…
depends on how it pans out… if I fell in love with a girl tomorrow…
I'm not scared of commitment." – Liam (17)

"So we have experience for when we are older, but I think it is also
a deeper thing for some people." – Rose (13)

"It's hard seeing all my friends going out on the prowl. I should be doing
that at this age. I haven't been able to. I was sixteen when I first went out with her. I didn't
really know what a relationship was about. I've been in a relationship for two years. My girlfriend is
totally in love with me and I've been thinking that maybe I should break away. She's a bit crazy – almost too
in love with me. Now it's more full on, I'm sick of it. I can't have my own life. I want a break but
she wouldn't let me. She's way too possessive. We are best friends.
I'll lose my best friend. " – Dave (18)

What is Real Love?

Love is one of life's mysteries. You may spend the rest of your life exploring it.

Real love is about two people's commitment to each other at a human level and it can also be about bringing as much that is sacred and spiritual into their relationship. It is special. Extraordinary as well as ordinary! Real love isn't a feeling that withers overnight or a fantasy that is never fulfilled.

A committed relationship is when both partners are prepared to work together to create intimacy and a life together. This involves dedication and a desire to grow together. Loving, considering and caring for each other also takes patience. Developing that patience may take time. The relationships you have before you commit to a partner can be a preparation for later on. Until then you can explore and learn about relating. You may spend the rest of your life with your mate. Wait until you are ready to deeply explore yourself with another.

Take time to think about the couples you know. Which ones have respect, honesty, open communication, closeness and caring for one another? Healthy role models can help you to learn what harmonious relationships are. If you know couples who have fulfilling relationships, it is useful to consider what special qualities they bring to them.

Qualities to develop with a loving partner include:

enthusiasm, stillness, independence, sexuality, energy, nurturing, loving, loyalty, honesty, spirituality, connection, freedom, sharing, patience, understanding, communication, giving, pleasure, compassion, caring, laughter, peace, dedication, commitment, touch, passion, joy.

Add to the list for yourself. Dream it up!

What are Fantasy Relationships?

For many people this scenario may be familiar:

You see him or her at a distance. You fall in love. You imagine what it is like to talk, to spend time with that person – the laughter, stimulating conversation, the first kiss. But you stay as far away as possible and don't take the first step of introducing yourself or finding out about her or him. Before long, in your fantasy, you're passionately in love, then married and having children. But the real person is just as far out of reach as ever.

Everything is under your control when you fantasise – it is safe. You make the story up and determine the outcome. The effect of habitual fantasising is that when you are with a partner, you wait for the romantic movie to play itself back. You don't know how to be real. The other is the pawn. She or he doesn't know what you are hoping for.

Fantasising can keep you separate and alone. You are unlikely to get close to the real person because you haven't learned how. There is a danger in fantasising. Reality might never come up to that level of experience and it might be disappointing. It is no substitute for being intimately involved with someone.

"If I see someone I'm attracted to I just go over and start a conversation. If we get on I say I'd like to be friends with him and we take it from there." – Kylie (14)

Very simple! If you do that before you start running the movie in your head, you may have a chance of a real relationship. Fantasies about knights on white chargers and princesses waiting to be rescued can get in the way. There's a whole bunch of human beings who have little idea about getting close. Be realistic in the way you relate and create meaningful relationships for yourself.

Our friendship is a forest of fears
and doubts of love and light.
Walking through we see only one bit
until we see another.
All the parts make up the whole.
Our love is a landscape
we choose to traverse for as long as it appeals.
The view is clearer from the top of a hill
and there's always higher hills.
And higher hills to come.

– Les Joyce

Unrequited Love

The unrequited love syndrome is where you love from a distance or you have a brief encounter, fall in love and she or he leaves. You think there could have been a lot more to it – an incredible potential. Then you get dumped. It's painful.

People who are prepared to give themselves away or lose themselves in relationships feel pain when they **fall** in love. It's possible to spend months wondering what went wrong, why he or she left. It helps to find ways of dealing with leftover feelings such as talking to friends, writing poetry or in your Journal.

If you are not getting what you are looking for or being mistreated, not feeling cared for or are unhappy in your adolescent relationships, you can always walk away.

The challenges you face in every relationship are a learning ground for your later life. Take brave steps and explore different ways to relate. At your age you have a lot to gain by receiving love from another and by sharing the love that you are. So go for it! As much as you can, dance and play – learn to relate intimately but don't take it too seriously. Become involved as often as you feel like it. Find out what works and feels right for you.

RISE up to Love, rather than FALL in love.

It's a lot less painful!

Romantic Love

Romance is the dream. It's the lace and the satin that can be the trimmings of a garment.

> *"The boy-girl romantic notion of love is but a small part of the picture, to think of that as the whole story of love is like reducing a jigsaw puzzle to one piece, a musical score to one passage."*
>
> – MAPS TO ECSTASY , Gabrielle Roth.

Romance is when you meet Mr or Ms Perfect. Your heart misses a beat. He brings her flowers. She adores him. He feels ten feet tall. You look and feel wonderful together. You are in a rose coloured bubble. You think about each other all the time and can't wait to be together. You live in each other's pockets. Everything about life takes on a warm glow.

In an article by Robert Johnson in CHALLENGE OF THE HEART, he says human love is like Stirring the Oatmeal – "... it shows us the principal differences between human love and romance. Stirring the oatmeal is a humble act – not exciting or thrilling. But it symbolises a relatedness that brings love down to earth. It represents a willingness to share ordinary human life, to find meaning in the simple unromantic tasks: earning a living, putting out the garbage, feeding the baby in the middle of the night."

Caring nourishes love. Doing things for the loved one that you don't always feel like doing strengthens the bond and the love between you.

Putting the other first at times.
Creating equality in the relationship.
Respecting each other's individuality.
Taking time apart...

all help to create a truly loving relationship.

Neediness

If you have been starved of love and affection or don't love yourself you may feel needy. An example: a dog comes up to you and won't leave you alone. You may get annoyed if it pesters you and won't go away. You may feel like kicking it because it is begging too much. The same thing could happen if you come across as needy in relationships. Sometimes people push you away if you become like a leech. This is painful. Find ways to love yourself first. That way you can relax and so can others.

Finding Happiness

Relationships don't work if you are looking to someone else to make you happy. It is not his or her responsibility. You do not find happiness when you are dependent on it coming from outside of yourself. There can only be a depth of love and true happiness when there are two people who are there for themselves as well as for the other. Each is fulfilled in her and his own life and brings that to the relationship.

If you love something
– set it free.
If it comes back – it is yours.
If it doesn't – it never was!

Crossroads
Adam (16)

Black and blue here we stand
Heart in heart and hand in hand
My love for life and living to the full
Take me far from this haze of foggy blue

For love is real and real can hurt
Torn into pieces I lie in the dusty dirt
But life goes on for some we think
And with hope and truth we make our stand
Take me from this old torn house
Stains in our bodies and fallen paths

What I am I to do here now?
You leave me here and let me drown
My love for you will never die
You are the soul jewel of mine eye
Friend for life and lover too
Maybe one day we can see right through

I know what I am to do here now
I will not let you let me drown
I will swim and I'll survive
I will breathe, I will achieve
I will swim and I'll survive
My life and soul will succeed
I will thrive!

Intimacy

In-to-me-you-see expresses what true intimacy is.

It is essential in any intimate relationship that you are open and listen to your heart. It's also valuable if you can feel into the other's heart. Your heart talk guides you in knowing when to set boundaries and when to allow yourself to melt and merge. To let go into the love you are. Intimacy is when you have created a bond on many levels. This is based on loving feelings towards each other.

Being intimate and close with another can take you into more pleasure, open-heartedness and ecstasy than when you are alone. This involves bringing all of your attention and being fully present with each other and feeling into the other's heart.

To create intimacy in relationships:

Love Yourself First

You cannot fully love another person until you love yourself. Building up self-esteem and being in touch with yourself is a good place to begin. If you have been hurt as a child or teenager, it is possible that someone else loving you may help you to love yourself. If you love yourself then you can accept your friend's love.

Know and Trust

Get to know yourself first and develop your knowing of the other. Trusting another is about opening your heart and allowing the other to see you from the inside. It is also about being playful, spontaneous, giving and caring. By taking risks, learning by trial and error you develop trust. If you are with someone you care about, who hangs in, you can become true friends and intimate lovers.

Communicate Clearly

Talk together. You can learn to communicate in open and honest ways with an intimate partner. Clearly ask for what you would like in your relationship. Ask for reassurance if you feel uncertain. Talking about your responses and expressing your feelings makes understanding possible. You may think you know what's going on with the other. That's unlikely – especially when you're first getting to know each other. Check in with your partner to find out. To be clear – communicate – it's the only way.

Drop Your Defences

Allow yourself to be vulnerable. This involves opening up the tenderest parts of yourself and allows your partner to get to know you deeply. Be prepared to have the other see your weaknesses as well as your strengths. It may involve tears or expressing your fears. In your vulnerability lies your strength.

Clear communication is a key

Face Your Fear

You may be afraid of being hurt or losing what you've found. It could be fear of betrayal, being misunderstood or abandoned. Fear responses can happen if you feel threatened by someone getting too close. If you have been hurt, closeness can trigger childhood memories. Fear is something to move through. Talk about what you are afraid of with your partner. Understanding where the fear comes from and discovering the truth about it can help it disappear.

Maintain Independence

Retain your individuality. Often at the start of a relationship people get entwined and sort of merge together. It's possible to lose yourself. This can create conflict when the honeymoon phase of the relationship is over. One person may start to do things separately. This can challenge the foundation of your relationship. Be open to the other but also maintain your friendships and your hobbies.

Questions for yourself and the other:

What am I asking you to give me?
What are you asking of me?
Do you have expectations?* What are they?
What can we do?
How can I make it better for US?
How can we make it better together?

* Having expectations of others can lead to pain if they are not met.

Just a note: Many adults attending my workshops have been married for many years. They have not experienced deep intimacy with their partners. They did not know what was possible.

By following the suggestions in this book you have every opportunity to create fulfilling intimate relationships for yourself.

LOVE

Sally (14)

It's floating on air.
It's feeling your heart flutter.
It's grinning like an idiot.
It's making a fool of yourself and hating it.
It's making your tongue feel like it's in knots.
It's sighing when he walks past.
It's writing his name everywhere.
It's wanting a picture of you and him together.
It's staring at him in class.
It's telling everyone about him.
It's making him hate every other girl alive.
It's daydreaming when you should be studying.
It's forgetting about reality.
It's hating the guy you used to like.
It's taking down your tacky posters.
It's your mother hating him, when she doesn't know him.
It's making you wish you were prettier.
It's only a crush.

I want to love you without clutching
Appreciate you without judging
Join you without invading
Invite you without demanding
Leave you without guilt
Criticise you without blaming
And help you without insulting
If I can have the same from you
Then we can truly meet and
enrich each other.

– Virginia Satir

Ways to Create Trust and Intimacy

Tenderness, soft touching, eye contact and breathing together, with your hearts open, can create connection. Relax while intimately exploring your sexuality with another. There are many gifts of an opened heart. Loving feelings, spontaneity and passion adds to the deliciousness. If you allow yourself to be danced in your love for one another, your intimacy expresses itself in all sorts of different ways.

The following exercises are ways you can increase your sensitivity and energetic awareness.

Energy

Shake your hands rapidly until they feel like they are dropping off. Now shake your arms, your shoulders, your head and all your limbs until your whole body is shaking. The longer you do this the more your energy moves. When you are ready, stop still! Observe the sensations moving through you. Something like this also happens to your energy field when you are making love with someone else.

Sharing Process

With a partner, close your eyes for a minute. Open your eyes. Take it in turns to talk while the other listens. Do this for five minutes. Then swap over. The listener practises being present and listens with the inner ear and the body. The speaker shares from his or her heart and allows the emotions and feelings to surface. This can help you get closer and deal with problems or misunderstandings that come up in your relationships.

If issues arise the following can help clear things up.

To go deeper: The following are sentence stems. Repeat them over and over again, adding what you wish to say at the end. Take it in turns until changes occur in how you are feeling. Listen and don't interrupt your partner.

Use one of the following sentence stems at a time, then swap over – until you've done all four. You can also make up others.

Something I'd like to say to you is…

Something that I would like from you is…

A way that I see you is…

Something I like/love about you is…

In any clearing process always end on a loving note.

Emotional Expression

You may have been taught to suppress or hide your feelings. Play around with different emotions – act them out and exaggerate them. Become emotionally expressive. It helps the other person understand more fully what's going on for you. It is false and confusing when people say they are sad when they are smiling. Be dramatic and play at showing your partner the different aspects of your emotional self. This allows you to see and be seen by another.

Breathing Together

Lie close in each other's arms and breathe together. Allow your body and mind to relax. Melt! Be super-sensitive and watch what your energy does.

Another way you can do this: one person lies down on his or her left side in a curled up position, you lie next to your partner's back against your front – sometimes called spoons. Get as close as you can. The person at the back reaches over and places the right hand on the belly of the person in front. Allow all sense of separation to disappear. This can be done with more than two people.

Eye Contact

Sit comfortably and face your partner. Close your eyes to get in touch with yourself. Open your eyes and look into your partner's left eye. Stay relaxed and calm. Keep eye contact. Keep breathing. This process can be powerful and sometimes confronting. You may notice your partner's face change into many different faces as you do this.

To go further – look and truly see: This can be done with or without clothes if you are with an intimate partner. Sit facing each other. One person spends time looking at the other. Take in details of things about his or her body you do not normally see. The person being looked at can check out his or her response to this. Swap over. Talk about it after both of your turns. This is a good way to overcome awkwardness and shyness.

Heads on Shoulders

This is a good position for sharing intimacy. Lie down on your backs and put the sides of your heads together, feet away from each other so that you are in a straight line. Put your head on the other person's shoulder. Connect with your breathing and relax. Feel the closeness of your partner. Talk quietly after some time if you feel like it or be silent.

Sensual Self Massage

Create a safe place for yourself. Give yourself a warm and relaxing bath.

Have cold-pressed oil for massage ready (for extra pleasure, warm it slightly). Massage the oil into one arm. Using long, gentle but firm strokes move up your arm towards your chest. Do the other arm. Knead your shoulder and neck muscles. Move to your torso and do the same, moving up towards your neck. Change the quality of your touch and become aware of what that feels like. Massage as much of your back as you can and then your legs. Rub your scalp rapidly and gently pull your hair. Slowly, perhaps with face cream, make small circles on your face.

If you feel like it, tenderly massage your genitals. Allow yourself to feel sexual pleasure.

With another: Massage can be a healing experience and also a sensual or sexual one. It is helpful to be clear about how far you are willing to go when you exchange massages with someone. Communicate so that you both know what the boundaries are.

Use oil on the skin and massage the whole body. At times you can be open to receive what the other chooses to give or the person being massaged can give directions. It's good to practise asking – then receiving what you ask for sometimes. If the massage is gentle and firm it can be therapeutic. Get to know your body and that of the other. Explore with sensitivity and discover your sensuality. There are many great books about massage and you can attend courses to gain more skill.

Use both hands when you are massaging yourself or others.

A suggestion: If you are an adult reading this, take yourself back to your own adolescence and feel what is stirred up in you. You may find it useful to write about your experiences in order to resolve anything that comes up. If you have unfinished business with teenage relationships or your sexuality, resolve it now.

Completion – Ending a Relationship Cleanly

When someone does not feel the same as you do or leaves you, there are ways you can end a relationship cleanly. If you stay emotionally attached, you sometimes suffer unnecessarily. Completion allows you to move on. It may save you repeating the same patterns in your next relationship.

Here are some suggestions:

- Writing poems and letters can be helpful in getting the things off your mind that have been left unsaid. You do not have to send them.
- Talking openly to the person face to face can finish things off cleanly. If the other person involved is not willing to do this, you can do it by yourself by talking to a cushion or a tree. You could write in your Journal.
- If you have love letters, photographs and other bits and pieces and are ready to let go you can create a ritual and burn them.
- Write letters thanking them for the experience you shared. You could express what you learned and what you are letting go of. You could also let them know the wishes that you have for their future. Wishing them well sets you both free. You can choose to send the letter or not.

Sensuality, Sexuality and Growing Up!

Hormones and your rising sexual energy, fuel the changes at puberty. Through your sensual and then your sexual experiences you create ever-deepening connection to yourself, your girl or boy friends and later your intimate partners. Your emerging sexual self is searching for its own expression and identity.

Both sensuality and sexuality have been considered wrong or bad over the last couple of centuries. These aspects of yourself and your increasing sexual energy are normal and a natural part of growing up. There is much to enjoy in discovering your sensuality, sexuality, intimacy, emotional involvement, spirituality and love.

Parents may find it difficult to talk about their own sexuality or yours. Sometimes parents believe that if they talk about sexual contact it may make you do it. If they don't talk about it, it eventually happens anyway. If you are left to learn about your sexuality by trial and error, it can be confusing and challenging, especially during adolescence when you are already experiencing so much change.

Premature Sexuality

Teenagers are often pressured to become sexually active too soon without any real friendship or love. Everyone loses! Some teenagers are not interested in playing this game. Even though feeling pressured, they resist the temptation and respect themselves enough not to go against their true feelings. Some lose friendships because of this. **If you are not ready for sexual contact – don't.**

If in doubt, don't!

Maturing from child to adult is relatively slow. Your body matures much faster than your ability to deal with the choices you are faced with. The results of your actions and what happens to you emotionally as you become sexually involved are not always obvious to you.

Hormone levels increase, creating natural sexual responses to be awakened. This can cause a huge surge of sexual energy in the body. Pornography, sexual misuse and sexual suggestions in the media, increase the intensity of this natural process. We add our own fuel to the fire when we have expectations, passionate fantasies, lustful thoughts and images. This can generate more sexual **charge** and can cause sexual over-stimulation.

The media, TV and movies usually show the romantic or lustful side of sexuality. They rarely present what sexuality in real relationships is about. Watching movies, idolising rock stars or being exposed to pornography may stimulate your sexual responses but can deaden your heart. You can't love screen images but you can feel desire for them. These characters are not real – they are acting. To move into your sexuality in a natural and spontaneous way, avoid movies, TV shows and pornography that over-stimulate you.

Your sexual energy can be activated too early. If the brain, hormonal and reproductive systems are not fully developed, your system can become overloaded. In early teens your body, social skills and emotional experience may not be mature enough to deal with this amount of sexual charge. It can greatly multiply the mental and emotional confusion that is going on inside. It supercharges the emotions of anger, depression, fear or guilt. Similarly if you are feeling love, joy and tenderness this also is magnified.

Sex education at home may be superficial, if at all. At school you are mainly taught about your biological sexual function, about contraception and sexually transmitted infections (STIs). With adequate preparation and education, the Journey into your sensuality and sexuality could be smooth running and safe – as well as fun and exciting.

Sensuality is one key. Being sensual with yourself and others allows an expansion into more intense sensually/ sexually connected, fulfilling and loving experiences.

Slowly exploring sensuality can be a gentle way to prepare your body for pleasurable, intense sexual experiences as you become older. Sensuality also opens and fine-tunes your bodily sense organ – your skin so that it is able to feel and enjoy more. Internal organs also benefit from sensuality.

Sexual fulfilment does not happen overnight. Lovemaking takes practice. It's exciting and thrilling and there is so much more to sexuality than meets the eye.

"...there would be a lot less... problematic teenage sex if kids were given ample opportunity and guidance in exploring the full range of their sensuality in non-sexual ways."

– MAPS TO ECSTASY, Gabrielle Roth.

The stirring of your sexual energy pot can be a slow and delicious one. There is a lot to be explored, long before you even kiss.

Find Out for Yourself

The following list may help you to know whether you are mature enough to deal with your increasing sexual energy.

If you are ready to:

- Sense when you are safe.
- Know what your boundaries are – when to say yes or no.
- Communicate clearly how far you are willing to go.
- Enter into a relationship where agreements about sexual involvement are respected.
- Take adequate care of yourself, using effective methods of contraception.
- Emotionally deal with the issues that arise in a sexually active relationship.
- Protect yourself from people who sleep around as this exposes you to unclear energy and confusion.

As you may be aware there are many opinions about sexual contact and sexuality. It stirs up a lot of emotions. It can be difficult to make up your own mind and heart on the subject. Take small steps. Stay relaxed and connected with your Essential Nature.

A loving sexual experience can be the single most exciting, most energising, most affirming, most intimate, most uniting, most recreational physical experience possible. Discover this for yourself, not too early in adolescence BUT when the time is right for you.

Do your best not to accept other people's judgements, opinions, condemnation and ideas about sexual expression and then set about convincing yourself that your experience of your sexuality must be wrong. Listen to adults and friends who have more experience than you if things get confusing.

You may have been taught from a very early age that you don't know what's best for you. For example, when you are playing and a parent tells you to put on a sweater when you are not cold or if you are forced to eat when you are not hungry. If your parent insists, you begin to doubt your knowing about your own experience.

Become master of your own life and your sexuality.

Questions to ask about sexual contact:

- Do I value and respect my body?
- Am I willing to be sexually active with or make love only with someone who is a friend – a person I can share my fears, joys and insecurities with?
- Can I listen to my inner voice before rushing into any sexual activity?
- Do I prefer to be intimate with someone who is taking responsibility for contraception and taking precautions against sexually transmitted infections?
- Do I choose to make love in comfort or somewhere uncomfortable, where it is rushed?
- Can I say No or Stop at any time I feel like it? Can my friend hear me and respect my wishes and still care about me? If not, do I choose to be sexual with her or him?

If most of your answers are YES, you may decide not to have sexual contact with someone you hardly know.

TEENSPEAK

"My first experience with real sex wasn't real! I was with a guy I didn't know. In a way I wanted to experience it, get it over and done with. But then I didn't want to. I didn't love or even know him. But I did it anyway. I regretted it afterwards and it felt yucky." – Nancy (16)

"It was a threesome, with another girl and a guy. It was when I definitely shouldn't have been doing it. It was fun. Excerpt from my diary: I gave my virginity to a guy whom I've only known for five days and I don't even know his surname. It was actually a threesome. He's got a crush on her and she would have made love with him but she was bleeding. It hurt quite a bit. The juices were flowing so it wasn't for lack of being horny. It's kind of exquisite hurting, so I don't mind." – Isabelle (15)

"On New Year's Eve I lost my virginity. I had a condom in my wallet. I met a guy at a dance and we went back to my tent and lay on a mattress. We got closer together until our hands touched. By this time I was so terrified I could hardly move. He asked me how far I wanted to go. So I took a trip to the toilet while I thought it over. I decided this was my only chance. I felt that I had to prove that I was attractive enough to get him to do it. The actual event was quite painful and unromantic. He was very understanding and when I kept apologising he told me I never had to apologise to any guy. He tried most ways possible to help me enjoy it but due to my fear he was unsuccessful. He had to give up. At one point he jokingly called me a tease. I felt bad for not giving him what he'd obviously been looking for, which was cosmic multi-orgasmic sex. I didn't enjoy it. The next day I awoke late feeling extremely ill and ashamed and thinking someone may have heard the whole event. I crept out of my tent and had a shower. I haven't had sex since. I hope that I don't get desperate or feel the need to prove myself that I rush into it again. I really want to do it in a loving relationship." – Lorraine (16)

"I decided it was time to do it. I asked a boy who was a friend if he would do it with me. He agreed. Mum said we could spend the night together in my bedroom. I made up the bed with clean sheets. I enjoyed my first time. I didn't love him and I didn't do it again with him. Not long after I met my current boyfriend. He was still a virgin. I love him." – Patti (16)

"My first experience was with my high school love. My puppy love. She was my next-door neighbour. We went out for a year and a half. We had a great relationship. We full on thought about it together for six months. We knew what we were doing. We made sure we loved each other. That we were going to have a future together for a while, before we got into it. We didn't know what we were doing because we had no experience. I knew she was the one for me. I was completely in love with her. In a way I think that her and I are still in love a little bit because of that first time. It was a great experience."– Dax (18)

The first time is special – your virginity is a gift that can only be given once. If you are a virgin (male or female) you can choose how you give that gift.

THE POWER OF SEXUALITY

From an interview with Julie Henderson author of THE LOVER WITHIN.

"During the years in which we are becoming sexually potent, whether we are a male or a female, the turbulence is particularly strong. Because we are becoming strong we are becoming powerful in ways that we can't imagine until they've already happened.

As a teenager it is important to discover what it is to be powerful without being harmful.

Socially, it's a real difficulty that we ask young people to postpone acting on their sexual maturation. For eight to ten years we ask young people to go on acting like children, when they are experiencing the strongest biological pressure they will ever experience to reproduce, as well as inappropriate peer group pressure to prove themselves.

This is one of the situations where it would be tremendously helpful to have social community, with a men's society and a women's society, whose function it is to provide a holding of the young people and instruction. As a culture we seem to spend a great deal of time in avoidance and denial of this change that is happening when children become socially adult. It's true they are not as sexually mature as they will be, given any real opportunity, but true sexual maturity can take twenty or thirty years.

A lot of people get sexual intercourse over with quickly – some of you will already know about that. The main reason, apart from a lack of education about sex, could be the inability to contain pleasure. You can expand your energies and your capacity for pleasure."

Allow yourself to dance and sing till you feel as big as your feelings.
It's all movement. Breath and sound!

Having Sex versus Making Love

Many of us are not educated about sexuality and how to be comfortable with sexual energy. In some cultures it is a well-practiced art with the motivation of meeting the divine in your lover and experiencing total union as a result.

Sexual contact can be many things. It can be a purely physical act to release sexual tension, a way of using power over someone else or a thoughtless and unconscious act, which is animal like.

It is selfish when you:

- seek sexual activity to only release your tension or gratify your senses,
- are more focussed on what is going on for yourself and forget about the other,
- get caught up in what is going on in your mind, off into fantasies,
- are no longer connected to your body's sensations,
- are in fear of opening your body or your heart and so close down,
- are afraid of being abandoned or hurt.

These things and many more stop you from being present with the other and also stop the pleasure and love from flowing between you.

Expressing your sexuality can also be a way to deeply connect and bond to another human being – a spiritually enlightening experience. This is making love. When you make love with someone you focus on the connection and love between you and become closer to the other.

You can access resource books through your local library. Look for Tantric Sex and Taoist Sexual Philosophy.

Different Ways of Being Sexual

Food has been used to compare the differences between having sex and making love. This may make it easier to distinguish between bad sex and making love in the most sacred way possible.

Grab, Grope and Grunt

Having sex like this can feel like someone is masturbating, using your body. He or she is not really aware that you are there. The person is there to satisfy his or her desire for sexual release. This is not a pleasant experience.

Grab, grope and grunt is where the person is eager for sexual release and doesn't care how he or she gets it. You are literally grabbed, sometimes against your wishes, your genital area is touched, you are banged at a few times, the person 'comes' and collapses.

Bad sex is like eating cold fish and chips. Unappealing, it's tasteless with the fat solidified and sticking to your mouth, leaving a yucky taste afterwards.

Words that describe this kind of sex: slimy, distasteful, dishonouring, disrespectful, awful, degrading, dirty, low, base and unfulfilling. Your thought might be – **never again**!

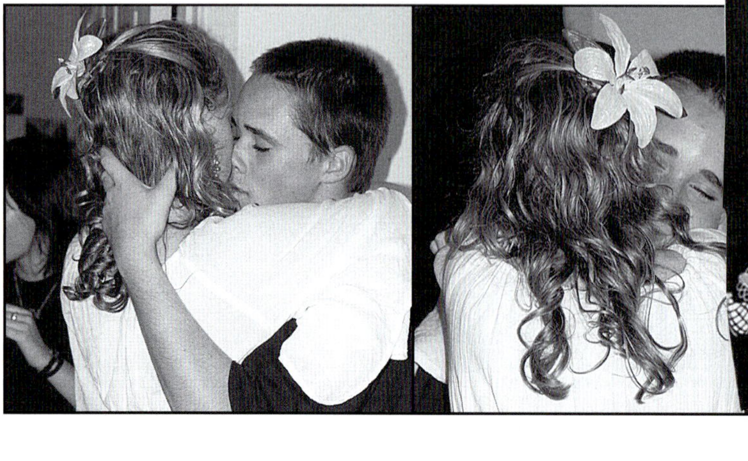

The TV Dinner Type

Ho-hum! Something to be over and done with as quickly as possible then he or she gets up and switches on the TV or something! The flavour doesn't count, but it fills a hungry appetite – though not for long.

There's a feeling of rush in this. There is definitely a goal and that is to 'come'. This sex is a means to an end. That end is penis in vagina or vagina around penis. Wham, bang, thank you ma'am! It's over before it properly starts. It may seem like you can be closer because you are physically close, but you may feel more distant afterwards. This can be painful and leaves you feeling empty and dissatisfied. You may experience sexual release but enjoyment and pleasure is minimal. No love is shared. It is hot but cold. It might be fun, but not much.

Words that describe this: used, hurried, rough, distant, alone, rubbished. It may be one step better than the grab, grope and grunt experience, but by no means good enough.

If the above two examples are how you experience sex on a regular basis it can create emotional emptiness, loss, grief or guilt for you and the person on the receiving end. It may also create feelings of shame, resentment or anger. This is what sex can be like without intimacy and love.

Spicy Sexy

Everyone gets dressed up for the spicy, sexy party. Dudes and chicks are out on the town looking for some heat. There's funky music playing and booze flowing and it's 'let's have a good time' time. Sizzling sausages, bursting burgers, topped with cheese, hot chips…

Everyone is on the make – eyeing each other up to see who goes with who.

The aim of the sex here is FUN! Maybe a one night stand and, "Will he still love me tomorrow?" Light, easy, playful with little responsibility and no thought for it to be anything else. The sex is simply for the thrill of it. This might be satisfying for a while but it is superficial and doesn't meet the deeper yearning for real connection.

The Sacred Feast of Love

Imagine this: You are on a beach or somewhere else in Nature at full moon or maybe you're in a warm candlelit room. You are surrounded by soft pillows and have fragrant oils for massage.

There is the most exquisite feast laid out before you. Everything is presented on platters and decorated with flowers. All of your favourite delicacies are there for your enjoyment. Your eyes boggle in wonderment at the delights before you. Your mouth is twitching with anticipation. You enjoy one taste explosion after another and share all these with your partner. You are relaxed and feeling heart connected. You smile often and feel the chemistry and magic flowing between you. Taking breaks between courses you feel deeply fulfilled and content. Over the next few hours you fill yourselves up and are electrically alive.

Making love, you move slowly, stroking, touching, with heart and eye contact you are enjoying the 'food of the gods'. Your bodies merge and are full of pulsating, blissful energy. Boundaries dissolve in the love making you share. You are totally ecstatic.

Words that describe this: divine, passionate, blissful, yuuuum, oneness, beautiful, thrilling, fulfilment, peaceful, awe, contentment. You have been touched by the wonder and Mystery of Life.

Sexual expression, when shared between two **conscious** people, who love each other, can be like shimmering waterfalls of pleasurable sensation taking you both to heaven. Spiritual sexuality and lovemaking can open both of you into an Infinite experience of Oneness.

These examples give you some idea of what is available and what you can co-create with someone else. The choice is yours.

"Sex is opening our hearts to one another, then opening our bodies. When we open our bodies to each other in sex and won't open our hearts, sex becomes a terrible pain."

– SEX. IF I DIDN'T LAUGH, I'D CRY, Jess Lair.

TEENSPEAK

"With teenage relationships it is important to have a friendship, I feel. You may not end up married but you might as well be buddies and have fun at this age. Have a relationship which is genuinely friendly and caring for one another." – Anna (16)

"I think sometimes society has the wrong attitude towards sex – it's far too casual. I think a lot of people abuse their sexuality. It has become more of a physical pleasure than a spiritual form of bonding and union." – Sam (15)

"I'd say yes we are all looking for a root. But not all the time. I don't go out on a Saturday night thinking I'm going to have sex." – Les (17)

"I thought boys were just out for sex with girls and now I think that girls are too. When I was on holidays I met a girl and she was in for that. She was trying to convince me to fool around with her behind my girlfriend's back but I wouldn't do it." – Dean (18)

"Sex is just physical. It is much more satisfying physically and spiritually when you love her. A good relationship should also have good sex as well as love." – Larry (16)

"Anyone can have sex, sex is just an action, but making love is a feeling deeper than the ocean. You lose your pride if you share your body and your soul with someone you don't love." – Tammy (15)

"My biggest problem has been that I thought everyone else had perfect sexual experiences. I thought I must be the only one who had funny feelings about it. Sexual relationships shouldn't be so hush hush. I'm now realising that other people have problems too. Making love is a learning experience. It takes practise. It takes time. It's not like in the movies. Fall into bed and everything is brilliant. I think because of all the rubbish there is about sex, porn videos, sex-related violence, that sex becomes an unnatural ambition. Young males want to do it to know they can. Young females want to know they're attractive. Everyone does it before they're ready. Not readiness in age, but before they know the right reasons for doing it. Only since I've been in a committed relationship have I learned what sex is about. I have sex when it feels good in my body and in my heart." – Jessica (19)

Setting Safe Boundaries

It is safer when exploring your sexuality that you are dating friends you know. You know where they live, who their parents are. Talk with them about where you're at before you get involved in sexual contact. For example, if you are dating someone and physically exploring your sexual feelings you could say, "I really like you but am not ready for full-on sexual contact with you yet. I would like to get to know you better first. I would like to kiss you and am open to some intimate touching. I choose to stay fully clothed and I would like you to do the same. Are you willing to agree to that?" Only go ahead if you sense the person is willing to agree. Check the response in your body to see if it feels right before going any further.

If you don't know how to do this or feel uncertain about communicating in this way, practice out loud in a mirror by yourself or with a friend.

You could find yourself in awkward situations that could go further than you intend if you are not:

- sure if this is for you,
- clear about your boundaries or trust the other person to respect these,
- sure about saying No or feel too scared to,
- creating safety,
- comfortable in yourself or with the other person.

Trust and respect take time to develop.

If you set limits on your sexual involvement with a partner, make sure YOU stick to them. You may feel like going further once you're involved – BUT DON'T! This is an opportunity to test her or his trustworthiness, as well as yours. Can you both keep your word? If you say, I am willing to go this far and you go further, the other person may not believe that you mean NO the next time you really do. If you change your agreements while feeling excited with your partner, you may regret it later. It's best to decide for yourself before becoming sexually active. If you break your agreement, you put yourself at risk now and perhaps later.

On your next date if you feel ready to go further, state clearly what your boundaries are. This way you can find out whether or not you can trust yourself and the other person. If and when you are ready to make love with your partner, make sure that you are both clear about methods of contraception.

Pay attention, listen to your body. The messages from your body can be trusted. Your mind can deceive you. Your body usually indicates what is true for you.

- If it doesn't feel right and good for you, say and mean NO!
- Make sure there are people around who can offer protection if you feel unsure or unsafe.
- Do not go to places that are isolated or accept a ride in a car with someone you are just getting to know.
- Don't feel obliged to say yes for someone else's sake. That can leave you open to being abused or abusing yourself.

Most people will not take advantage of you, some do! Be aware. Be careful!

Before Sexual Intercourse

If you can do the following things with your friend before having sexual intercourse you are well on your way to being ready.

- Talk about your sexual experience so far – briefly. Also talk about any history of sexually transmitted infections and successful treatments.
- If there is a chance that your partner has HIV/AIDS have a test. It takes three months for the virus to show up as positive. Keep that in mind if your partner is from a high risk group – intravenous drug users or homosexual males or someone who has had many sexual partners.
- Make agreements about what you are ready for and not ready for. Honour the agreements you make.
- If you prefer that your partner is not sexually active with someone else while he or she is with you, make this clear before getting involved.
- Use effective methods of contraception. Condoms prevent pregnancy and offer some protection against STIs.

Be prepared to stop what you are doing as soon as one of you does not feel okay about what is happening. If the person you are with cares about you, he or she is prepared to wait for you to be ready.

Double Standards

There was so much anger in a classroom of fifteen-year-olds when the subject of sexuality was raised. The place was in uproar. The adolescent females were angry because the males were pressuring them for sex. Some of the guys were angry at their friends for doing this. The females were called frigid if they refused and sluts if they agreed. These double standards cause a great deal of tension.

Many males boast when they **have** and feel insecure if they **haven't**. There's a lot of showing off. This pressure is unbearable for some teenagers. The real value of male/female relationships is often lost and many are doing it for reasons that are questionable. Even if it doesn't look like it, everyone loses in this situation.

Generally males seek physical contact and release. Females seek emotional closeness and intimacy. Another way of saying this is – a male finds love for his partner through sex and females come to enjoy sex through feeling loved. There are exceptions, of course.

Sexual Preference

During adolescence you find yourself to be either:

Heterosexual – that is, you are sexually attracted to members of the other gender. Sometimes called straight.

Homosexual – that is, you prefer to have sexual relationships with people of the same gender. Some people use the term gay to describe this.

Bi-sexual – that is, you enjoy sexual relationships with both males and females.

You have the choice to share your body and sexual energy with the same or the other gender. You are an individual and what happens in the sexual development of one person may not happen for another. Your choice of intimate and sexual relationships is up to you.

Many homosexual people experience pain about parental rejection, lack of social acceptance and separation. It can be unsafe to come out and be honest about sexual preference for fear of being hurt, attacked or left out. Some people shame and blame those who have a different sexual preference to them. This causes a lot of suffering. In some parts of Indonesia, India, Africa and some Scandinavian countries, sexual relationships with either gender are socially acceptable. To love someone sexually in ways that are not harming others is quite normal to them.

If you are attracted to members of the same gender – homosexual or bi-sexual:

- Understand that this is normal.
- There are many people who feel like you do, so you are not alone.
- Find places that feel safe so that you can express your sexuality.
- Be clear about how you approach people of the same gender if they are unaware of your sexual preference.

If you are feeling alone and unsupported about your sexual preference there are organisations that offer help. Look in your phone directory or on the Internet for Lifeline or the Gay and Lesbian Counselling Services.

"A girl seduced me. She was my best friend. We got pissed. I didn't know she wanted to seduce me but apparently she'd wanted me since the last time we got drunk. She got me to give her a massage and a hickey (love bite) because she thought it would be interesting. Then she put my hand on her breast. So I thought, 'Ah well, okay.' I was drunk, but I would probably have said yes anyway. This past year has been a learning experience for me. I am enjoying finding out and learning about myself. Being 15 is fun!" – Delilah.

Mucushla (16) on bi-sexuality and queers

"Our society doesn't deal with childhood sexuality very well. Even the most enlightened parents tend to shy away from the issue. But rather than obliterating the problem, repression leads to psychological trauma and feelings of alienation. It is exceedingly easy, as a child or young adult, to pick up the idea that you are a mutation and a freak – that you are simply wrong.

Adults are nervous about childhood sexuality because it can be easily manipulated by the more perverse and predatory members of our society. However, ignoring the fact that children are sexual beings does nothing to change the fact. Children's sexuality should be acknowledged, but adults should not be involved in it. We work it out, as long as we aren't made to feel somehow criminal for it.

I can't technically claim to be a queer kid, since I decided long ago that I'm indecisive, but I can say that my decision to be a sexually aware and an undecided young woman was not aided by the people around me. During high school, I was already alienated and ostracised for being staunchly individual and then becoming aware that I was not strictly heterosexual made me into a feared figure. People fear that which they do not know. From someone who is entirely hetro, a queer kid is intimidating and frightening. Girls who had been friendly acquaintances became paranoid that I was going to pounce on them and so steered clear of me.

Both my parents are enlightened people, neither of whom have any homophobic tendencies, but I never talked to them about my dilemmas, it didn't seem to be any of their business. They are both comfortable with my decisions. They trust me to be aware of all the safety issues and behave intelligently. For someone from a more conservative background, the whole process might have been very different. The transition into a sexually active and independent adult can be confusing enough for a heterosexual, but to be in an environment which fears sexual relations altogether, not to mention same-sex relations, a young adult could be traumatised.

I am a person who has to offload whatever I am thinking about, regardless of how it fits into the value-systems of those around me. But many young adults dealing with these issues lock them up and carry them around. Instead of confronting them, the issues fester. They may be festering and rotting away unacknowledged for indefinite lengths of time. Possibly forever.

For young queers who are open about themselves, you will inevitably face some hostility from your peers. For people who are themselves confused, a brave young queer who knows exactly where he or she is coming from is confronting. Usually the most panic-stricken homophobes are repressed queers themselves. This is natural, we bring up their issues and they resent us for it."

Masturbation and Self-Pleasuring

Masturbation usually releases sexual tension. There are many old fashioned sayings about it. Like, it makes you blind or that your hand or penis, if a male, will fall off. These are not true! Some religious groups condemn sexual self-pleasuring and have made people ashamed about doing this. Masturbation is defined as self-abuse in some dictionaries. These ideas have stopped people from sensually enjoying their bodies for centuries.

Understanding about masturbation can change the motivation for sexual contact with someone else from sexual frustration and tension, to loving and sharing.

FOR MALES

Perhaps your first experiences of your sexuality involved masturbation. If all you give to yourself is jerking off then you may be robbing yourself of something special.

David Deida, an inspirational teacher says: "Masturbating over and over ends up conditioning your body and nervous system to a habitual sequence: genital stimulation, mental fantasy, building up tension and ejaculating. Teenage masturbation is essentially an exercise in fantasy, done alone, without much love or even human intimacy. By the time most men are having sex with women, they repeat the same sequence they learned while masturbating. Sex has become a road toward ejaculation, a road paved with internal imagery, self-enclosure and the desire to release tension.

To realise the full potential of sex, you must learn how to re-condition your body and nervous system. You must learn how to unhabitualise the mechanics of your ejaculation and convert your orgasm into a massive profusion of energy that deepens, not ends, the lovemaking session.

The first step is undoing the habits you learned while masturbating as a teenager. Instead of tensing your muscles as you become sexually stimulated, learn to relax them. When you notice your face squinching up, relax it. When you notice your breath getting fast and shallow, slow it down and deepen it. When you notice your belly tight and your chest hard, open your belly and soften the area around your heart." – THE WAY OF THE SUPERIOR MAN.

"I masturbate when I am not in an active sexual relationship with a woman. It is a way of giving myself pleasure, of loving myself physically when no one is around me on an intimate level.

I have overcome the built-in guilt that society, mostly through religion, attaches to pleasuring myself. I have a healthy sexual energy that usually leads me to masturbate two or three times per week – but this can vary to each day for a few days, usually when there's a lot of stress in my life – to once in several weeks. This keeps me balanced energetically, so that I don't get over-sexed and go out looking for sexual activity, nor do I lose my sense of sexual health and fitness.

Through this practise I've found that I can prolong love-making with my partner and can experience multiple orgasms with her without ejaculating." – John (56)

FOR FEMALES

There are some who naturally masturbate. There are many who are unfamiliar with their genital area. You can explore your body and allow this to lead onto sexual self-pleasuring if you like. You may discover different ways to bring yourself to orgasm. You may not know that females can have several types of orgasms.

This is what Jude writes: A clitoral orgasm is the most superficial. It is a genitally focussed pleasure that you can have with or without a partner. Vibrators are usually more effective than penises for this. It is a personal, tense, lightning bolt orgasm. Over quickly – but it can happen many times.

Although the following is not speaking specifically about masturbation it is useful to know what's possible. You can have a multiple **G-spot orgasm** without a partner. The G-spot is the spongy area of tissue located on the front inside of the vagina up behind the pubic bone. It is usually sensitive. It can hold a lot of tension and may take some time to relax.

This area opens me into my vulnerability and requires a lot of trust for me to allow my partner to go there. It is what I most yearn for. This orgasm is interdependent with my partner. Surrendering to him with eye-to-eye contact, allowing all the emotions to flow. I am not afraid, I trust him. The longer we make love the more I open and pleasure radiates from my vagina throughout my whole body. I am gone. My mind is stilled and I am just an oozing, moving, ever-opening surrendered mass of nothingness and everythingness all at once.

A cervical orgasm is the deepest and most blissful dissolving into oneness with my man that I have felt. It is truly a spiritual experience where we recognise the godliness in each other clearly. No mind, no ego. Pure heart connected, passionate, **perfect merging of two bodies into one love.** We are opening each other, going deeper and deeper together. The skin dissolves, the edges melt and I sink into a void in total body ecstasy. This is the fireworks orgasm that blooms over and over again. The body pulsating, it feels like the melting never ends. It is an unbearable fullness. This one lingers and I carry the glow of being loved around for days!

FOR BOTH

Allow your masturbation, self-pleasuring and love making to be a way of loving yourself. Take it slowly and enjoy learning about your body. The more you are able to be sensual with yourself and also when you are with a partner, the more open your body becomes and the more pleasure you can share with him or her.

Contraception

Sexual intercourse is Nature's way of making babies.

It also offers a deep openness, pleasure, sensation and love for everyone. You can make a conscious choice as to whether you are ready to bring a child into the world. It is not wise to do this if you are still in your teenage years.

Parenting is a long-term commitment and an enormous responsibility – many adults are unprepared for this. Many say that if they had any idea about what child rearing involved they would not have had children. For others having a child is the best thing they ever did.

Make responsible choices around your fertility to avoid unplanned pregnancy. Find a method of birth control/contraception that suits you before becoming sexually active.

Educate yourself before choosing any one method – read books, check out the Internet. It is also advisable to see a health care practitioner.

If you are petting – kissing, touching, fondling and there is no contact of penis with vagina, the female cannot become pregnant. If there is penis to vagina contact, live sperm in the male's fluids can be transferred and a female can become pregnant, even if he doesn't come (ejaculate) and even without full erection or penetration.

You may be uncomfortable talking about contraceptive methods with your partner. He or she may be unwilling to take precautions.

If this is the case why are you choosing to be sexually active and running the risk of unwanted pregnancy?

By taking responsibility together for contraception you can create a strong bond and closeness with your partner.

It can bring confidence and safety into your relationship.

TAKE RESPONSIBILITY...

for your own fertility. Do this even if your partner is willing to take care of his or hers.

Janine decided that she was ready to become sexually active when she was seventeen. She also made a decision that she would not make love with any man that she would not be willing to have a child with if this accidentally happened. It took her three years to find such a man. That is taking full and conscious responsibility for her fertility!

Be conscious about your fertility as a young woman and take responsibility for your sperm as a young man.

If it is challenging for you to get to a doctor or clinic because you:

- live in a remote area,
- prefer that no one knows,
- are embarrassed or uncomfortable,
- have other personal reasons,
- are having underage sex (which is against the law),

then look in your local library for books or on the Internet for Websites on Birth Control/Contraception. You may know a nurse, an aunt or uncle, a school counsellor or someone nearby who you can trust – ask for information. Make sure you are fully informed.

It is cool to be in charge of your body and uncool to become pregnant or get someone else pregnant when you are not ready. Take care of yourself...

Get contraception handled

Different Methods

A condom when used properly is a fairly reliable form of contraception. It can be 98 percent effective if one is used every time you have sexual intercourse. The added advantage of using a condom is not only can it stop pregnancy, it can also protect against sexually transmitted infections. Young people often ask how to put one on. It is pulled over the head of an erect penis with the bubble pointing out and rolled down the shaft. There are usually diagrams on the packet to help you. Condoms for females are also available.

Males are strongly encouraged to participate in contraception. The following methods are used by females:

The contraceptive pill when taken regularly is a way of chemically interfering with the natural menstrual cycle. It prevents you from ovulating. Pregnancy can only occur when you ovulate and sperm contacts the ovum (egg).

The Pill is 98% effective and a convenient form of contraception for a female who is sexually active and doesn't choose to use natural methods. The Pill interferes with the natural functions of the body. There are potential side effects that have been well researched. Find out about these so that informed choices can be made.

Taking the Pill alters your experience of the emotional ebb and flow of your monthly cycle. It reduces your connection to your body, cycle and your fertility. Other methods of contraception require more education, care and active involvement.

If you see a doctor, it is more likely that the Pill is recommended rather than any of the natural methods. It is not the only choice available. Some doctors may prescribe the Pill for you if you are having an irregular cycle or menstrual discomfort. This does not deal with the cause of these symptoms.

Note: If natural methods of contraception are not suitable at this time in your life it is better to use the Pill than risk unplanned pregnancy.

A **diaphragm** or **cervical cap used with spermicidal gel** can be 95-98 percent effective when used properly. The gel kills live sperm cells. A diaphragm or cap is a device that is inserted into the vagina. It covers the cervix to stop sperm from entering the womb. When used with spermicidal gel it is a harmless and effective method of contraception. Family Planning Clinics, doctors or Women's Health Centres can measure, fit and teach you how to use it. If it is not inserted properly it is not an effective method of contraception.

Fertility awareness if used properly is a natural method of contraception where mucus flow and menstrual cycle are taken into account. This can be 95-99 percent effective. You can get specially designed calendars to help keep accurate records. After some months of recording your cycle and checking your mucus (vaginal fluids) you can become familiar with your fertility pattern. It takes practice. You can back it up by using other methods of contraception, like condoms or a diaphragm, at the time of the month when you can become pregnant. Get professional advice if you intend to use this method.

You can use a thermometer. By recording your basal body temperature daily you can know the precise timing of your ovulation. Knowing this assists you in using other contraceptive protection and deciding not to include sexual intercourse in your lovemaking.

Lady Free Biotester is the name given in Australia for a new device that helps you to determine the time of ovulation. It has a mini-microscope and is a bit bigger than a lipstick. It magnifies the crystals in saliva and when a fern-like pattern shows, you are about to ovulate. It's very simple. It is not a method of contraception but tells you even before your mucus indicates whether you are becoming fertile. It is obtainable at Pharmacies.

If you choose to use fertility awareness, seek professional help. Natural Fertility Management and Family Planning Clinics can teach you about this method. These clinics may also give you a Lunar Cycle chart.

Be conscious about your fertility. You can do this by keeping accurate records of the date you begin to menstruate. Over the months it becomes easy to recognise when you are ovulating, when you could become pregnant and when you may bleed. Sperm can live for up to five days in the vagina. If you make love anytime during the five days before ovulation and five days after, you can become pregnant. During this time you can take extra care by not having sexual intercourse or by using a safe method of contraception.

Most methods of contraception have a 95-99 percent success rate but when not used properly they can result in a high failure rate. When we become conscious of our fertility there could be less unplanned pregnancies, abortions and babies in the world.

A Note: With the arrival of the Pill in the 60's, it became fashionable to be sexual with many partners. This is called promiscuity. There has been an increase in sexually transmitted infections because of unconscious sexual contact and a weakening of the immune system. Take care of yourself sexually!

Whoops!

If you don't use contraception or a condom breaks or slips off the penis, there is a pill that you can take the next morning if you think you might be ovulating and may become pregnant. It can have side effects – headaches and vomiting. You can get this from a doctor, Women's Health Centres or Family Planning Clinics. **The Morning After Pill is for emergencies only** and is not to be used as a regular method of contraception.

Some Reasons for Pregnancy

Some females decide to get pregnant because they feel empty inside and long for something to love. This is not a good reason to bring a child into the world. Another reason is to keep a partner. This does not usually work. Many females are literally left carrying the baby. Consider deeply the responsibility you are taking on by having a child before you get pregnant.

Decide with your partner when it is the right time to bring a new life into the world. It helps to have a steady income, a home and a committed relationship. The baby then has a responsible mother and father and a settled start to life.

Birds make their nests before laying their eggs.

Be aware: The world is over-populated. It is a valid choice not to have children.

Abortion

There is a lot of disagreement about this issue.
Some people think that:

- it is a woman's right to have this choice available to her,
- this is taking a life,
- no one has the right to make this decision.

It is not an easy decision for any girl/woman to make. There are emotional, ethical or religious issues involved as well as the physical effects of choosing to abort an unborn child. If you become pregnant when you are not ready to give birth, abortion is one option you have. This is something to be considered carefully with a caring adult or with professional guidance.

DO NOT have abortions as a method of avoiding giving birth or instead of contraception. Multiple abortions can damage your health, your ability to conceive and your emotional and spiritual wellbeing. Abortion may also be against the law where you live.

Underage Sexual Intercourse is Against the Law

Many teenagers are not aware that laws have been made to protect them. It is not easy to determine at what age you are mature enough to make your own decisions about becoming sexually active. This law makes it an illegal act for anyone to have sexual intercourse before the stated age. It is saying that the law considers you too immature before then. The legal age varies in different countries. It is usually around sixteen.

This law is designed to stop older people from having sexual intercourse with someone who is under the legal age. This may not stop them from doing this. If this happens they can be imprisoned.

Check out the legal age where you live by calling your local doctor or a Kids Helpline.

My Story

Because of early childhood experiences I was afraid of males and did a good job of staying unattractive to them. I did have one or two boyfriends, but when it came to kissing and petting I didn't feel comfortable at all. I was given no preparation about sexuality from my mother or father.

Sex was something that happened behind closed doors and was not talked about.

The message I got sub-consciously from my mother was that as a female it was my place to please men. That was common in her days. No one had explained to me that some males are not trustworthy, that I could protect myself and that my virginity was a precious gift.

In my twenties, much of my sexual activity was motivated by a longing to feel close to someone. I went against my true feelings out of a desperate desire to be loved. Sex with that motive always left me feeling alone and empty. Just having sex has never been satisfying for me. By doing this I was actually sexually abusing myself. Making love is something I didn't discover until I was older.

I've had powerful sexual encounters when I was fully clothed and the man was also. The first time was when we were lying together after a camp. As we lay holding each other our breathing changed. I felt an incredible rising energy. It was as if we were about to get fully involved in sexual activity, but without even kissing or moving. Whew, the energy got stronger as the sensations rose and fell. Wave upon wave of surging ecstatic energy rushed through my body. I was moved to what I can only describe as multiple energetic orgasms over and over again.

A whole new avenue of exploration with sexual energy had opened for me.

In another relationship I experienced real love for the first time. Our lovemaking reflected the depth of feeling that we had for one another.

Sometimes if one of us felt like making love we spent hours talking about what was happening in our relationship – clearing our minds, hearts and bodies of anything that did not allow total surrender to each other. At other times we made love to heaven and floated in bliss for hours.

SEXUAL ABUSE

Sexual abuse is something that is happening all over the world all of the time. Statistics show it affects up to one in four females and one in six males at some point in their lives.

Reading about sexual abuse may stir up hidden memories or remind you of experiences that you have tried to forget. You might not be in touch with any feelings about this. On the other hand you might feel hurt, uncomfortable, nausea, anger, disbelief or fear. These are all understandable. Make space in your life for your feelings and accept them. They are part of you. For some of you it may bring a sense of relief and understanding.

What is Sexual Abuse?

Sexual abuse is any sexual behaviour that is forced upon you by another person. It is unacceptable when something is being done to you by any person that involves sexual feelings that you do not like and that you have not given permission for, or if you are too young to make a choice about what is happening to you.

Someone who is sexually abusing you may be playing with your genitals or any part of your body in a way that sexually excites him or her. Some of these behaviours are crimes. You may have allowed people to do things that you didn't like because you didn't know how to stop them or didn't know that this is unacceptable behaviour. Sexual abuse is extremely complicated and it can be confusing and scary. It may seem like a person who is abusing you is caring for and loving you. If you have been abused you can do something about it.

Sometimes abuse starts with something that seems small but feels yucky. This can still be sexual abuse and should be dealt with because it can gradually lead to more abuse over time. If it feels yucky – it is most likely to be wrong.

Trust your instincts!

If you have been sexually abused, your experience of the world has been changed forever.

Sexual Abuse is Not Okay

If you have been or are being sexually abused or if you suspect that you are or sense that someone close to you is, then read everything in this part of the book. Any sexual behaviour instigated by an adult with a child or under-age teenager is wrong. Teenage sexual abuse is covered early on. Everyone could read this. By knowing about sexual abuse you can take care of yourself and do what you can to protect yourself or others. It may stop sexual abuse from happening. Child and teenage sexual abuse is covered in detail. If you have been abused, you are not alone! Reading about it may help you understand what has happened to you.

For more information about sexual abuse and its related issues you can find support groups and professional people who are recognised experts, to further inform yourself. There are also many useful books:

OUT IN THE OPEN – A Guide for Young People Who Have Been Abused – Q. Bain and M. Sanders, Virago Press.
THE ME NOBODY KNOWS – Barbara Beana and Shari Bennett, Lexington Books.
THE COURAGE TO HEAL – L. Davis, Harper and Row.

Sexual Abuse is a Taboo

Sexual abuse is taboo all over the world. People feel uncomfortable, don't talk about it and prefer to pretend it doesn't exist. It happens in schools, churches, parks, hospitals and children's homes, at camps or any activities where children or young people are. It often occurs in the home, by people who are known to the child or teenager.

Sexual abuse is coming out into the open. It used to be kept a secret. Abusers could get away with it more easily. The fact that sexual abuse is more in the public eye may help to stop some people from abusing others. One of our challenges as a society is to find ways to prevent this from happening so that we can make this a safer World for everyone.

If you are someone who has been sexually abused, the existing taboo may make it hard to talk about and you might prefer that other people don't know. Some reasons for this are that you may feel ashamed, dirty, tainted, spoiled or afraid. You may believe that if people know what has happened, they may not like you or be your friend. By not telling others you may be trying to protect yourself or the person who has abused you. If you tell others, it could be difficult for some people to hear what you have to say.

You may have tried to tell people but they did not believe you. You may have never told anybody because it is too painful to talk about. If you tell others, they may pretend that you are having bad dreams or making up stories. They may be unwilling to face the truth of your pain or theirs. When this happens you might think you can't get help from anyone.

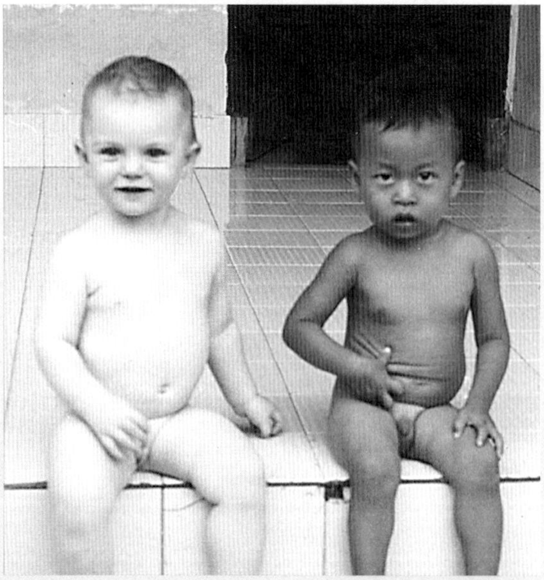

Healthy Sexuality

It is usually innocent when young children play with their own or each other's genitals. This is natural childhood behaviour. Young children are interested in exploring their world. Their bodies are a part of their world and they may play games like doctors and nurses with each other. Young children innocently playing with each other's genitals can be just like playing with any other part of their bodies to them. This is natural and feels good and is not the same as sexual abuse.

Teenagers and Sexual Abuse

Teenage hormones kick in between about twelve and fifteen years of age. This stimulates an upsurge of sexual energy that can lead to curiosity and exploration. This is natural. Emerging sexuality makes young people appealing. There is often a magnetic pull sexually from and to them. They may be unconscious of it. This is called sexual attraction. This can make young people vulnerable to sexually abusive adults and abusive teenagers. Because of a lack of experience or because most teenagers are innocent, they may not be aware of the dangers. **For many children and teenagers the World is a safe place.**

Exploring your sexuality is healthy and natural. It can be fun and is a part of growing up. Forcing someone to be sexual with you, groping, being violent and abusive or raping someone is not **natural** and is not acceptable sexual behaviour. Young people sometimes abuse themselves and others. It is essential to know how to take care of yourself. It is wise to avoid situations where you are at risk.

If sexual contact doesn't feel right to you, it may be because:

- contact with that person is not acceptable to you,
- you are not enjoying what is happening,
- you have been told that expressing your sexuality is wrong,
- society's taboo about sex may be interfering with natural sexual responses,
- someone is sexually abusing you.

If you are unsure about your feelings talk to a responsible adult about them.

If what is happening to you does not feel right in your body – it is wrong for you.

Take responsibility: If you are aware that someone is about to or is being sexually abused in any way, do something about it. Find a helpful adult or call the police. It is not cool for this to happen to anyone. If you do not take any action, you may be allowing a crime to occur.

Sexual Abuse Outside the Home

Friends or acquaintances may make sex seem cool. You may be pressured by them to be sexual when you are not ready. They may not respect you or themselves. There are risks in any social situation. Take care of yourself whenever and wherever possible. You can do things to reduce the risk.

You are at greater risk when you:

- are feeling weak, vulnerable or lonely,
- are desperate for love and looking for affection,
- are becoming sexually active, exploring and curious about sexuality,
- are walking alone without a clear and confident purpose,
- accept a lift anywhere from a stranger or someone that you do not know very well,
- are on a date with someone who is not trustworthy,
- are left alone by or leave your friends at parties. You can be sexually abused or raped at a party in a toilet, in a bedroom, garage or garden – even when there are people around,
- are under the influence of alcohol or drugs and therefore not in control of all of your faculties,
- run away from home with nowhere to go. You may be leaving yourself open to people who kidnap teenagers, get them addicted to drugs and then make them sell their bodies for sex. This is prostituting them. It happens!

Things you can do to look after yourself:

- stay alert and be aware,
- develop an attitude of confidence to let people know you are not the type of person they could overpower,
- avoid situations where you are vulnerable that could become dangerous,
- follow your intuition. If you have strange or uncomfortable feelings about someone, don't trust that person,
- if you invite someone home make sure there is a responsible adult around,
- be aware of your surroundings – know where you are going and with whom,
- make sure your parents know where you are. Stay in touch with them while you are away from home,
- set time lines with parents so that they know when to expect you home. If you don't come home, they are alerted,
- attend a self-defence class and learn simple methods to fight off an attacker,
- if attacked, make loud noises – screaming, shouting or breaking a window. Noise can frighten off attackers. Carry a rape alarm or whistle if you feel unsafe or are in an unfriendly neighbourhood.

The Effects of Alcohol and Drugs

Taking drugs and drinking alcohol affect your ability to think logically. That makes drinking and drug taking extra dangerous when it comes to sexual abuse. Drugs and alcohol can reduce your capacity to know what is right or wrong.

Some people who might not normally harm others, can do so when drunk or when on drugs **because they may be out of control.** Some people get others drunk on purpose to sexually abuse them. The chances are that the people around are also drunk or on drugs and therefore don't notice or care if someone is being sexually abused. Sometimes it is considered cool to abuse someone in those situations. Many teenagers have been raped when under the influence of drugs or alcohol. Some people do not even remember what happened until they find themselves in disarray once the effects of the alcohol/drugs have worn off. They may feel ashamed when they become conscious that they have been raped and don't remember what happened.

As you get older, if you're drinking alcohol, do so with trusted friends. Do not mix drinks. Limit the amount you consume. One of you could agree to stay sober and remain aware of what is going on. Looking out for each other can keep you safe.

Be careful! Nowhere is one hundred percent safe unless there are responsible, caring adults around who are willing to protect you.

What is Rape?

Rape is the crime of forcing anyone to have sexual intercourse without that person's free consent. Rape is a violent act. The rapist can physically threaten and/or use blackmail. Rapists can be charged and imprisoned for this. When rape happens to children or teenagers they may not tell anyone about it or go to the police. Let someone know if this happens to you.

TEENSPEAK

"I was 15 when I met this guy who was a hairdresser. He could tell I was adopted and knew I was gay. That freaked me out. I was just coming to terms with being gay myself. He gave me his number. I rang and he invited me to his place – half an hour out of town. We sat around and talked. He said I looked tired. He kept asking if I'd like to lie down and take my clothes off to be more comfortable. I said NO! He asked if I'd been with a guy before. I said yes. It didn't click. He offered me a drink – it tasted a bit funny. I started to feel strange. He got frisky and pushed me into a chair and sat on my lap. He tried to kiss me. I didn't enjoy it. Then full force he tried to take my jeans off. I got him off. I said NO. I tried to go home – he wouldn't let me.

I jumped off the balcony and he raced after me. I ran towards the road and there was a big hedge. He tackled me – I fell. He hit me over the head with something. That's the last thing I remember. When I woke up my shirt was torn and there was mud all over me. There was blood, I didn't know where from. I had no jeans on. I didn't feel right. I found my jeans and got to my car. He started yelling abuse and stopped me from driving away. He said, I love you and you were great.

I drove home and mum asked me what happened. I told her I got into a fight. She believed me. I didn't go to the police. I was too scared to see a doctor until a lot later. They did lots of tests. I could have caught HIV/AIDS or Hepatitis. He wanted me to see a counsellor. I didn't want to talk about it. I wanted to close that part of my life. It impacted heftily on me. I don't really trust people. I have issues with my sexuality. I can't be intimate with somebody. It's caused problems. Guys can't understand why – they think I should get over it." – Mike (24)

Date Rape

Date rape usually happens when you put your trust in someone you go out with and that trust is abused. You may be grabbed and forced to do things you don't like or raped. Some people still don't see this as a crime. When it comes to date rape it's not usually the sleazy stranger hanging about in the street to fear, but someone who offers you a ride home or invites you back to his or her place after a date. Some people think they have a right to sex if they have taken you out to a movie, bought you a drink or dinner or given you a lift home.

"My parents had never talked to me about sex. I was thirteen when I was raped. I had not learned much at school by this point either. I had low self-esteem so when a sixteen-year-old boy showed me attention at school I was quite flattered and felt special. I invited him to a party. It was in the basement of a friend's house. We played games like spin the bottle and twister.

The boy took me into another small room, closed the door and started kissing me. That was okay, but I didn't like him touching my barely visible budding breasts and groping at my crotch. It all happened so fast. I didn't know what was going on. He pinned me down on the floor, pulled off my shorts and panties and stuck his hard penis into my tight, dry vagina. It hurt so much. I tried to push him off but he pinned my arms down and kept up the thrusting. I was too afraid to scream for help and too ashamed. It did not take long before he ejaculated and let me free. My undies and shorts were soaked with blood.

When I was dressed he picked me up and carried me over his shoulder back into the party room. As I was carried in, my brother, who was at the party, smacked me on the bottom in a friendly manner. I worried that he'd see the blood. This was my first intercourse experience and I didn't understand what had happened to me. When writing about my story I can't believe I still feel so much pain, thirty-four years later." – Brenda .

If anything like this happens to you – make lots of noise. Tell someone you trust. Don't allow people to get away with any other kind of abuse or rape. It is a crime and deserves to be punished. It may take courage and a sense of justice to tell, but it may stop it happening again to you and to others.

A note from me: How do you feel when reading these stories.? I feel sadness and anger about these stories and others like them. Please do everything you can to protect yourself. Listen to your intuition. Don't go to people's places and don't let them know where you live if you do not know them very well.

Legal Action

If you have been raped or are being currently abused and you choose to press charges, call the police or go to your local hospital emergency room or a rape crisis centre. When charges are made, a medical examination is required by law.

Take a support person with you if you can.

A medical examination may be necessary to:

- make sure your body has not been physically damaged,
- gather legal evidence that may result in charges being made against the abuser,
- prove that there was sexual contact.

Do not bathe or wash after being sexually abused until after the examination as this may remove evidence that could support your case. A medical examination may be uncomfortable. It's okay to tell the doctor if it is painful.

The authorities will write down the details of the abuse. You may be asked questions that are embarrassing for you to answer. With evidence of abuse your case is stronger if you decide to press charges. Sometimes people are set free, even when everyone knows they are guilty. They may not get punished because there may not be enough concrete evidence to prove their guilt.

If you're not going to press charges, you can still go to your own doctor or a health clinic to make sure everything is okay.

Teenagers Abusing Children

If you know teenagers who are sexually abusing a brother or sister or a child who is younger or smaller than they are – report this to an understanding adult.

If you are a teenager who is or has sexually abused a younger or smaller child – seek help. It is likely that you have been physically or sexually abused and may not even remember. You may think this behaviour is acceptable. Whether you have been abused or not, sexually abusing someone else is wrong. **STOP IMMEDIATELY!** Let someone know. Be brave enough. To be that honest is a big ask and takes courage. Find someone who is compassionate, willing to hear you and who recognises what it has taken you to own up to what you have been doing. Help is available for you and the other child. If you are sexual abusing a child, you are harming him or her!

Some teenagers sexually abuse other teenagers. This happens a lot. If this happens to you or someone you know, make sure he or she does not get away with it. Speak to someone you trust. That may prevent the abuse of others and yourself.

Who is Sexually Abused?

It does not matter if you are black or white, yellow or red, rich or poor, boy or girl, teenager or baby, intelligent or simple, beautiful or ugly, fat or thin. If you are quiet or outgoing, a loner or sociable, live in a city or the country, come from America, England, Hong Kong, Australia or any other country in the world. Whether your parents are unemployed, working or wealthy or still married or divorced. Get the picture?

Who Sexually Abuses?

Some adults abuse babies. Some abuse children. Others abuse teenagers. Some abuse others of any age. Some adults only abuse their own children and others abuse as many children as they can, even if they don't know them. Sometimes teenage males or females sexually abuse children and each other.

What Does an Abuser Look Like?

You cannot tell who abusers are by looking at them. Sexual abusers can be in their late teens, an old man, a young woman, a teacher, a doctor, a housewife, a babysitter, an uncle or an aunt, a neighbour, a youth worker, a priest, a policeman... **anyone!**

The only way you can recognise a sexual abuser is when something is being done to you that you don't like. Check out how you feel emotionally and in your body. A person who sexually abuses others may seem like a nice person most of the time, but this is not the truth.

Adults of either gender who sexually abuse boys or girls are generally called perpetrators, victimisers, molesters or abusers. They are officially called paedophiles.

If a person in authority is blackmailing you and/or if he or she is bigger, older or stronger and is abusing you – it is not your fault.

Sexual abuse can happen to anyone, by anyone, anywhere, at anytime!

Incest

This is when a blood relative has sexual intercourse with (or molests) another family member.

This often occurs within the home when biological fathers sexually abuse their daughters, sons, nieces and nephews. Some biological mothers sexually abuse their daughters, sons, nieces and nephews. Some grandparents have sexually abused their children as well as their grandchildren. Some aunties and uncles also sexually abuse young relatives. When step parents, adopting and foster parents interfere with, molest or have sexual intercourse with young people in their care, this is sexual abuse.

As a child or teenager you are dependent on parents or carers, for food, shelter, transport, love, education, safety – **everything!** If the people responsible for looking after you are also abusing you, it can be hard for you to speak up or feel safe. You may be too scared because you have relied on them to look after you.

If you have known someone for a number of years, perhaps since birth and you are used to doing what you are told AND if he or she is inclined to sexual abuse, you are more vulnerable. You have little protection if she or he is a paedophile and are at greater risk from a relative you know than from people who are not connected to your home. You may feel loyalty to the person who is abusing you and be unwilling to speak up.

If you are living with someone who is sexually abusing you – or if you visit or an abuser visits your family – **you are not in a safe place.**

Get help. Tell someone you trust **immediately**. If nothing is done about it, tell someone else. If there is no-one you trust, call the police, Family and Community Services or a Kid's Helpline.

The most frequent form of sexual abuse is from father to daughter. Some teenage girls become pregnant to their fathers.

Brothers and sisters abuse younger or smaller siblings in some families. Sometimes they have been taught to do this by a parent or family friend. They may have been abused themselves.

Thank you Kate

for the courage to share your story and reveal who you are.

Kate's Story – 16

What do you remember about living with your Dad?

I remember how he used to spoil me. Take me places and buy me things. The abuse started when I was about 5 or 6. I got used to it and put it into the back of my mind, thinking it was just normal. My older sister left when I was nine. I think he abused her as well. So I was living on my own with dad for four or five years. When he came home from work he would get stuck into beers, but he didn't get violent.

I stopped living with dad when I was fourteen. Just before I left, I had what I thought was a dream. It was like midnight and I was in a really deep sleep when he got home. Drunk! He came into my room and got on top of me and raped me. I was struggling. I think he may have hit me across the face a few times.

I was really scared when I woke up the next morning.

I told the school nurse. I was upset and started crying. I was in class and the school counsellor took me into her office. A police officer was there. A Department of Community Services (DOCS) lady took me to this place to see what I was like mentally. I didn't know what was going on.

Someone from DOCS came to the house to see dad but he wasn't home.

Dad told me he would never do anything like that to me. I had to believe him. I felt confused. I'd like to ask him why he did that to me.

Mum didn't know until I visited her in the next holidays. I decided to live with her. I had a bit of weight on me but now I am losing it and I think I'll lose more. Mum said when you are being abused you usually put on weight around your buttocks and thighs. I started to put on weight when I was about five when the abuse started.

I thought dad loved me. I don't think he does.

The teenager in these photographs is not Kate. This story in no way relates to her. Kate appears on Page 173.

Has abuse affected your sexuality?

I think it might have. I always need sex and things like that. I like sex only if it's in a good way. My first boyfriend was when I was thirteen. I felt I needed to be sexual, but we didn't do much. Later, I went out with a boy and we slept in the lounge room. We woke up at about two and started mucking around and it just happened. It hurt a lot. I thought it would. It always hurts the first time, even if you've been sexually abused. I had to try and relax as much as I could. That was the first time I willingly had sex.

How do you feel now?

I'm glad I got out of that sexually abusive situation. I feel a lot better about myself now that I am free of my dad. I still have a long way to go. I feel a bit tired, even though I go to bed early. Just feel stuffed. I always feel so hungry. I eat virtually anything.

What would you say to teenagers about sexual abuse?

If you know you are being sexually abused, get out of there as soon as possible. If you think you are being sexually abused, go and talk to someone about it, a counsellor or a friend. Ask what you can do. Try and get over it. Otherwise you'll probably end up really screwed. You might make some stupid decisions when you are older.

(Kate's father was imprisoned for breaking the law)

Sexually Abusive Behaviour

The following list may help you recognise sexually abusive situations if they occur.

This can give you an idea of what to look for.

- The way some people look at you. You may sense they are undressing you with their eyes. For example, your P.E. teacher or a fellow student may perve at you while you're undressing in the changing rooms. If you are sensitive you may be aware of this and be uncomfortable. It's okay to say that you don't like it.
- If someone is fantasising about being sexual with you, imagining things he or she would like to do, you may sense that something creepy is going on. But because it is not happening physically it may confuse you. If someone is psychically abusing you, you are being energetically invaded and insidious damage is being done to you. Learn to trust your instincts.
- People speaking rude words that you don't like. They may be asking you to do sexual things to their bodies, making comments about your body, saying that they would like to do things to you or telling you what they would like you to do with someone else or to yourself.
- Adults making a child or teenager wear revealing, sexy clothing or asking you to see them dressed up in a way that sexually excites them. If it involves relatives, it can be confusing because you may be used to pleasing and obeying them. They are taking advantage of your trust.
- People showing their bodies to you, this may include a woman showing you her breasts or vagina or a man exposing his penis. These people are called flashers. This can be scary even if they are on the other side of the road or in a park and they never touch you. You don't know what is going to happen next.
- Someone leaving pornographic magazines around so that you can see them. They may be trying to get into your mind or planning to do something to you at a later time.

If any of the above things are happening to you or have happened, find someone you trust to tell.

Child Sexual Abuse is Illegal

Children are considered under the age of consent until they are sixteen. In some places this may be eighteen.

Look at the list below. If any teenagers or adults blackmail, physically force you, threaten or make you believe you have to do these things, they have broken the law and can go to jail.

- A person making children or teenagers have sex together.
- People making you watch them while they touch or play with themselves in a sexual way. They may tell you they are showing you what you can do. For example, an adult man showing a boy how to masturbate. You may feel sexually aroused and curious while they are making you watch them. You may also sense that something is wrong as well. Keep checking in with your body and listening to yourself.
- People taking pornographic photographs or making pornographic movies using children or teenagers.
- People making you watch pornographic movies. They may be trying to make you feel sexy so that they can then do sexual things to you. They may then blame you for what they did, saying that you must have liked it because you were feeling sexy.
- People making you touch them when that includes kissing or touching genitals, breasts or bottoms or any other part of their bodies.
- People asking you to use any object to touch their genitals or any other parts of their bodies.
- People touching you in any way that your intuition or body tells you is wrong. It can be something like stroking your leg, hair, breasts or your genitals with their hands or any object. Even if the stroking feels pleasurable but you feel bad – it is wrong. If you are uncomfortable with what they are doing with any part of you – they are abusing you.
- Adults or older teenagers arranging for other people to do sexual things to you, even if they are not touching you themselves. They are breaking the law. If they are getting money for this, they are prostituting you. They are called pimps.
- Ritual sexual abuse is something that very disturbed adults and sometimes older teenagers do. Ritual abuse can involve more than one adult and often more than one child. It can involve brainwashing and

violence and occasionally results in death. These people sometimes make children abuse other children. There can be religious connotations or talking about the devil, Satan, etc. This is rare, but it does happen. If you are in any way being ritually abused get help immediately. It can be hard for other people to believe you. Keep trying until you find someone who does.

Advocates for Survivors of Child Abuse (ASCA) is a voluntary organisation in Australia. These people know that sexual and ritual abuse happens and they offer any support they can. They may be able to refer you to someone who lives in your area or country. They can be contacted on 1300 657 380 in Australia. Email: asca@hunterlink.net.au or the Website: www.asca.org.au

You can also contact them if you are being abused in any other way.

There are other forms of sexual abuse – not all are mentioned here.

Be aware: If someone is abusing you or feeling sexually aroused, some or all of the following signs may alert you.

Signs of sexual arousal are: breathing changes, pupils get bigger, hands may shake, temperature rises, the voice may change, a male may have an erection… you may feel bad about the way you are touching or being touched.

What If You Like It?

This can make sexual abuse even more confusing than it already is. On some level you know that what is happening is wrong. On the other hand your body may like it and experience pleasure. You may also be feeling loved by the person who is abusing you, if she or he is gentle with you.

If you are enjoying the feelings, it does not mean that you are not being abused. If you sense that the sexual contact is wrong, some parts of your body may still respond and may even seek out more sexual activity, even though it feels uncomfortable in other parts of you. If you enjoy it you may think that your body is betraying you. In your body you may have painful and pleasurable sensations. In your mind you may know that something isn't right. Many children/teenagers say they do not like it at all.

There is nothing wrong with you if you do or you don't like it.

Getting to Know the Difference

Sometimes adults are genuinely being affectionate by touching your arm, hand or shoulder or by giving you a hug. Even if you are shy, you may not like it and yet feel okay about it. Your gut feeling may tell you that they are not harming you. But if you do not like them hugging you and you move away or tell them to stop and they insist, they are abusing you. They are using the fact that they are stronger than you to do things you don't like.

So as an example, let's look at a visit to the doctor. You may be having problems with your genital area. The doctor, who could be a man or woman, may physically examine you. He or she may look at your genitals for a long time and have a strange look. You might be touched for longer than is necessary. If the doctor is gaining any sexual pleasure from this examination, you are being sexually abused.

If it is not sexual abuse, you may feel uncomfortable or shy.

How can you tell if it is sexual abuse? You may feel hurt, offended, invaded or afraid. You may feel like kicking him/her and running away. You may also feel yucky. Inside your body you may sense that something is not right. If you have been abused often you may be numb. Trust yourself. You are able to sense the difference.

If you are a young male and an adult touches you to make you have an erection you are being sexually abused. If he or she is a doctor who medically examines you and you feel shy and uncomfortable but safe and you have an erection, you are not being abused. You are not wrong for having an erection if someone is sexually abusing you, but **he or she is wrong for trying to make you have one**. It is not your fault. It's like seeing a piece of chocolate cake and your mouth waters. **You can't help it.**

Why People Sexually Abuse Others

Many studies and interviews have been done with adults who abuse children. There doesn't seem to be one common reason to explain why they do this. A minority of abusers are medically diagnosed as being mentally unstable. Some abusers have been abused themselves as children and may not remember. Some people do not understand the amount of pain and wounding they are causing. However, some people do and seem to enjoy this. There are some people who have evil intentions to harm others.

There are no **excuses** for anyone sexually abusing someone else. There are some **reasons** for it, but it is unacceptable and goes against the laws of Nature and it is cruel. Some sexually abusive behaviour is illegal and is described in criminal codes.

People sexually abuse you to make you:

- feel smaller than them. To have control over you,
- feel scared or sad or desired and loved or ashamed,
- do something to yourself you don't like or get you to do something to them that you don't like,
- feel guilty and responsible for the abuse.

Or to harm you.

Sometimes children or teenagers are told by their abusers that they cannot help themselves or that it is their fault.

They may:

- tempt you with lollies, money, favours or gifts. When you accept what they offer, they may expect you to do them a sexual favour in return,
- make you believe you owe them something,
- tell you that they are educating you or that you are somehow asking for it. This is manipulative and is not true,
- threaten you quietly or violently and make you promise not tell anyone about what has happened,
- say really bad things can happen to you or someone you love if you tell.

People who sexually abuse others are psychologically disturbed.

Sexual behaviour by an adult with a child or under-age teenager is NEVER appropriate.

Do You Remember?

If you have already been sexually abused and you don't remember, it is called traumatic amnesia. You already know the world is not safe. The messages from your subconscious mind affect your body and go out like a radar signal, you may keep people at a distance or you may attract further abuse.

If you are having strange feelings when reading about sexual abuse: nausea, headaches, panic attacks or feeling afraid, it may be that buried memories are resurfacing. Or it may be that just knowing that this kind of thing happens in society makes you feel ill. You may not be able to tell the difference at first.

If you have been sexually abused you may remember the details, the place, the person and what happened. You can deal with it as soon as you are ready because you know it happened. You may remember everything that happened during the abuse, but don't consciously experience any feelings about it. This is because they seem too big to feel. You might feel like eating, taking drugs or drinking. So you stuff them down. This can exhaust your system. You may also think that you are going mad and don't know why.

The mind and body are clever. When you have a traumatic experience like sexual, physical or mental abuse and it's not safe to deal with it at the time, the mind takes the memories and stores them in a safe place. They are hidden inside your body.

It's like everything gets packed up into a suitcase and put into storage in your body/mind until you are ready to heal it. Even though the memories are buried, it is like trying to bury a suitcase under a carpet. You keep tripping over it. You see a lump but it has been there for so long that you don't even realise it's there. You walk over and around it without seeing it as something that shouldn't be there. If it has been under the carpet for a long time, it can take a while to come out again.

You may find at some stage that your memories resurface. If you seek counselling or group support, this can happen sooner, rather than later. Some people who have been sexually abused, whether they remember it or not, can live a relatively normal life until they get close to someone. At that point they can become unravelled. This can be a cry for help from their body/mind.

For example if strange things are happening to you:

- you are having terrible nightmares for no obvious reason,
- you are in love with someone who is kind to you and you love her/him, but you can't stand being touched or not being touched,
- you crave having sex or you avoid having sex all the time.

It could be that some of your feelings or emotions are coming from your subconscious mind but you don't remember the details of what happened.

If you experience memories and feelings resurfacing all at once, your life may feel like a nightmare. This may be because you are remembering the nightmare that you lived through when you were younger.

Sometimes the memories are buried so deep that they can stay hidden until you are much older. When memories resurface your mind is now ready and you are old enough to feel and heal your abuse.

The Effects of Sexual Abuse

If you have been sexually abused you may:

- experience physical pain - back, pelvic, neck or headaches,
- cut yourself off from your emotions and feelings,
- feel unsafe and be afraid to take risks,
- live in fear of unfamiliar situations and environments,
- be tense and your life feels restricted.

Before reading this list you may not have known why you were affected in this way.

Other effects of sexual abuse can be that you:

- experience fear, go numb, space out, have difficulty concentrating,
- try to control things in your life all the time to feel safe,
- become ill, suffer from nausea, headaches, trembling, nervousness or anxiety,
- become violent and express antisocial behaviour,
- harm your body,
- find your body does not develop normally. Sexual abuse may have frozen your physical development,
- put on weight. Extra fat is one way the body protects itself,
- take drugs or alcohol to suppress the pain and escape your feelings,
- feel depressed or suicidal.

You may also:

- become obsessed by changing underwear many times a day because you feel dirty,
- not be able to sleep in a room without the light on,
- not be able to touch your own genitals,
- hate your body and do all sorts of things to control it – overeating, dieting, obsessive exercising,
- experience pain when your body or sexual organs are touched,
- develop phobias that seem irrational to you or to others. For example, you may hate the smell of rose perfume without understanding why. It might be because someone who abused you when you were young always wore it. You may not remember this.

Closed down or sexually over active

There are different kinds of responses to having been sexually abused:

You may either be a loner, go numb, be depressed OR you might be over emotional and like to be at the centre of attention OR seek frequent sexual experiences.

Some people close down and don't become sexually active until later in life. They may never like being sexual or have healthy sex lives. Their bodies don't have a clear sexual response and they may not have orgasms. They may be afraid of all sexual contact and avoid intimacy at all costs because it may remind them of childhood sexual abuse. They avoid situations that they know can trigger that response in them.

Being around friends who are sexually active may confuse them because they may not feel normal and may not understand why. Some people stuff their emotions down by being very busy, either by working long hours, having a demanding hobby or are always socialising.

If you have been abused you may have been over-stimulated sexually at an early age and become overly sexually active. Sex can become addictive, like a drug. Your body may be addicted to having sexual feelings. People who have been abused may use sex as a way to avoid feeling the pain, which is true of any addiction. This addiction can make you have sex with people that you would rather not be sexual with. Even though you are saying yes or even initiating sexual contact, you may still feel bad about it and have no idea why. This is not a healthy way to express your sexuality but it can make you think you are getting some power back. You may not have had power or any choice when you were being sexually abused as a child or a teenager.

People who are promiscuous may have been sexually abused in some way. They may become involved in the sex industry – become prostitutes, striptease artists or escorts. They may not know why they are doing this. They may not remember having been sexually abused.

What Can You Do About Sexual Abuse?

If you are presently being abused, for your own safety and wellbeing, do something immediately to protect yourself. If the abuse is in the past, it is wise to deal with it as soon as possible so that you can be healed and live a fulfilled life.

If you have been abused in the past:

- If the sexual abuse was a mild incident that happened once from a stranger, you may still feel upset about it. You can talk to someone to help resolve your feelings.
- If the abuse was a mild, one-off experience that happened with someone who is still in your life, find the courage to talk to a helpful adult about it, you may save others from being abused.
- If the abuse was a regular occurrence, mild or strong in the past, then it is likely that it is a wound that is buried deep inside you. If it sits there unrecognised, it can make things go wrong for you in your life. It could even make you sick.
- The more regular the abuse and closer the abuser is to you, the stronger the effects can be. It is important to seek professional help.

If any of the above things have happened to you, talk to somebody you trust about it. You can benefit with professional help if the abuse was strong.

If it's Happening NOW

If you, your brothers and sisters or a friend or anyone you know are being sexually abused, get help immediately. You can stop the abuse from happening.
It takes a lot of courage.

If it seems too hard to talk to someone, write down everything you remember when you are ready to. Keep it safe, away from any place that an abuser might find it. This writing can make it easier for you to share about your abuse with someone else and if necessary, the authorities. It is also a step towards healing the abuse. If the words don't come out right, you could draw a picture or make up a poem. You can then give this or post it to an adult you trust, if you are unable to speak up.

If You are in Danger

If you know that when you go home you are at risk of being harmed or raped, going to the police can provide some physical protection. If the police don't help, contact Family and Community Services and explain what is happening. They sometimes take children and teenagers away who are being sexually abused by family members in order to protect them. This may not seem like a good idea to you at the time but leaving home may be the only way to keep you safe. Then you can start to face your feelings. You may be scared to trust someone again after being hurt and betrayed. You may feel tough and think you can get through alone without any help. It is wise to get help, even if you think you can handle it.

Find Someone to Help

Talking to someone you feel safe with is an important step. When you speak to him or her, if you have written something down or drawn a picture, have it with you.

The person who could help you might be a friend's parent, your local librarian, the person who works in the grocery shop, your doctor, a relative or a grandparent. In fact, it can be anybody, so long as you trust her or him.

If you tell a teacher or school counsellor, legally the authorities must be informed.

Some adults may not be willing to help you.
This could be because they may:

- tell you that it is your fault,
- be sympathetic but not know what to do when faced with your story,
- not listen to you because it is unbelievable to them,
- try to avoid dealing with the issues because they have been abused and are unconscious of it OR have unhealed wounds from childhood sexual abuse and are not ready to cope with yours,
- be abusers themselves and feel guilty or ashamed,
- feel guilty about not noticing what was happening and helping you before you approached them,
- be friendly with the person who is abusing you. They may not believe that someone who seems so nice, who is a friend or husband/wife (if it's one of your parents) could do this,
- not have hearts that are open and so they may not be ready to help or understand what you have been going through.

If adults do any of these things they are not being kind or helpful.

Some adults are able to help or can find others who can. If you can't find someone you trust, phone a Kid's Helpline, Family and Community Services or the police.

Don't give up!
Keep trying until you find someone.

Healing Sexual Abuse

It is possible to heal yourself. One way out of the emotional and psychological pain is feeling it until there is no pain left to feel. The sooner you begin this healing the better. This is because if left, the pain sits inside you and can make you sad, angry or depressed. It can cause you to become ill. The pain is waiting to come out. Find someone you feel safe with and know you can absolutely trust. It may take time.

You are not alone!

THINGS TO DO!

Some things you can do:

- Journal writing is an excellent way to explore your thoughts and feelings.
- If you can, find an understanding friend. She or he can provide backup when you ask for support and offer you feedback about your progress.
- Spend time with people who love and respect you.
- If your body has been damaged in any way or you experience back pain, menstrual problems or headaches, seek help from a health practitioner - a doctor, naturopath, physiotherapist, osteopath, accupuncturist and/or a bodyworker.
- If you feel safe, professional work on your body helps to release memories from your cells.
- Professional people can support you in moving through what comes up. They can suggest ways to cope and can help you to keep your life on track.
- Find a counsellor, therapist or an ongoing support group. Community, Women's Health or Men's Resource Centres sometimes offer these services.
- Some organisations offer residential programs.
- To assist the healing process you can attend personal development courses, Yoga or Tai Chi, art therapy classes or meditation classes.
- Find a hobby to focus your mind on something you enjoy. Read informative and inspiring books.
- Do anything that makes you feel glad to be alive and which opens your heart and body.
- If as you grow older you experience difficulties in sexual relationships seek help.

PAINFUL MEMORIES

Katrina (17)

In the oracle of my mind
There was a single being,
Trying to get out.
This being was a child.
A child that had never had the chance
To grow or be the way it wanted to be.
Now that I have released many dangers
By letting it feel and see
What for many years
Reluctantly hid away,
I am experiencing emotions
That I never thought were possible.
Emotions that have been playing games
With my mind.
Games that force me to understand
The painful memories that once were
hidden.
Hidden from you and many others.
But the most hurtful realisation
Is that I was also hiding them from myself.
I now understand that even though we
must forget the past
We must not forget the memory.
This memory isn't there to hurt
Or punish us.
It is there to remind us that we cried
And that now we can live.

Katrina was sexually abused as a child by her brother. No one in her family believed her. She thought she was going mad.

My Story

I was physically and emotionally abused as a child. I wondered if I'd been sexually abused as well. I had no conscious memories of this. In my mid-twenties, a doctor told me I had a small cyst on my left ovary I had no symptoms so thought nothing of it.

Years later a deep tissue bodywork session triggered memories of the sexual abuse that had been buried deeply, both into my subconscious mind and my left ovary! was 47 when these memories surfaced and I'd done a great deal of personal development work by then.

The sexual abuse I experienced as a child has affected my life in many ways.

When I was 18, I was at a so-called friend's flat. We were kissing. When it was going too far for me I asked him to stop. He didn't! As a sexually abused child I didn't have protective boundaries so I couldn't say NO loudly enough to make him stop. I was used to having things done to me that I didn't like. It was many years later before I realised this young man had raped me. As a child I knew that the abuse was wrong but I couldn't do anything to stop what was happening.

Until a few years ago I wore baggy clothes to hide my body. I didn't feel safe enough to be seen as a sexually attractive female. As a teenager I didn't go to parties. I didn't explore sexual relationships until in my late teens. I didn't understand why. I was too shy and afraid. My body did not respond sexually and I was emotionally protecting myself.

For almost twenty years I have seen chiropractors and osteopaths to relieve chronic back pain. My posture was out of alignment, I suffered headaches and tension in my jaw and neck. My kidneys had been weakened. My upper and lower body looked like they belonged to two different people.

I have still not fully recovered. I follow a self-care regime which is helping. I am freeing myself of the effects of sexual abuse on my life.

I honour Lisa Bingham,
and her healing journey.

Lisa, is a rebirther and has assisted me to unpack the suitcase that's been hiding under the carpet. Her experience, clarity and understanding about sexual abuse has helped this section to be clear and informative.

Thank you!

On the day we worked together it rained.

It felt like God was crying
...It hadn't rained for months!

AN ADDICTIVE SOCIETY

Some young people use drugs and alcohol to loosen up socially – to free-up and relax with friends. For fun! They have a good time in mind. It can make socialising feel easier for people who are uncomfortable with themselves, shy or inhibited. This may seem harmless.

Some do not have any inclination to use tobacco, drugs or alcohol. Others may decide to dabble now and again socially and not become addicted. Only a small proportion of teenagers who are having problems turn to damaging substances. At the other extreme some young people become addicts, can overdose and **DIE**!!!

This section has not been easy to write. I love working with young people. I have strong feelings about the damage teenagers are doing to themselves when they abuse drugs, alcohol or sniff petrol or glue. I've seen the suffering these things cause. In our world harmful substances are easily available.

Adolescence can be confusing enough without the added danger that drugs and alcohol can bring. I've heard too many heart-breaking stories to sit back as an uninvolved observer.

If you have no intention to use drugs, alcohol or tobacco and none of your friends have, you may wish to read this section to become more informed.

This information is important if you are thinking about trying out harmful substances or are already using them.

Many Addictions

Many people take some kind of addictive substance everyday – legal or otherwise. Tobacco, alcohol, painkillers, tranquillisers, caffeine and prescribed drugs, are all legal. Some prescribed drugs, excessive drinking of alcohol and smoking cigarettes damage health. For the majority of the population they are acceptable, even though it has been shown how harmful they can be when used in excess for a long time.

The manufacture of medically prescribed drugs, alcohol and tobacco are multi-billion dollar businesses. These substances are doing a great deal of damage to human health. Some prescription drugs are over used. Antibiotics, the contraceptive pill, Valium (tranquillisers), Prozac (an anti-depressant) and Ritalin (given to children diagnosed with ADD) account for millions of prescriptions throughout the world every month. Taking medically prescribed drugs in this way may not deal with the cause of the problems for which they are recommended. Many people become dependent on them.

Starting Early

Illegal drugs, such as Marijuana, Speed, Ecstasy and Heroin are condemned by many people. How many of these same people take prescribed drugs, smoke or drink alcohol and have introduced their teenagers to some form of legal drugs early in life? While there is a lot of concern about illegal drugs, sometimes the most harm and the greatest risk to young people comes from using legal drugs such as alcohol, cigarettes and some prescription medicines.

These days drug taking, smoking and drinking starts early for many. Teenagers are a direct target in the tobacco, alcohol and drug market. They are its biggest potential consumer group. They are the focus when the advertising industry is aiming its pitch.

Watching TV and playing video games in excess can be another form of addiction. Too much time in front of a screen, while growing up, dulls senses and slows down brain and motor skills development.

Research has shown that the ability to relate and communicate is lessened. Often people are not informed about the damaging side effects of seemingly harmless activities.

If you are taking illegal drugs, smoking and drinking too much alcohol, spending hours passively in front of a computer screen or television set, be aware! These things can take you away from your Essential Nature. They can destroy what is life-giving to you.

It's your body!

Are you choosing life or death through the choices that you make?

Any dependence or addiction indicates there are issues that are crying out for attention.

Note: If you are found guilty of possessing, using or selling any illegal substance you can get a criminal record.

Abuse of drugs and alcohol are not the CAUSE of society's problems. They are a symptom showing that society has problems.

It's Schoolies week – celebrating leaving school by getting drunk every day!!!

A Drugged Culture

Society creates the drug culture. People use drugs believing they can cure their ills. The drug industry continues to create and supplies this demand by inventing new drugs and by investing enormous amounts of money into advertising campaigns. That's a vicious cycle!

Births, depression, painful menstrual periods, headache, stress and dying are some of life's many experiences where drugs are prescribed and socially acceptable. We expect, when taking drugs at these times, not to feel pain, to avoid the physical sensations or to side-step fear or emotional issues.

We live in a drug-induced culture! Using drugs at birth or during pregnancy is common practise in western medicine. At some stage during pregnancy or birth, many babies are having a drug experience. A large percentage of hospital births are interfered with by the use of prescribed drugs.

There could be a connection between drugs used during birth and drug use later in life. If, during birth a mother is given any drug, the baby may be programmed that in painful or stressful situations, later in life, drugs can be used to get out of it or avoid feelings. This could be setting the scene for today's drug problems.

Examples of drugs used during birth are an epidural (which numbs the body from the waist down), amphetamines or painkillers to reduce the intensity of the birthing experience. Sometimes the use of drugs may be essential to save lives, on other occasions they may be used for convenience.

Ask your mother about your birth to find out whether drugs were used. See if that is affecting you now.

It has only been in recent human experience that synthetic (man-made) drugs have been available for medicinal or social use. Before that, only natural herbs were used. Our systems are adapting to many changes in our modern world. Taking chemicals and sitting in front of radiation emitting screens is relatively new to us. How well are we adapting? We as yet don't fully know what damage is being done.

The use of drugs that take us away from our direct experiences reduces the power for Initiation through life changing passages such as birth, adolescence, dis-ease and death.

Drugs, Alcohol and Other Stuff

Some young people try out new things to test limits. Of those who do, not all go on using drugs regularly and only a few develop serious problems.

Alcohol, tobacco, Marijuana, amphetamines and Ecstasy are readily available. It is wise to learn about their effects on your body, mind, heart and spirit – if possible before you are even tempted to try.

If you're already experimenting, it may be hard to accept the information in this section. You have highs and lows that can influence your choices. Reading this may bring awareness to what you are doing to yourself and your body.

Alcohol and some drugs kill brains cells. No brain cells are grown after puberty. Are you taking care of the ones you've got? You can rethink! Education is better sooner rather than later.

Some Reasons for Substance Abuse

People do drugs or drink alcohol for different reasons. Some make educated and aware choices. They know what they are doing and why they choose to use substances. Others don't consider the long-term effects or the consequences that substance abuse can have on their lives. Some are in so much pain they don't even care.

You may use drugs and alcohol – for the fun of it – and later find that you depend on them to relax, feel comfortable or socially acceptable.

Tobacco, drugs and alcohol can numb out your real feelings, offer you a temporary fix, but you can become physiologically and psychologically dependent.

Some of the reasons young people try out drugs:

- curiosity,
- it's cool – the popular thing to do,
- easy availability,
- they offer new experiences,
- to see the world in a different way,
- they relax and loosen you up OR give you a buzz,
- they can be a means of asserting your independence,
- to rebel if your family/society is against them.

Young people likely to become addicted to substance abuse are those who:

- don't like or value themselves, have low self-esteem or are shy,
- find it difficult to say NO and give in to pressure from others, become followers, belong to a self-destructive group of friends,
- may be avoiding – feeling pain, making decisions, emotional upset, dealing with boredom, being motivated, anxiety (drugs can cause more), facing a difficult family or life situation or feeling stuck in their lives,
- have been wounded during childhood or experienced a traumatic birth,
- may be feeling disconnected and alienated from those around them,
- know there is more to life than their current experience,
- are seeking an expanded sense of reality,
- believe nothing can harm them,
- do not understand the effects of substance/drug abuse on their lives,
- may have been dealt blows in life that they find challenging to deal with and so have little ability to handle stressful situations,
- may think they have no reason to live.

If you become dependent on drugs, then who's in charge of your life – you or the drugs?

Young people who are vulnerable to substance abuse do not usually associate with friends who have high self-esteem. That can make them feel worse. If you don't feel good about yourself and are afraid you may fall into a self-destructive life cycle, find someone to talk to. You may benefit from adult support if more than two or three of the statements in the list above describes you.

If you know people who drink and take drugs, take time to observe them. See what you discover about them and the way they live their lives. Is this what you choose?

A famous surfer said:

"I don't take drugs. I may need my body tomorrow."

TEENSPEAK

"If you're in with people and you don't do it, that's cool if they don't care. They say stuff. But if you're not in and you get bullied, it's really bad. If people want to do drugs themselves it's their choice, but they shouldn't tell people it's wrong if they don't do it. Make your own choice." – Chelsea (14)

"My friend asked me if I wanted to smoke dope but I said, No. She was cool about it. I reckon you can be cool and popular without drugs being involved." – Kate (15)

"Kids who are ten get stoned. That's really stupid! Sometimes it's their parents as well. They see older people taking drugs and see parents doing it, so they say to themselves, okay we'll do it and be cool. They don't think there is anything wrong with it 'cos they've had it in their everyday life." – Angie (14)

"At times I have used alcohol to deal with stress but I don't now. I haven't used it to drown out problems. I don't agree with getting smacked all the time. When I tried pot for the first time I thought I'll see how it is. Recently I smoked dope every day for a month. I don't hate drugs but I never thought I'd end up smoking every day. Maybe at first it was due to friends. It came on and we did nothing to stop it. I made a decision consciously not to smoke any more. Now I smoke only occasionally. It's a bad habit but it's not worrying me. I've been into sport for a long time. I was starting to worry about the effects. I wasn't 100% in my lungs – getting colds and then I thought if this goes on much longer I could end up losing my mind. A friend became schizophrenic." – Ben (17)

"Due to the fact that I've given up drugs I am healthy again after two years of being sick. I finally cried – I can't remember the last time I did. I cried about everything – about my mother's death, losing my virginity, about the way I think about myself. I let out everything that was really pent up. Now that I am more in touch with the way I feel, I realise the reactions I have to my own thoughts and often cringe away with loathing at some of my memories. I have been facing those memories instead of just putting them out of my mind. I can now think about a lot of things freely and openly. It makes me feel legitimate and worthy to be able to do that." – Laura (16)

"The age where young people get into drugs is getting much lower, because they think it's cool. In some cases it can buy them a place in the group. I find it disappointing in a way that sixteen-year-olds are into cigarettes, drink or dope. I can't really relate to anyone. It divides me and the rest of my class, because I don't socialise with them. They come to school and talk about what they did on the weekend. I can't contribute. It would increase my understanding if I did but I don't want to be around them when they are doing that. Drinking and doing drugs affects the way they communicate. The long-term effects for those who become addicted may be a lack of intelligence. It gets dulled. In the case of strong addiction, a lack in physical ability. Those that don't do it, don't fit in to the scene. I try and find other activities. I like model painting, skateboarding, playing computer games. I spend a lot of time on my own. There's times when I don't enjoy it but at times I feel that it is actually good for me. I try and motivate myself. I feel okay doing my own thing. It's my choice. It is a bit of a setback sometimes. People could give it more thought. Don't do drugs just 'cos you think it's cool." – Jacob (16)

How Addiction Starts

Getting out of it or drunk does not solve anything in the long term. If you are emotionally insecure, unsupported and fragile or if you are susceptible to self-harm – drug and alcohol use can cause a great deal of confusion and damage. This could be emotionally, physically, psychologically and socially as well as spiritually.

People who are drawn to addictive substances may currently experience trauma or stress in their lives. This could have happened on one occasion in the past or accumulated over many years. By taking drugs or drinking alcohol they feel relaxed, at ease – more normal. This could be for the first time in their lives for those who have experienced physical or emotional abuse in their childhood.

When children have experienced major birth trauma or separation from their mothers at birth or are badly abused, their bodies may not function properly. They may be emotionally unstable as well. If major issues are not resolved and released, drugs may be used to get out of it and not deal with what's underneath. They may think that drugs help them function in some ways.

If you have been badly wounded, dealing with your issues may challenge you. It is not an easy path to recovery. Once issues have been resolved it may be possible for the system to re-balance itself. But this can take time. It may take all of your will to bring yourself into a place of wholeness. You can connect with your Essential Nature. By finding substitute families, support groups and therapists it is possible to overcome feelings of isolation, loss, abandonment or not being cared for. You can ask for guidance and support from Spirit, God, Power – anything but drugs.

"It is important to remind you that the universal law that has allowed anyone to ever overcome a serious addiction has not been repealed. It does not matter how far down you have gone. You have within you the ability to make a miracle of your life and rid yourself of addiction."

– REAL MAGIC, Wayne Dyer.

Turn within for guidance and strength

Tobacco and its Abuse

Nicotine found in tobacco is a strong repressant. It dulls responses and helps suppress feelings and emotional problems. You don't have to face issues that are going on for you. Like most drugs tobacco does not offer long-term solutions. Cigarette smoking is generally socially accepted. But it is just as damaging, if not more so, than some other dangerous substances.

Tobacco is deceptively harmful. If you start smoking at an early age it can inhibit physical growth. It also causes damage to the brain, respiratory system, the lungs and other vital organs of the body. This damage may be irreparable if smoking is long term. One result of smoking is cancer. The body's cells cannot sustain their vitality with the constant onslaught of the 3,000 toxic substances in cigarettes. It has been said that nicotine is harder to get off than heroin.

It is estimated that a quarter of a million Australian school students aged twelve to seventeen smoke.

"Well I sometimes look after my body. I do in some ways but not in others, because I look after my body from getting sick and most of the time I eat healthily, but then I don't because I smoke cigarettes. That is something I wish I never started because now that I am addicted my body depends on them." – Sharmane (15)

"I don't like the idea of it destroying your lungs and stuff. I think that's really ugly. There was an ad on TV showing this man getting something squeezed out of his lungs. Yuk!" – Chelsea (14)

"I knew someone who was coughing up tar.
That's disgusting." – Kintasha (14)

Note: A lifetime of smoking equals a cup full of tar.

Some young people think its cool to smoke!

Cigarettes are harmful. They are relatively easy to get. In some countries it is illegal for under eighteens to purchase them.

If you are smoking why are you choosing to destroy your body in this way?

Alcohol and You

Do you know that drinking large amounts of alcohol is poisonous and addictive? It is illegal in most places for young people under eighteen to purchase alcohol or drink it. Even so, it's easy to obtain. If alcohol is being consumed around you, you may believe it's harmless.

Adults everywhere use alcohol to celebrate special occasions, to loosen up at parties and some drink after work or every night at dinner. Drinking in moderation for adults can have health benefits. But many people are addicted to it and have a drinking problem even though they deny it. Because it is socially accepted it is not so easily recognised when there is an alcohol addiction.

Alcohol can bring out the worst in people – aggression, violence and a lack of human feeling. It can also be used as a way to escape what is going on in life. Alcohol has a different effect on the brain compared to other drugs. It can be used for shutting down, not dealing with reality and may result in a level of unconscious behaviour.

The fear of illegal drug use makes some people blind to the dangers of alcohol. Alcohol causes a high number of injuries and deaths to young people.

Some parents drink, smoke, watch TV, get out of it and don't take responsibility for their addiction. Some don't take proper care of you because they are addicted. This is a poor example for you.

It is smart if you:

- don't consume alcohol while your body and brain are developing,
- don't accept pressure from friends who choose to drink when you would rather not,
- stay together with friends at parties where alcohol is being consumed,
- do not drink and drive. It is illegal to drive when your blood alcohol level is over a certain limit. This may occur after one or two drinks,
- do not get into a car when the driver has been drinking.

Being unaware of your actions can get you into serious trouble. The number of young people injured or killed in alcohol-related road accidents is much higher than that of adults. It is a serious problem.

Sometimes, when drinking:

- young people lose control,
- teenagers have been sexually abused or raped,
- females get pregnant because they don't know what they are doing,
- stealing, car theft, fighting or life-threatening behaviour occurs,
- young people may develop mental diseases because of mixing addictive substances. Young males are more prone to develop schizophrenia if they do this.

Make sure there is adult supervision at parties you attend until you and your friends are responsible enough to keep yourselves safe. Adults can protect you even though you think they may spoil your fun. Car accidents, violence and rape are not fun!

Set limits on yourself so that you are able to stay conscious of what is going on around you. The harmful consequences of alcohol and drug use can be unforeseeable to you. You are unprepared for what may happen because you have not experienced enough of life yet.

Alcohol can have a stronger effect and is harder to handle for young people than for adults. The body weight of a teenager is not as great as an adult's, so the alcohol is assimilated quickly into the system.

Binge Drinking

Regular binge drinking impacts on your health. During adolescence your body and brain are still in their developmental phase. They are fragile to the onslaught of damaging chemicals and mind-altering substances. Your brain, stomach and liver are damaged first. Binge drinking can lead to alcoholism. This is when more than three standard drinks are consumed regularly. A standard drink is a measure of spirit (a shot), a wineglass of wine, a beer glass of beer.

My Story about alcohol

A celebration dinner with my grandparents, brother and sister. Look at the booze!

I was a teenager during the '60's in England. It was famous for its pub life. I was raised in an alcohol drinking culture. From about eighteen onwards I got drunk at weekends. I talked too much, laughed loudly and often made a fool of myself.

I changed my drinking habits drastically when I could have died of alcohol poisoning on my 21st birthday. I was celebrating at lunchtime with friends in a bar. I was quickly becoming dehydrated after drinking brandy and coke. An irresponsible male acquaintance did a stupid thing. He gave me a pint of orange juice laced with three vodkas. I drank it straight down. Mixing drinks like this could have been the death of me. I passed out in the toilet and don't know what happened next.

I'd organised a big party to celebrate my coming of age that evening. Every time I moved I felt like vomiting. But at least I was alive!

Not long after that someone told me that drinking alcohol kills brain cells and that they are the only cells in the body that don't regenerate. Yikes! I'd probably already murdered trillions of my brain cells. I stopped drinking immediately!

I have very little personal experience of drug use. When I was in my late teens drugs were just coming into fashion, big time! People where I worked were told that if we got involved in the drug scene we would lose our jobs. That was a clear line for me. One I was not willing to cross. I am grateful for that. I've been free of drugs, prescribed or otherwise for most of my adult life.

Cannabis, Marijuana, Grass, Hemp, Dope

If drug use becomes regular, it can be used as a means of getting out of it and not dealing with uncomfortable or painful situations. It's a delay mechanism and is not a cure for anything. Unresolved pain and personal issues are only cleared up when they are faced and dealt with in some way. Dealing with pain, stress and uncomfortable situations, even if they seem intolerable, provides an opportunity to fully embrace life.

The stuff of life is not always sweet!

If you don't allow yourself to feel pain –
how do you develop the strength to bear it?

If you don't relate and so get out of it –
how do you learn to connect with life?

If you don't know what you are feeling –
how can you deal with what's going on for you?

If you are not feeling – how can you be whole?

Some young people resort to methods used by adults to deaden their experience of life by smoking, drinking or taking drugs. That some drugs are illegal becomes irrelevant. Sometimes this makes them more appealing. Drug and alcohol abuse weaken society.

Paul, an ex-drug user says, "It started in the fifties and now it has escalated to epidemic proportions. The disease is: Let's avoid – pain, difficult situations, emotional anguish, social inadequacy, avoid being on the planet, avoid responsibility for what is going on inside and around us. Getting out of it works for a while. It eases the symptoms of the disease."

He went on to say that over time taking drugs takes every value out of life other than taking drugs. He was addicted to cannabis for twenty-five years. He justified his use of cannabis on the basis that it was helping his depression. He was not as angry, he noticed. Instead, he suffered from fear, anxiety and was often panic-stricken. He said it was directly related to his cannabis use.

He is concerned that cannabis is a problematic and subtle substance that is portrayed as harmless. There is a large amount of evidence that there is psychological dependence, that its use causes personal trauma and has severe consequences. Cannabis he said, isn't supposed to be addictive, but it does reinforce its own use. Some people become consumed by using it. They feel driven to get it and the obsession takes over. It seems to bring relief but it is actually avoidance. As the effect wore off he craved more and more dope. Caught in a hopeless spiral it was difficult to step out of drug addiction. His situation became intolerable.

He believes drugs are destroying the fabric of our society. It's important for people to be educated, he said. In order not to have a problem, don't use drugs in the first place.

For every reason to take drugs there is a non-drug solution!

From a Researcher

Dr John Anderson, a Consultant Psychophysiologist from the Brain and Behaviour Centre, Westmead in Sydney assesses people for psychological disorders. He said that there are a significant number of people with problems that are directly related to cannabis abuse. We have made drugs fashionable. As adults we are faced with the responsibility for that and for taking some action to change the situation in society today.

He said the level of a young person's self-esteem at the age of ten is the best predictor of substance abuse later in life. Young adolescents, especially if they have low self-esteem, are not able to make informed and life supporting choices.

Doing the exercises in GETTING REAL... about growing up! can raise your self-esteem and support you to make choices that improve the quality of your life.

Is Cannabis Use Harmful?

Cannabis is a herb. It contains THC (Tetrahydrocannabinol). It has an effect on the mental function of the brain and on the liver. It also contains substances that interfere with the reproductive and immune systems. These are mutogenic. They cause changes in the genes and chromosome formation in the body.

Cannabis decreases levels of testosterone. As these levels drop, serotonin is reduced. This results in a lack of motivation. Serotonin affects eating habits. This is why people using cannabis get the munchies.

Cannabis is fat-soluble. It is stored in the body fat and slowly excreted. Its half-life is seven days, so that seven days after using cannabis, half of it is still in the system. Compare that with what happens after taking heroin. It has a half-life of four hours. In three days it's all gone. With cannabis it takes up to three months to leave the body. This makes it a hard drug to get off because it stays in the system for so long.

Cannabis contains fifty percent more carcinogens than tobacco, so it is much more likely to cause cancer. It can affect lung function and the respiratory system. The effects of these disturbances can last even longer than the after effects of tobacco. There are significant dangers in cannabis use.

Cannabis Affects the Brain

If you stay stoned twenty-four hours a day you may feel good when using cannabis. When you stop, the chemical reaction in your body changes the high into a low. The reason for this mood swing is that the brain is constantly balancing two specific hormones. These are called dopamine and noradrenaline. Too much dopamine can be a cause of schizophrenia. Dopamine is increased with the use of cannabis. The reward factor of dopamine is that you feel good.

Noradrenaline on the other hand causes physiological disturbance. It causes feelings of anxiety, anger, hostility, depression, fear, paranoia, frustration and stress. Under normal circumstances the brain strives to balance dopamine and noradrenaline so that we can live normal lives.

When using cannabis, dopamine gets increased so you feel good but if it gets too much, the brain cannot bring it back into a balanced state. The natural metabolic process has been blocked. The only way to feel better is another joint or cone. People then may find it difficult to sleep and so smoke more dope to relieve that stress. By using cannabis, you are actually creating stress, so it becomes a physical, psychological as well as chemical addiction.

A vicious cycle!

Using cannabis changes behaviour over time.
You can become:

- depersonalised, disorientated and paranoid,
- unhappy with yourself – you'd rather be someone else,
- depressed and suffer from increased anxiety.

It alters perception of time and space.
Things look further away than they are or closer.

It takes twenty-six years for the brain to fully develop. When you are eighteen your brain is only two thirds developed. Cannabis use causes damage to the developing brain. Its long-term effects are as yet unknown. Research has shown that even fifteen years after giving up cannabis, people show subtle brain dysfunction.

At what stage of development is the brain at twelve years of age? Some young people use cannabis or drink alcohol at that age. They don't know the damage it causes to the body and brain. They may not even care. They believe themselves to be invincible, that nothing can harm them. **Wrong!** Young people can suffer badly from drug abuse. Some have been damaged for life.

Hard Drugs

Hard drugs are a big topic and except for Ecstacy and Heroin are beyond the scope of this book. Some young people experiment with all sorts of chemicals. You might like to educate yourself about how they affect your developing body and brain. At least then you can make informed choices.

Ecstasy/E/Eccy

Young people have easy access to Ecstasy. It's become popular. Teenagers may be unaware of the dangerous effects of taking it.

Ecstasy is an illegally manufactured drug. It can contain dangerous chemicals that are not Methylene Dioxy Methamphetamine (MDMA).

Ecstasy tablets usually contain one or more of:

Methylamphetamine (Speed), Ketamine (Special K), Heroin, Dextromethorphane (Cough Suppressant), Methamphetamine (Ice), Caffeine, Pseudephedrine, Talcum Powder, Baking Soda and Lactose...

and therefore there is no safe dose.

Regular use can cause permanent damage to the liver, heart and brain. The immediate after effects are headaches and tiredness. Depression is common. Some people experience other bad effects. If it is mixed with alcohol or any other drug it increases the risk of serious health problems and the chance of death. When used while dancing for several hours people can become dehydrated. This also increases the risk of death.

"When I lived in Sydney one of my brother's friends died at a rave party. He was only sixteen and died from an overdose of drugs. And the worst thing about it was my brother's friend didn't really have a family. His mother and father died in a car accident when he was fourteen. He was living with his aunt and uncle. After he died my brother refused to be friends with anyone who did drugs." – Sharmane (15)

Ecstasy can help people to feel happy. It lowers inhibitions because it releases large amounts of serotonin. Very high doses of Ecstacy kill serotonin cells. It may make you feel great for a while. Any change experienced is temporary and can lead to emotional disturbances or depression.

Natural highs are possible, harmless, a buzz and strongly recommended. Any changes in your experience as a result of a natural high can be permanent. See page 192.

All drug experiences come at a price!

Heroin

Heroin is highly addictive. Like most other drugs the more you use, the more you crave it. Buying and using heroin can take over and control your whole life. Eventually, you take heroin in order to feel normal.

Heroin reduces your appetite. You become sick very rapidly due to poor diet. It can contain unsafe chemicals, legal or illegal. There is a risk of getting deadly diseases such as AIDS, hepatitis, liver and kidney failure or blood poisoning by using dirty equipment. There is a risk when taking heroin of overdose regardless of how little is used.

Drug habits can be expensive and young people are driven to get the money from somewhere to pay for them. Beg, borrow or steal! Stealing is illegal.

MISS HEROIN
Rahni Newsome (16)

So now little one you've grown tired of grass,
All that damned acid and cocaine and hash.
Then someone pretending that he is your friend
Said, "I'll introduce you to Miss Heroin".
Well honey, before you start fooling with me,
Just let me tell you how it will be.
For I will seduce you and make you my slave,
Believe me I've sent stronger people to their graves,
You think you could never become a disgrace
And end up an addict of poppy seed waste.
You'll start by experimenting one afternoon
And end up asleep in my arms very soon.
Then once I have entered deep in your veins,
The craving will drive you nearly insane.
You'll need lots of money as you have been told,
For darling, I'm more expensive than gold.
You'll swindle your mother just for a buck
And turn into something vile and corrupt.
You'll mug and you'll steal for my narcotic charms,
And feel so content when I'm in your arms.
Then you'll realise the monster inside you has grown
And you'll solemnly swear to leave me alone.
But if you think it's easy and you've got the knack,
Then sweetie, just try getting me off your back.
The vomit, the cramps, your gut in a knot,
Your jangling nerves screaming for just one more shot.
The hot chills, the cold sweat, the withdrawal pains,
Can only be saved by my little white grains.
So now you return, just as I have foretold
And I know that you'll give me your body and soul.
You'll give me your morals, your conscience, your heart,
And now you are mine till death us do part.

Drugs and Spirituality

Some people feel the emptiness and isolation in their lives so acutely that they search for something to fill themselves up with. Sometimes drugs seem to offer more meaningful levels of awareness. Once you have experienced chemically induced highs it may be more challenging to let them go.

Sally once believed drugs could give her spiritual awareness.

"Drugs may not give you a real spiritual experience but they may offer another point of reference. If you are not careful you can crave these experiences and become their slave. The down side gets more extreme and you can come under their power. It can be an illusory dead-end street. It does not lead you to where it promises. Or to where you think you want to be. That's its trap and its temptation."

For every reason to do drugs there are hundreds of reasons not to!

Some people argue that drugs can open levels of spiritual awareness and consciousness. Others say that any drug induced experience that you have has to happen again without drugs for it to have any lasting value in your life.

In all traditional cultures where drugs were used for spiritual or healing purposes, the greatest care was taken.

"Native Americans felt horror that white people would take peyote with no elders present, no one to clear the air or protect the souls from invasions by those spirits who do not wish us well." – THE SIBLING SOCIETY, Robert Bly.

Author's note: Peyote is a plant that has the effect of a psychedelic drug.

Many people don't realise they have a subtle energy body. This is called an aura. It surrounds and protects our physical body. Cannabis and some other drugs are said to be harmless, this is not true. Taking drugs can make holes in the aura. These holes leave people open to influences and spirit entities that may feed off, drain, control, agitate or manipulate them. Some people using drugs look grey or washed out and it looks like their life force is being sucked out of them. They don't know how to protect themselves.

Jonathan, a Metaphysical Counsellor says, "If people have been invaded by dark forces or spirit entities and they have sexual contact with others, these energies can be passed on. This may account for the growing number of females who have ovarian cysts, cancers of the cervix and other reproductive difficulties. Another thing that can cause dis-eases is when people have unresolved anger and pass the effect of this onto their sexual partners. It happens both ways. When they have sexual contact without honouring and respecting each other, disease is more likely to occur."

How does that grab you?

If Your Parents do Drugs or Alcohol

If your parents are cigarette smokers, use drugs or abuse alcohol then your challenge may be great. They may not have values that protect you from going down the same track. The messages you get can be unclear. Your parents may be unable to give you helpful guidance.

If they are severely addicted to drugs or alcohol, they may not be offering you emotional or physical stability at home. This is the case for some children of substance abusers. Addictions can be passed down from generation to generation.

If you have grandparents or a caring neighbour who can care for you, get as much support as possible from them. There are Government Services assisting young people in distress. They may not provide ideal or easy solutions for you but they offer you an option. You don't have to become an addict. Alcoholics Anonymous (AA) has been supporting people for many years. AlaTeens is especially for young people – check your local telephone directory. Or go to www.alcoholics-anonymous.org

Do your best not to sink into shame if you have inherited addictive behaviour. Find out what you value. You can make other choices. Learn how to protect and love yourself. **You are special!**

If You are Wounded

For those people who have been so badly wounded that life offers no hope, drugs may be used as an escape from facing these wounds for a while.

Our characters becomes weakened if life's tests are avoided. We can stop ourselves from maturing by avoiding the processes necessary to grow up and develop. If we cushion ourselves from painful and challenging situations we may slowly die. It takes a willingness to give it a go. It can also take loving support.

Ultimately we have the capacity to deal with everything. Life is sweet and also sour. Let's embrace and dance with it and allow ourselves the strengthening that happens when we face reality and get on with it.

Healthy Children

Most parents enjoy seeing their children grow up healthy, contented and fulfilling their potential. They have their own values and often they would like to pass these on. These may not become your values. Mature parents can become your guides as well as your friends during adolescence.

Let your parents know:

- that you understand something about harmful substances,
- when you are in danger. If they are willing to support you – ask them,
- that you are okay, if you sense they are concerned about you,
- what is going on in your life, so they don't worry unnecessarily,
- how it is for you growing up,
- that you are able to protect yourself, if this is true.

As you get older you get to make your own choices. Be willing to negotiate with your parents and gain their trust. It gets easier the more trustable and mature you become.

Life is your greatest gift – how are you living it?

The information for this section was found in:

The HOW TO DRUG PROOF YOUR KIDS Seminar at Mullumbimby High School.

A BOOKLET FOR PARENTS, Talking to Teenagers about Drugs. Author unknown.

PARENTING – THE MOST IMPORTANT JOB IN THE WORLD, The Department of Community Services, NSW. The Alcohol and Drug Information Service, NSW, Australia.

TEENAGERS AND ALCOHOL, A parent's guide. National Alcohol Campaign. Australian Government.

IT'S TIME TO TALK STRAIGHT, Australian Government.

A GUIDE TO QUITTING, National Drug and Alcohol Research Centre, University of New South Wales.

Getting Off It

Are you using addictive substances? If so, it may be hard to let go of them. If you feel the truth of what has been said and are ready to get off them – and GET REAL! Read on.

Drop any guilt about your drug or alcohol use.
Don't leave it until it's too late to change destructive habits.
Do not replace one harmful substance with another.

If you are ready to change your tobacco, drug or alcohol use, ask yourself:

What are my pay-offs?
What am I gaining by their use?
Am I ready to quit?
Am I becoming a slave to drugs rather than their master?

You may have become addicted:

- because you did drugs for fun and weren't aware of the consequences,
- to relax – find other ways to de-stress yourself,
- to make socialising and conversation easier. Be brave in these situations without the influence of substances.

Give it a go! In this moment you can make another choice. It only takes one thought, then an action to start with. Then keep going. It can be challenging and also life saving!

Does this feel difficult for you? **Can you accept the challenge?** Identifying your reasons for smoking, getting drunk, stoned or high is a starting point.

Lifestyle Changes

You can set new routines to know you are doing something differently. This could be eating healthy foods, playing a team sport or finding a new hobby. Give yourself a chance to enjoy life without using harmful substances.

Find people to support you by telling you that you're doing well by stopping.

The more you practice the easier it becomes.

The best results are from people who go cold turkey and give up in one go. If you are serious about quitting – STOP!

Your thinking may get clearer and your life has more chance of coming back into balance. Get reliable people to support you in this. In some circumstances you may benefit from medical advice. Attend a de-tox program if necessary.

If your smoking, drug or alcohol abuse has harmed you or someone else in any way, seek help – professional or otherwise – so that you can talk about what happened and deal with it. Free yourself of the effects of guilt and blame and take a step towards your own wellness.

If at first you don't succeed – keep going until you do. The only moment to do that is this one!

There are other exercises in this book designed to support you to look after yourself.

The choice is yours.

It's your life and also your death.

THINGS TO DO!

Use your Journal:

- Write down a list of reasons for using substances – what are you getting and what you may be avoiding. All the things that are bothering you and that make you feel unhappy, inhibited, unable to socialise and whatever else.
- List your reasons for giving up – they could include health issues, financial, social or spiritual.
- Become clear about your reasons for giving up and what you are letting go of?
- Imagine your life drug or alcohol free. What is that like for you? How do you feel? Write about it!
- Think about what to say to your friends who you drink, get stoned or smoke with. Practise before you see them.
- Make new friends with drug free people.
- Find life enhancing alternative behaviours. Write a list of them.
- Make a promise to yourself to follow through on these. Write them down and set a date for each of them.
- Then write about how it feels for you once you've achieved your results.

Natural Highs

Natural highs are possible, healthy and preferable to substance use. They come from an intense experience of life while doing something you love or enjoy – appreciating the beauty in Nature, watching a sunset or sitting by waterfalls or simply having fun with friends.

You can also experience natural highs through a sense of achievement – if you have done a job well or have stretched yourself in your life. By exerting more physical energy than you thought you had, by opening yourself up, by taking risks in your relationships or by stretching beyond your usual capacity – you get enjoyable natural highs.

Many young people experience natural highs and know there is no real substitute for them.

"Drugs have always been readily available to me. I didn't actually enjoy being high or tripping but it's the social norm, being part of the group. After the camp I realised I didn't need drugs to make me happy. I could be happier without them. I actually enjoyed myself more with friends when I'm not stoned.

You can get high on life. Like one night down on the beach – we were on this amazing high and thought we were tripping. It was like we were with the best friends we'd ever had in our whole lives, walking along the beach in the starlight, phosphorescence and waves. We did some twirling. We laughed and laughed. More than I'd done in a long time. I felt wonderfully free! I felt like I wasn't being judged. Whereas a lot of my life I've felt like people are criticising me.

Well it certainly initiated a big change in my life. I see the whole experience of drugs in a different way. I can look at it objectively and realise why I was doing it. I can see it for what it really is. Being a teenager and fitting into a certain crowd, being part of a mould that I have to fit into. I was doing it to get away from my problems and to fit in and now I'm facing my problems – I'm empowered." – Honey (15)

Do whatever gives you natural highs!

Natural highs are achieved through release of tension and pressure in the mind and body, as well as by being connected, loving and physical with the people around you. You can let more of life's energy in and experience joy, excitement and love like never before. Like climbing and reaching the top of the mountain – after all of the exertion there is the opportunity to appreciate the view.

Massage, singing, touching, painting, drawing, riding a surf board, dancing to your favourite music, initiating intimate connection with another person – are some of the ways that you can enjoy natural highs in your life.

Embrace your life and give yourself more. Through natural highs you experience your Essential Nature. There is a potential for you to live all of your life like this.

Open your mind to the possibility and your heart to the experience.

SUICIDE
The Silent Killer

A taboo exists around suicide – it is a problem that is not openly talked about.

Suicide is a major social problem. It is complex and dealing with it can be difficult. There is justified community alarm at the level of suicidal behaviour among young people. A lot of lives are touched when a teenager takes his or her life.

Many more young people make an attempt on their lives than actually achieve the end result – death!

Australia has one of the highest teenage suicide rates in the world. America and England are not that far behind. Countries like Spain, Italy and Greece have the lowest. People in those countries sing and dance in the streets, take siesta time and seem to balance work, relaxation and fun. Families seem close knit, with an extended network of relatives, grandparents, aunts and uncles. They have a passion for life that filters down to the young ones.

Things may have changed since I visited them but recent statistics reveal that something healthy is happening that keeps the suicide rate so low.

An old woman came and sat beside me in a park in San Francisco. She told me about her grandson who had recently committed suicide. I asked if she knew why. Shaking her head she said, "These young ones they don't know how to live."

The stresses of living in our technological and industrial world press upon us. Body image and achieving at school have become over-emphasised. Consumerism and the pressure to own material possessions has increased ridiculously. The world is speeding up! Suicide figures have escalated alarmingly in the last two decades.

Thank goodness for good news – teenage suicide rates have decreased in the last couple of years.

Life is unpredictable

We are constantly dealing with change as well as emotions that may be difficult to cope with. It is normal for us to experience a whole range of them – from feeling good and excited, to feeling rotten and at times, being in crisis. All of these arise from the experiences of our lives. Most of the time we are able to cope, using the skills we have learned.

If we don't have these skills and no one to turn to, we are at increased risk of:

- suppressing emotions or becoming depressed,
- becoming socially isolated,
- creating eating disorders,
- bullying, antisocial or abusive behaviour,
- having unrealistic expectations,
- conflict with friends or family,
- running away from home,
- losing touch with reality, unable to cope with life,
- substance abuse,
- self-harming or becoming suicidal.

At these times it is crucial to reach out for help from friends, parents, counsellors, relatives or a doctor. Doing this can save greater suffering and perhaps a life.

Coping with life becomes difficult, especially if you:

- have conflicts with parents,
- are living with parents who have unreasonable expectations,
- have parents who constantly fight, drink or are separating or divorcing,
- have a parent who becomes seriously ill or dies,
- are not getting on with friends,
- experience the death of a loved one,
- experience stress at school or fail exams,
- break up in a relationship,
- are being physically/psychologically/sexually abused in some way,
- are growing up in a world that is not always friendly,
- feel hopelessness about your situation and the future,
- experience increased stress for any reason or some other challenging event occurs.

It is normal in these circumstances that some young people become depressed, feel downhearted or alone. They may think that things can never change or get better. At such times they may feel in crisis and become suicidal.

When teenagers' lives are already in crisis it may only take one more problem or loss for them to become suicidal. Normally, this event may not be significant, but when they are in crisis it might take something relatively insignificant to tip the scales.

Stopping the Pain

When people become suicidal they usually go into fear-driven survival mode. This radically changes their thinking processes and body chemistry. They may become obsessive about suicide and find it impossible to see that there are other alternatives. Caught up in escaping the pain of living, they think of death in terms of an existence free from pain.

Dr David Bennett in his book GROWING PAINS, says with suicide the focus is on the end point, but there is a process involved. Reaching a point of desperation does not occur overnight.

What underlies increasing suicidal behaviour is an awful lot of adolescent depression and only recently has this been widely accepted as existing.

Teenagers generally reveal their depression in three ways: sadness, physical symptoms or antisocial behaviour.

Suicidal people:

- are normal people whose thinking has changed,
- have run out of options and are desperate,
- are crying out for help,
- may be considered weak, selfish, attention seeking or consider themselves to be,
- have not usually thought about how long death lasts,
- are dying. Slipping away. Faltering, they have temporarily lost touch.

Suicidal people often don't want to die. They are trying to stop the pain. Ninety percent of suicidal people don't follow through if their pain is released. Suicidal people have the capacity to relearn their ability to cope.

In this culture the terminally ill are given great care and attention. Millions of dollars are spent on seeking a cure. Little is spent on suicide prevention.

Someone who is experiencing suicidal tendencies is like a dying person. It's almost like he or she has cancer. The pain eats away at self-esteem, the will to live or to see life in a positive way. So that particular cancer grows.

There are three ways in which adolescent suicides can occur:

- indirectly when young people choose to take drugs or directly by deliberately choosing a lifestyle to slowly kill themselves. Eating disorders fall into this category,
- an accidental death, say through a car or motorcycle accident can be a disguised suicide in a depressed teenager,
- by taking his or (less commonly) her life through a deliberate and obvious suicidal act.

...and full of CHALLENGES

TEENSPEAK

"I dreaded going to school each morning. I felt like I was crashing up against an almighty wall. So much so that I'd stay awake all night to make the time seem longer. If I slept the crash would come sooner. I was desperately trying to hang on to not being suicidal, hanging on to my will to live. It was like being trapped in a prison. If I hadn't got out I would have become violent and turned to drugs. The drugs would have helped me not to feel it but would have got me in a lot of trouble. It would probably have led to suicide unless someone had intervened. I am out again. I thought I might not come out of it that time." – Lee (14)

"Drugs affected me and I think it was half their fault. I didn't even know it was happening. My girlfriend told me how I'd changed. I got angry and depressed. The pot made me so paranoid. I wanted to kill myself. I thought there was nothing worth living for. Things like: no one liked me – everyone had turned against me – when no one had. That once I finished school and everyone drifts off or once my family dies, I'll be on my own. I was petrified. I thought there would be no one to comfort me. I'd think crazy things – push myself too hard. Sometimes accelerate in my car and think that I could do it that way. Surf the biggest waves I could, even if I knew it was dangerous – not caring if I get hurt. Seeing my mum going through what she went through freaked me out. I thought I would get cancer. That if so many people get sick I'm sure to. So I thought I should end it now. It was my fear about death." – Derek (18)

"I experienced dissatisfaction with life, negativity. Conflict. Confusion to do with love and relationships. Mum's problems. I was looking for answers. I was suffering with depression! I guess I was suicidal because I didn't feel that I had any purpose or that anybody would notice that I was gone. Well I was hiding it away – nobody noticed! I think it's because I am over-sensitive about my experiences and problems that happen. I just let everything affect me too easily. I guess I wasn't very strong but I don't feel that way anymore. I know that lots of people attempt suicide and don't do it. I wanted to do it right if I was going to do it at all. I felt all sorts of things. Then I thought about it and saw there was a possibility that the way I was thinking wasn't true at all. That people did love me." – Honey (15)

"For a long time I'd been feeling low self-esteem and asking what was the point of my life. It all began when I went to the beach. I began to swim. I knew at the back of my mind what I was doing. When I was far out to sea I turned round and thought, 'I'm going to die.' But it was like – so what! I waved my arm and called out, just once, out of obligation. I gave up my life and it was extremely beautiful. Letting myself be pulled further away by the rip, I was beginning to sink under the waves. I saw a friend coming over on his surfboard, heroically to rescue me. I arrived on the beach and everyone was crying and going over the top. Nobody wanted to know or understand what it had really been like for me. The next year was the most agonising year of my life. I was suicidal most of the time. I couldn't explain why I felt so terrible. I became an addict to medication. I would take large amounts of tablets every time I felt upset – simply because of the words PAIN RELIEF on the packet! I knew it was illogical and a stupid thing to do, but I didn't care. When I had enough of life I would take as many tablets as I could. But it never worked. I would wake up in the morning and be annoyed that I was alive. One time I decided to take an extra amount, about two packets but they didn't work either because they made me vomit. I'm now very glad that it didn't work." – Laura (15)

A Cry for Help

Many people who are suicidal attempt to communicate that they are considering it. They are not always heard. Some families are genuinely astonished following the suicide of a loved one – they had no idea there was anything wrong.

It is important to keep our eyes and hearts open to cries for help. Suicidal people often tell us in several ways, directly or indirectly:

Writing – Sometimes by writing a poem, story or in the words of a song. They may leave their Journal lying around hoping someone finds it.

What they say – Things like, "I'd be better off dead!" or "I can't live like this any longer!" or even, "I've decided to kill myself." In a not so obvious way they may say, "What's the point of going on? Who cares if I'm dead anyway? The world would be better off without me in it."

Giving things away – Suicidal people may prepare for death by giving away their favourite things. They usually give them to someone they respect and like. Usually that person can help them the most.

Changing behaviour – You may notice a change in their behaviour – what they are eating, their sleeping patterns, they may stop socialising, experience dark moods and become depressed or use drugs.

Suicidal people operate from emotions rather than from rational thinking. They may feel depressed, fearful, overwhelming guilt or shame, hopeless and helpless, isolation, being trapped, sadness, anger or desperation.

Most suicidal people are looking for a way to STOP THE PAIN rather than to die.

Facts about Suicide

- **Eight out of ten people who kill themselves give definite signs of their suicidal intentions. People who make suicide threats and attempts must be taken seriously.**
- **Most suicidal people are undecided, often right up until the last minute about living or dying. They gamble with death, leaving it up to others to save them.**
- **Most people who wish to kill themselves are suicidal for only a limited period of time. They often go on to lead meaningful lives.**
- **Suicide does not run in families.**
- **Most suicidal people are extremely unhappy! They are not generally mentally ill.**
- **Research shows that nine out of ten suicidal people do not really intend to die.**

In most cases the person does not have to die for the pain to stop.

DEPRESSING POETRY
Grace Lily (16)

When she was sick
Dearest
Dearest
Dearest
Rain
My Mother
Thinks I am
Insane

Sometimes
Times like today
When both my parents
Hold very queer
Expressions
On their faces
I feel a
Controllable
Urge to laugh.

Written while I was sick and my parents were asking me why I wanted to die.

Stay Tuned In

Follow your feelings, trust your judgement and stay closely connected to anyone you think is at risk. As a caring person you may be able to help. If you are feeling vulnerable and don't think you can help, tell an adult about what is happening. Reach out on the suicidal person's behalf.

You may be able to help suicidal people:

- if you have a sense that something is wrong and take action,
- if they let you know that they are thinking about hurting themselves and you do something about it,
- if you don't abandon them. Don't leave them alone to make up their own minds when they feel isolated, desperate and unsupported.

The world is not a reasonable place to someone who is suicidal. Don't be lulled into believing that the risk of suicide is over when a person appears to rapidly recover. This is one of the oldest bluffs used by people contemplating suicide. It has been shown that most suicides occur within three months after a period of improvement. This is when suicidal people have more energy to turn their thoughts and feelings into action. Be particularly watchful during this time. Be aware that people who have attempted suicide in the past are likely to try it again.

Suicide Prevention is Everybody's Business

Would you like to make this a more caring World?

If so, then be aware of what is going on around you and to help those who are in pain. Be willing to give more than you get at times. One of these times is when faced with a suicidal person.

In a crisis moment don't attempt to discuss the situation. It is not possible to reason with someone when his or her world is hitting the wall. The problem is big enough. Don't promise that things will be better. Don't try to offer solutions. The more a suicidal person cannot do what you suggest, the more useless he or she may feel.

Because talking about suicide is taboo and because it is personal, asking suicidal people if they are suicidal may be awkward and difficult. If you think someone is suicidal, you can't be sure until she or he tells you. Even then you can't be sure. Be willing to step out of your comfort zone to help.

Care enough to help!

Things you can do if you have a friend who is suicidal:

- Be willing to open your heart and be compassionate towards the suffering she or he is experiencing.
- Let her or him know that you are not burdened by what is happening.
- That your friend is talking to you may mean that the decision to suicide has not been made. If you suspect – Ask, "Do you feel suicidal?" It brings the subject out into the open. This may be the most important question you can ask at this time. Asking may not increase the risk of your friend suiciding and it may save a life. Then ask, "Now that you have told me, what would you like to me to do?"

If the answer to the first question is NO but intuitively you sense it is not the truth, you have options. You can suggest that your friend talks to someone else and you can tell someone else yourself.

If you can, enter into his or her world. Remember it's about the pain. Be compassionate. Do your best not to get too involved in the dynamic of the pain or story. Go with what's driving him or her, the hopelessness, despair, disempowerment or anger. Stay optimistic if you can. Be clear about what your job is – **to get the suicidal person to someone who can help.** If there is a plan, do your best to stop the plan from happening.

Ask your heart what you are willing and able to do. Seek other help! Talk to a school counsellor, to parents or relatives. You can ring Lifeline or other Helplines.

Practical Suggestions to Help

Open-ended questions give your friend the opportunity to experience choice, power and personal responsibility.

- Approach your friend by saying, "I notice you've seemed down/unhappy/depressed lately. Would you like to tell me what's going on?" or, "I'm concerned about you, is something on your mind?" Your friend then knows that you care and perhaps can help.
- Be aware not to be judgemental. Do not tell your friend what to do and be careful not to make her or him feel guilty.
- Listen for what drives the pain, in that moment. Listen and don't give advice.
- Ask open-ended questions. These ask for detailed answers rather than a Yes or No. Some examples:

  You feel desperate because you think nobody loves you. What does that feel like?

  You feel pain because your mother died. How are you feeling about that?

  You feel lonely because you have no friends. What's that like for you?
- Learn to give feedback. Repeat back what is said to you: "You feel… because…" to get clear about what the feelings are. Do your best not to be like a parent.
- Ask if there is a plan. See if there is a set time and if he or she is willing to talk to you about it.
- Discuss the subject of suicide without shock or disapproval with your friend who seems seriously depressed. When you do this it shows that you are taking him or her seriously and responding to his or her pain.
- Find out if there is anyone your friend trusts to talk to.
- Ask for agreement not to harm him or herself until meeting with someone who can offer more help than you. **Never leave the conversation without a no-harm agreement.**
- Make a time to meet with your friend again within a few and not longer than 24 hours – negotiate a time. This is to see how things are and to let him or her know that you have time and you care.
- Ask your friend to help you find suitable support. If he or she does not know where to turn ask an adult for assistance to find a professional counsellor and make an appointment. Offer to go with your friend if this would help.

  Check in your telephone directory for other services that are available in your area or on the web.
- Always tell an adult, a parent, neighbour or counsellor what you are doing and allow him or her to support you both.

By following the above suggestions your friend may feel more connected, safe and respected, also relieved.
If thoughts of suicide decrease, your friend is likely to see other options in the situation.

If You are Suicidal

To go on living or to die is a choice only you can make. The world is worse off if you're not in it, whether you believe it or not. No one can give any guarantees that things will get better. But remember that once your body is dead, this life is over. Right now that may seem like the only answer. But death goes on forever.

Death may not be an end to your pain. Your body may be released from the trauma of your current situation but you are more than your body.

A Message From Me

This is to anyone who is thinking about ending his or her own life.

My tears I shed when I think of you. I am not close to you but I care. I cannot hear your words and I cannot feel you, because you are not physically close to me. But I love you. When I feel your pain, tears stream down my face. That you are suffering and perhaps there is no one close by you, touches and hurts me, because I love you.

The depth of your loss or despair touches me as I weep for you and for the world where one person feels so alone. I reach out my hand and my heart. Can you feel it? Can you imagine the tears I cry for you? Can you feel my love, even if it's hard for you to imagine it? I love you even though we haven't met. Do you believe that? Your pain matters to me. You are connected to me. My heart weeps for you.

I wish to comfort you wherever you are. If I could hold you in my arms and stroke your hair, I would. Please know that you are not really alone. That even though the world right now seems bleak and loveless and you feel like dying rather than living, it can change.

I speak to your angels. I know they are around you. I ask them to hold you, protect and keep you safe. Your angels see your tears and mine. They are close. They are waiting for your invitation. Call out to them so that they can reach you. Ask them to be there for you.

Don't die! I know that somewhere, not so far away, there is someone who has enough love in his or her heart to care about you. Even if that person is someone you don't know yet. I believe it is true because I know there is GOODNESS in the World.

There is a God who loves and cares about you. Also that, for whatever reason, you are meant to be here on this Earth, whether you accept it or not. You have a right and a reason to be here. Your gifts are great, as great as any master, teacher, scientist, artist, professor or rock star. They are as great as anyone else's. You are so very special and a precious part of the whole of life.

I encourage you to live, to feel connected to all that is good and to find love in your life

I love you. I hold you close to my heart and catch your tears. Shed them willingly. The snake sheds its old skin. Shedding skins makes us new and tender again. Are you shedding a skin, a layer, to be lighter, changed and cleansed from your pain? Is that what is happening for you? Is it enough to shed one skin, rather than to take your whole life?

I give you the salt of my tears so that when it comes your way again you can taste the sweetness that is life. Even if sometimes it seems too hard to bear.

So let me hold you just a while longer. My love pours out as my tears flow again for you. I love you. Don't die. Hold on. Find someone NOW who has extra love in his or her heart and can listen to your pain. See if you can find a glimmer of hope in your mind that someone can hold and love you. Maybe, just maybe, what you are going through right now can open a door for a different experience of life for you.

As my tears stop flowing, I imagine you feeling a stirring of warmth. Just a little bit of hope that maybe you can believe in yourself – so that you can cope and live through this.

I love working with teenagers and it touches me deeply to think of any one of you in that much pain. I truly do believe it can be different for each one of us personally and also as a planet. That it is time for change.

A One-way Ticket

A mother, whose daughter suicided sends this message:

"If you are a teenager reading this, don't give up on life. Death is a one way ticket, marked Not Negotiable. The body in the morgue is no longer yours to make choices with. Suicide is a game where everybody loses – your parents, your friends and most of all you." – GROWING PAINS, Dr David Bennett.

Ending the Pain

Right now if you are suicidal you may be asking yourself how you can end this incredible pain. You may believe you have no other choice but to end your life.

I ask you to accept that:

- your emotions are spinning out of control,
- you may not believe that significant people in your life value you,
- you may have completely lost hope because it seems unbearable,
- you are losing your will to live,
- nothing is that big that it can't be fixed,
- it's okay to talk and reach out for help,
- everyone is unhappy at some point in their lives, some desperately so. It is normal.

Ask yourself if there is one reason to live today. See if there is one. If you can't find one, make one up!

Do you know that:

- you are good at the things that mean something to you? Even if these things are not what other people value.
- you can have control over the important aspects of your life?
- it is possible to live through this regardless of what happens even if right now you have lost it? Your sense of handling your life can come back sooner or later.
- you are not a burden to others who care about you?
- you can be valued for who you are, whatever you are, whether you are good at school, come from a desperately unhappy family or even if you have been badly abused? You are still worthwhile with your own unique gifts to bring.
- you don't have to be anyone but yourself?

You are Special!

The Paw-Paw Tree

"When I doubt my power, my ability to grow and expand, I think of a paw-paw tree I know. It is growing out of a tiny crack between a brick wall and a large concrete car park. There is no visible soil or water storage. It seems miraculous!

How much more miraculous then is Life in all its awesome variety and energy. Our World BURSTS with life and so can we. Express life, power, energy and humanity. Life is ours to fully express. That is why we are here. GO FOR IT!"
– Andrew Williams.

Seek Professional Help

If you are suicidal or know someone who is, find out where you can get qualified help.

You can usually find a Helpline listed in your local telephone directory. You may have a Neighbourhood Centre or Community Centre close by which could recommend someone who is a good counsellor. Look for a person who has a kind heart as well as the skills to support you. You may have a family doctor or natural therapist who may be able to help or lead you in the right direction.

Check out this web site: www.wesleylifeforce.org

Look for others.

I'M GONNA BE FREE
Shelly (14)

Chorus:
I'm gonna be free, free, free,
I'm gonna be free, free, free,
I'm gonna be free.
I know I'm meant to be happy,
Cos I'm me and nobody else,
And that's the way it's meant to be.
I'm me and nobody else
and that's the way it's meant to be.

I'll be a Light in the sky,
Without ever knowing why,
Rising high above the cloud,
I am proud.

Chorus.
Swimming like a silver fish,
I can be anything I wish,
And I know life's not so bad,
I am glad.

Chorus.
Like a bird on the wing,
I can do most anything,
I am free, yes, I'm free,
To be me.

My Story

As a teenager I felt alone, emotionally isolated and sometimes desperate. I had occasional thoughts of suicide. In a healing session years later I recalled sitting in the back garden behind the shed when I was 14. I thought about suicide. I didn't have any idea how to go about doing it. I don't think I've ever really seriously considered taking my life.

In 1993, I was living in a one-roomed cottage, planning to write. Having gone through a major personal crisis, I believed my work with teenagers was over. I was devastated!

My work had been one of my main passions. My drive, will and enthusiasm for life left me. I lost the plot! Over three months I sank into a mild depression, unable to write or focus on anything. One clear memory I have was sitting by the river. I wished I could have fallen in, sunk to the depths and not got out again. I allowed the thought but didn't do it.

Out of that dark hole a whole new direction in my life and work emerged. For me the depression was the muddy ground that was telling me something was not right. New seeds grew from that painful time. I felt compassion after that for people who had no sense of purpose or direction in their lives.

Having seen myself go from a motivated, powerful woman in a relatively short time of depression, I could not imagine how it must be for people who suffer over a long time.

I am grateful for that experience and to be alive.

Some of this information is taken from: LifeForce – Suicide Prevention Programme which is an activity of Wesley Mission, Australia.
Web site: www.wesleylifeforce.org

You can also check out: www.reachout.com.au

YOUR SPIRITUAL JOURNEY

By working with the suggestions in GETTING REAL… about growing up! you may have expanded your awareness of your Essential Nature and moved beyond your beliefs and conditioning about how life is. Things may seem different to you now. You may find yourself achieving goals you didn't think you could before. Your relationships could be easier to handle. You may have become self confident and able to create things you enjoy in your own life. Changes may not have happened yet in the outside world but from the inside your life may be easily manageable and enjoyable. You may have love available to you from within and from the World. You may have gained greater understanding about your Essential Nature and what it means to be REAL.

You may have learned the art of Inner Listening that offers guidance, support and direction in your life. When you hear the whispers of your heart, a secret key opens up the Great Mystery to you. You are totally connected to this Mystery whether you are aware of it or not. Listening to your heart gives you access to Love – the greatest Power available on the planet. Love Is. Following your heart frees you and sustains the gentlest part of your Nature. You can experience Wisdom, Peace and your connection to the Great Intelligent Source of all Life. Connection with your Essential Nature offers you the strength to walk your spiritual path and fulfil your life's purpose.

"Our religions and our technology have conspired for too long to put the divine out of our reach – in the eternal hereafter… and in so doing have made a terrible mess of the planet. So if we are to undo the mess, we must once again understand that God is in the leaves of trees, the banks of rivers and the wind blowing through our hair; that ethical work is a sacrament; that raising sane children is a sacred task; and that fully loving and accepting another person is an act of the profoundest magic and power. We must connect again." – WOMEN AND RITUALS, Celeste Fremon (Yoga Journal).

The BIG Picture

As young children we are naturally connected to something that is greater than our awareness of ourselves. If that connection is not nurtured it hides. Do you have memories of feeling something special and mystical when you were young?

When you clean out the excess clutter from your mind and have a strong sense of who you are, there is room for creating an expanded picture of yourself, your World and the place you have in it. When that becomes clear you may realise there are universes beyond this one… The picture is getting really BIG then!

If you keep yourself busy all the time with the little things of life and take no time to reflect on the big picture, you may believe you're small and live your life small.

Gardeners of the Soul

What is Soul? Soul in some ways is beyond words. It is not a thing – not physical. You cannot touch it. It is an invisible aspect of you. It subtly exists beyond your thinking consciousness in the realm of your imagination. It can be likened to an unfocussed camera. The images we see are blurred and perhaps unrecognisable. This makes the camera useless.

Your Soul responds to images, beauty, to the sense and feeling of things. It is intelligent and although not physical it can be subtly experienced.

When we bring our Soul into focus, our sense of colour, texture, softness and the depth and yum of life becomes more defined. We experience rewarding relationships, an increased sense of peace and power. We naturally move toward activities that fulfil us and our feelings are enlivened.

"I'm trying to live in harmony with my soul. My dad always says: 'Just live in harmony with your soul and don't ruin another's life.' I'm trying to do that because I think that this is very wise." – Olga (16), Wroclaw, Poland.

If people are soul-less they may act inhumanely. They can commit horrendous crimes – atrocities in the eyes of others because they are out of touch with feelings and conscience.

Other symptoms of disconnection from Soul are isolation, emptiness, depression or disillusionment about life. Lustreless, there may be a lack of energy and natural vitality. These people may live their lives like the walking dead. There is no spark in their eyes or spring in their steps. Life has become meaningless, dreary and drab. They do not have heart-felt life experiences.

When you are soul-full you deeply value life. You are not caught up with only the material aspects of your life. When you feed and nourish yourself, your Soul life is enriched. The Soul is fed by beauty, heart connection, intimacy and a sense of belonging. The Soul is strengthened when your imagination plays a part in your life. This could be through artistic or creative activities – story, poetry, painting, dancing or music. Ritual, ceremony and celebration also enliven the Soul and add meaning to life. Only you know how to nourish your own Soul.

If your Soul is well you are generally positive and enthusiastic about life. When challenges weigh heavily on you, you do not sink into a dark hole of hopelessness and depression. You still see the sunshine. You wake up in the morning ready to get into your day. Life is full of exciting possibilities and you are vital in it. You may not feel this way every day, but with a Soul that has been nourished, you often experience peace within yourself.

Your Soul's Purpose

Your Soul has a goal that serves and guides you to your highest good and also that of others. Written in its depths is a memory of the purpose you came into this World to fulfil. It may not be what you think you are here to learn or experience. It might differ from your personal desires. If you stray from its plan, uncomfortable events may occur to get you back on track. If you follow its messages your life can flow. Like a river that naturally moves towards the sea you are moved towards what is best for you.

We Are All Gardeners

Gardens take time to grow. You plant the seeds of your choice and then look after them. What seeds are you planting in your now fertile mind? Be careful once your seeds are sprouting not to step on them by being overly worried or concerned. Do not over-water, over-fertilise or try to make them grow faster. Mulch the seeds of your Soul with a sense of humour and the compost of the old beliefs and patterns that you clear out of your mind now and again.

Your plants grow strong when you tend and take care of them. With the right conditions they grow and you receive the harvest of your efforts. When you live your life from your Essential Nature the Miracle of your life unfolds like a flower blooming. Nature takes her time. Be kind to yourself. As you move along your path you harvest what you have sown. Fruit ripens on the tree of your life.

"The finest qualities of our nature, like the bloom in fruits, can be preserved only by the most delicate handling. Yet we do not treat ourselves, nor one another thus tenderly."
– Walden.

A relationship with Spirit and everything around you is possible as you nurture the seeds that bring consciousness to your Soul. You can do this by spending time in Nature, by listening to music that inspires you, by surfing, by painting pictures, reading or writing poetry, by eating beautifully prepared food and anything else you can think of that makes you feel buoyant, alive or passionate.

"…We are here primarily for the growth of the soul, for the enlightenment of the spirit self. We have a responsibility to the world, to our friends, to our neighbours. Responsibility starts with us. I would say, each man, each woman and each child is the 'mother' of the world. We hold the world in our hands." – Rosemary Althea from an article in THE NEW TIMES, Seattle, USA.

Note: Spirit and Soul are different – but one. Spirit creates the body, mind and Soul. These are all aspects of Spirit just like ice, liquid and steam are aspects of water.

Battered and Bruised

Think of different kinds of fruit and see what a symbol for life and people it can be. Take an avocado, which is a fruit, as an example. Sometimes it is just right – ripe, ready and appetising. At others, it is battered, bitter, bruised and inedible. That can be disappointing, especially if it looks good on the outside. At times in our lives we may also look or feel battered and bruised. No use to anyone – ugly and unappealing. Sometimes fruit is bitter and off. At times too, life has knocked people around so much that they are repulsive to themselves and to others. Never give up – no matter what the mill wheel of your life has made of you.

Within each battered avocado, there is a seed. That seed has the potential for a tree that could produce thousands upon thousands of new trees and new fruits. It takes time, of course and the right circumstances, but the potential is there. It's the same with human beings. With love and nurturing the most battered and bruised of people can blossom and grow.

I ENTERED THE WORLD
Vanessa (15)

I entered the world with peace of mind,
unaware of what I would find.
But the drama of life that people fear,
soon began to reappear.

The anger and hatred of their lives
was what I soon began to despise
and sitting here watching the sky,
I wonder why we have to cry.

But now I sit and look at the trees,
flowing freely in the breeze.
They stand tall in the Heavenly Kingdom
sharing with us their ancient wisdom.

Now I see the love I must share
with people that just don't seem to care,
For if I share the peace I'm experiencing
I'll help the world to begin loving.

Dark Times of the Soul

At times life challenges us to the core. We may have become lazy, fallen asleep or are caught up in the material aspects of life. We may not remember that we are spiritual beings having a human experience. If life knocks us hard we may feel lost and abandoned. When we fall into depression or sadness our trust may be tested. We can forget that God is available at these times. Sometimes, it may be our Soul's cry that is making us feel so bad. Perhaps there are lessons we are not learning.

Without experiences that deepen us we remain superficial – dancing over the waters of our life rather than diving to the depths.

FOOTPRINTS

If you feel down and alone remember this story:

"One night a man had a dream. He dreamed he was walking along the beach with God. Across the sky flashed scenes from his life. For each scene he noticed two sets of footprints in the sand; one belonging to him and the other to God.

When the last scene of his life flashed before him he looked back at the footprints in the sand.

He noticed that many times along the path of his life there was only one set of footprints. He also noticed that it happened at the very lowest and saddest times in his life. This really bothered him and he questioned God about it.

"God, you said that once I decided to follow you, you'd walk with me all the way. But I have noticed that during the most troublesome times of my life there is only one set of footprints. I don't understand why when I needed you the most you would leave me."

God replied, "My precious, precious child I love you and I would never leave you. During your times of trial and suffering, when you see only one set of footprints in the sand, it was then that I carried you."

– FOOTPRINTS IN THE SAND, Author unknown.

Sometimes on your spiritual Journey it seems hopeless and as if nothing good can ever come out of your life. That's never true. Everything constantly changes. When you think of it that way you can always keep your sense of adventure alive. You can always begin again. Nothing is set in concrete.

Every moment is a new beginning

TEENSPEAK

"God is everything. The trees, birdies and me! I am God. I think there is no distinct figure of God; there is a Spirit but there is no actual way to picture this. You can't really. The bigger your problems are, the smaller God gets. When you are troubled, you lose faith. The smaller the problems you have, the bigger God is. You think he always has a reason for having bad weather or making us have bad days but he never makes mistakes. I think of God as a 'he' 'cos that's the culture we've been brought up in." – Angie (13)

"I don't believe in God! But as soon as anything really bad happens I swear at him. I was in a really bad mood this morning. I couldn't go out. I locked my mum out of the house for a while. I sat on the couch swearing at him, calling him names. I was really angry. I stick my finger up and tell him I hate him. So I don't know if I believe in God or not." – Chelsea (14)

"My mother is Nepalese. She is spiritual but does not believe in one religion. She believes in a Higher Power and she doesn't have a preference where she gets it from – whether it's your Christian God, Buddhism… anywhere. It doesn't bother me whether I am Christian or Buddhist. I do believe there is someone there. One problem with Christianity is that they wouldn't agree with that. I do genuinely pray. " – Les (18)

"To me God is myself! It's a clarity and an infinite depth, which I know holds every truth, which is in me. But this idea of God is not just me. It is part of everything. So God isn't just inside me, God is also a power outside of myself that affects my life. This idea of God is very helpful to me. I really enjoy it when I feel this God feeling. The joy of that has inspired me to keep going many times when I felt like giving up." – Jessica (19)

"The world is covered by human beings believing in different things which may be their reasons for crying, dancing, loving, joining, cleaning and the celebrating of life, eating in a special way, loving, embracing the earth, or the reasons for feeling special, becoming sensitive, reflecting inside on the soul, or covering themselves in mud and leaves. Those things are all really wonderful to experience and to do, but being religious usually means more than some or all of these things. You do what you want to do, be what you want to be." – Bindi (16)

OH GOD! – Mel (15)

God was depressed. A question kept popping up in his mind:
How could I have picked Earth to rule over?

Finally he decided to call his counsellors together to discuss the matter. "Oh!" Cried God. "What can I do? I made man for happiness and learning and look what they do! I give them an apple, but if it's not red enough they pour chemicals and pesticides over it to make it look beautiful. Then people eat these chemicals and pesticides and become ill and pray to me to cure them.

So I offer a rainforest full of beauty, life and fresh, clean healthy air and what do they do? They cut it down and replace it with grey buildings and factories that pump pollution into the air that people breathe. This pollution of course makes everyone sick so they pray to me to make them better.

So I give them an ocean, cool, clear fresh, full of life and extremely healthy. Instead of swimming and bathing in it, they pump pollution, garbage, oil and just about everything you can imagine. Then instead of being full of life it becomes dead and unhealthy. Everything I give them they seem to waste or kill. It's no good! I feel like I'm having a nervous breakdown." The counsellors had never seen God as anxious or worried before became quite distressed. "God," one of them began, "Why don't you go on holiday?"

God considered this for a second or two and then said, "Yes, a holiday is a fine idea. I could hide somewhere until Earth has a hold of itself. But where could I hide? I'm God remember? What if humans found me? That would be a disaster."

Then Buddha suddenly stood up, cleared his throat, "God! I have it. You could hide on the moon!"

"That would surely be no good for people have already invented rocket ships to travel there. People will be living there soon! They will find me in no time at all." God muttered gloomily. Then Florence Nightingale stood up and announced, "I have an idea God. You could hide on the top of Mount Everest."

"Auugh, that is not good enough either, for people climb the mountain already.
They would find me in no time at all."

"God," said another, "You could pay Mother Nature a long visit.
You know you would always be welcome at her service."

"But Mother Nature is too busy; she's at battle trying to protect her rainforests," God explained. "They would find me in no time at all." Everyone in the room was silent for not one could think of a single place for God to hide that had no fault. Suddenly, an old, old, counsellor, who had been silently observing the entire conversation, stood up. "God, do not fret," he said, "I have it."

"Yes?" God beckoned anxiously. "Why don't you hide inside of humans, they'll never ever think of looking there!"

What Does God Mean to You?

This is an opportunity to find out for yourself who or what God is to you. If you have a clear idea about this, it may bring a great sense of peace, trust and love into your life. You may discover a deep connection that could become a source of understanding, courage and strength to you.

Some things you can do to clarify this for yourself:

- Spend time getting clear about what you think or know God to be.
  Write down your thoughts and feelings.
- Having written down your ideas, read them and reflect on them.
- Examine your list and separate the ideas that come from:

  What other people have said or believe God is.

  What religious organisations you have belonged to, if any, have said.

  Your family – if they have strong views and opinions that you have taken on.

If you do this, your perception of God as a Presence in your life, can change.

THINGS TO DO!

Write a letter to God

This is a powerful way to connect with the Wisdom that normally may seem unavailable to you.

Writing this letter can help you to:

- solve problems,
- receive clarity and guidance about things that are on your mind,
- understand more of what is going on in the World,
- find out why you are here,
- discover the Mysteries of life.

This can be done with a friend, in a group or alone.

- Have a notebook or your Journal ready.
- Find a quiet place to sit where you won't be disturbed.
- Think about the Universe – and the Intelligence and Power throughout it.

  How millions of cells are brought together to form a flower, a bird, a tree – you!
  What creates the wind, the water and the mountains?
  The infinite variety of experiences that life has to offer.
- Imagine a vastness beyond you.

  How a Great Intelligence moves within you, bringing synchronicity, blessings and unexpected surges of love or peace. Let scenes from Nature wash through your mind.
- Consider the Miracle of your life.
- Ask yourself how this Intelligence could operate in your life and become easily available to you.
- Allow yourself to become quiet inside.
- Call upon the Presence of that Great Intelligence to assist you in understanding about the many aspects of your experience, your relationships, your body, any problems you have and why you are here. You can ask questions about anything you like.

Now begin to write your letter:

- Address it: Dear God, Dear Wise Person or My Big Self – whatever feels right for you.
- Write down everything you would like answers to. Ask and allow your questions to come in their own way. Just write until you have finished your letter.

Don't read any further than this until you have completed your letter.

Next step:

- Take a few minutes in silence. Connect with what you consider God to be.

  Accept that all that is Wise is within you. It can give you the answers that you seek.
  It supports you with understanding that is usually beyond your own thinking.
  Your connection with God is possible.
  Relax and open your mind and heart.
- Now write your reply. Go for it! Write as much as you like.
- When you have finished, spend time considering your reply.
  Go back to your questions and see how well your answers fit.
- If you have been doing this with a friend or a group it is powerful to read out your letter and the reply to each other. Then you become aware not only of what you've gained by asking for help but also how it is for others. This can be awesome.

You can write letters to God at any time, whenever there is something in your life you'd like answers to or to understand what is going on.

"The aim or purpose of following the spiritual path is not to be able to name God, but to experience God and then let God be to us whatever It unfolds Itself as, because to each of us God will disclose and reveal Itself in an individual way."

– GOD, THE SUBSTANCE OF ALL FORM, Joel Goldsmith.

Constant Change

The one certainty in this life is change. Everything changes all of the time. The more easily you can deal with this change the more easily your life flows.

Have patience, allow your humanness and accept all aspects of yourself. By observing, enjoying and rejoicing in them – you are fully alive. Even if you feel terrible!

Life is a process of constantly letting go of old habits that no longer work for you and friendships that you've outgrown. Don't fear this. If you mix with the same people doing the same kinds of things over a period of many years, it may be something inside that's stuck. Staying small can hold you back. Your mind may tell you all sorts of stories to fool you. Listen, say, "Thanks, but no thanks" and then let your body and your heart direct your life.

What you gain from your spiritual Journey is – **YOU, YOU, YOU and more YOU!**

It's all YOU – and it's all God, the SOURCE or whatever you wish to call it. As you live more from your Essential Nature, you know that it's okay to be who you are, all of yourself, even the bruised, bitter and battered bits, because they make up your sum total.

Allow your growth to occur naturally.
Build your character.
Establish your values and a moral code for yourself.
Love and accept yourself as much as you can in each moment.
Take the steps. Stay as awake as you can and listen to your knowing.
Do not underestimate your potential.
Keep your heart strong and let your love-light shine by staying open and sharing yourself with others.

Be still and at peace with yourself

Living on the Edge

Being on the edge – living your life from the inside, according to your own spiritual guidance and vision – is different from life in the ordinary sense. You may not fit in. People may harass you because you aren't what they expect you to be. You are not behaving the same as them.

The benefits are perhaps not in the ordinary ways of money, material possessions or fame but even better, there is a sense of fulfilment, achievement and Inner Peace. This way of creatively living brings a sense of true aliveness and alertness.

There's no falling asleep on the edge!
"Come to the edge", he said.
"We are afraid", they said.
"Come to edge", he said.
They came.
He pushed them.
They flew.

– Guillaune Apollinaire.

We can all Wake Up
We can all Fly
It's our True Nature

Completing the Journey

A Message from Raithe Handiman, author of THE FINAL CHAPTER.

"Adolescence is an essential part of the life process; the transition from childhood into adulthood. It is a wonderful stage that must be passed through on the way to maturity. But the purpose of life is not to mature, grow old and eventually die. The real purpose of life is to awaken to the Truth and that can take place at any stage in life.

In fact, the first taste of awakening very often takes place at around the age of sixteen or seventeen, when the young adult has an experience of the true Nature of life. It can be triggered by something as simple as watching a beautiful sunrise or sunset or by holding a flower or an animal.

Some profound realisation takes place. Because we are not prepared for it, we almost invariably shut down to it and then spend the rest of our life trying to recreate it in the external, material world. That never works! Many turn to religion or spiritual paths to try to recapture the magic of it.

Real awakening has nothing to do with prayer or meditation or sitting under a pyramid holding a crystal, although such practices can help us to expand our awareness. Real awakening takes place within the heart. It takes place the moment we surrender our wants, needs, desires, beliefs, preferences, expectations and judgments. It happens the moment we allow ourselves to rest, openly and softly, in whatever we might have become.

When we do that, we make way for our Essential Nature to have the experience of that moment – then and only then, there is an awakening in the heart.

Our Essential Nature never judges us. It loves us exactly as we are. So when we allow our thoughts, feelings, desires and physicality to be as they are, we are actually living up to our highest and true potential as human beings."

If you express all that is good, inside and outside of yourself – the Journey home to your Essential Nature unfolds, and you fulfil yourself. You make it a better World.

My Story

My spiritual Journey began in 1979 on my arrival in Australia. I experienced a spiritual awakening through a set of weird circumstances. I saw that life, as I believed it to be, was not what it seemed. As I looked out through my eyes and saw only material reality I realised that was only one aspect of what actually IS. It was like I had been asleep. It began to dawn on me that there is something much more powerful going on underneath the surface of everyday existence.

It has taken courage to walk my spiritual path. I've stepped out and been a loner. My relationship with my family and friends changed because they couldn't relate to me in the old way. They distanced themselves from me and I from them. This allowed me to emerge with a new sense of myself. We are close again now and have deepened trust and understanding of each other.

I have been aware of my connection with God since that time. I listen for the whispers which give my life meaning, direction and purpose. My writing is inspired and so is my work. I could not do what I do without that spiritual support and guidance.

I am in awe of the Great Mystery – how it unfolds. I see a plan in motion. The signs become obvious to me and all sorts of cosmic coincidences take place. People show up out of the blue in answer to my questions. The deeper the knowing, the easier the flow and the more magic I have in my life. When I let go fully, I sense myself being danced by life. When I forget – and I sometimes do, I feel separate, struggling, alone and unsupported.

Feeling a part of the big picture and being in contact with the invisible Source has enabled me to be of service to others and fulfil what has been my purpose up until this point.

I am truly grateful… I AM blessed!

We don't always know where our Journey takes us. We can only take the steps.

**Sometimes it's challenging not knowing where we're going.
Standing still and trusting, the next step can become clear.**

ONE STEP AT A TIME

Amrita

As I was walking up the path tonight,
This message came to me
Take one step at a time, my friend,
The rest will be clear to see.
I pondered this and as I walked,
It became obvious to me,
By taking one step at a time,
The path was revealed to me.
At times the darkness overcame me,
My path was not clear to see.
Obscured by rocks and by fallen trees,
The next step was invisible to see.
I stopped, was calm and waited.
And saw before my very eyes,
The next step was revealed to me.
Oftentimes in future, when things are looking dim,
I'll remember this message, walk in confidence,
Sure each step takes me one step closer to my goal,
One step closer Home.

WE LIVE IN CHANGING TIMES

Today, in our World, His-Story is colliding with itself! Political events shake not only the foundation of buildings, but also the economic, social, psychological and legal foundations of the world. They are not as solid as we believed them to be. In the world we are regularly faced with the imminent possibility of war – religious, economic, terrorist or for reasons of revenge. This all adds up to a world under threat. We cannot continue moving in the direction we are going. It is not sustainable.
It's time for **big change!**

Recent events impact on us whether we are aware of them or not. They give us an opportunity to take another look and to move forward in a new direction – a giant leap for humanity.

In Times of Trouble

We are facing troubled times. How we deal with this is entirely up to us. Each one of us reacts according to our conditioning, upbringing, belief systems, how we feel about ourselves and the world in which we live. We can go beyond these. With awareness we may see that many of our reactions are dictated by outside influences – parents, friends, the media and the culture in which we live. The media are easily manipulated and are also used to manipulate. It is unwise to believe all that is reported on television or in newspapers and magazines.

Many people are not working for the good of the world. Some believe they are. Others are selfishly destructive. Some politicians are leading from a true place of wisdom. Others may not be. When connected to your Essential Nature you no longer believe all you hear and see. You can hear the not-truth when it is being spoken. Do not get caught up in the drama of events or hooked into the fear. Discover a deeper level of truth.

Let's open our eyes, wake up, speak up, tune in to all our senses and listen with all of ourselves. We can learn to hear with **both sets of ears,** both inner and outer and see with **both sets of eyes.** In these times it is vital for the continuity of life on Earth that we begin living from our Essential Nature. It can wake us up and help us feel deeper than the superficial level of life.

It might not be easy for some of you who read to do this right now. It could be that you have lost people you love through natural disasters, wars or political events. Some of you may be lost in a fog of confusion, may be numb and not know what to think or feel. GETTING REAL... about growing up! has offered ways to change that.

However things appear in the world, remember, we are in a process of purification. It's like a pimple. The puss builds up until it bursts. Very quickly the skin heals over and it might not be obvious there was a pimple there. That's a bit like what is happening in our world at this time. The pimples are bursting to heal. Are you ready to get real and make a difference in the World?

Looking through Windows

As we look out into the world through our windows of **fear** we see the world as we have known it, to be crumbling.

If we look at the world though our windows of **judgement** we see bad guys and good guys. We see fools, murderers and greedy people who are grasping more – more land, more arms, more money, more goods. We see people who say they are good and say that others are not. Who is what and what is who can confuse us.

What is true? If we use our judgement how can we know what is true and good?

If we look at our world through eyes of **hate** who can be right?

How can people hate so much that they wish to destroy stability in our lives?

If we look out at our world through windows of **disbelief** we wonder how can people murder innocent people? How can one person wilfully harm another? How unbelievable is it that the world can be ravaged in the hands of those who take power and destroy. Who can we trust?

When you look at the World through windows of **love** your heart sheds tears of sorrow that people do not love each other. That pain and suffering exist at all in the World is a crime against **love's tender heart**.

If you look with eyes of **love** you can see the beauty and bounty of the Earth. There is enough – enough love to create a peaceful planet, enough food and water for everyone. Looking with **love** you melt and there is no room for anything but goodwill to all men, all women, all girls, all boys – all life.

The World of love is rich and full. You feel peaceful because of love.

You become whole when you love. All is good in Love.

The Soul of the World is healed when you live as love…

Love shows you the way… guides you to the Light of the World.

Looking through the windows of love you are not deceived.

You know that love and truth, goodness and grace, miracles and metamorphosis spread

through the Earth and change The Story as you have known it.

If we look out at the World through the eyes of God:

"Ah my children how can you destroy creation? How can you wage your battles in My name?

Do not fight your wars in My name. They are not based on truth.

I am One God – not many.

Do not harm another in the name of religion. So many of you do not hear My voice.

Too many of you carry everything but the love in your heart that I gave you.

Many of you do not love your neighbour as yourself. Many of you crucify the messengers

I send to you. For I am the One God.

The All One in Everything.

In My will there is no separation. If you listen carefully enough for the still small voice

you would hear Me calling you into your hearts, into love. Love one another as I love you.

Do unto others as you would have them do unto you.

Create the Kingdom of God on the Earth.
Allow Peace on Earth!"

Looking through the windows of our **Soul** – we can see them opening.

They are being cleaned to reveal a **New World**.

They have been so soiled that we have not been able to see a different way to be.

There is one! The way to Paradise on Earth is being unlocked.

We have the opportunity to live a spiritual life on Earth.

Dream your dreams of a brighter,
clearer and lighter World.

This was inspired by Lois Hunt, a presenter at Bay FM Radio Station, Byron Bay and also from articles received on the Internet after 11th September 2001 – the terrorist attacks on America.

TEENSPEAK

"War against terrorism is not a solution. I think that powerful governments are neglecting international responsibilities in not attempting to recognise why there are terrorist attacks. We as humans are going on overdrive with consumerism and fear. I hope that humans wake-up to their responsibilities to the world and to other human beings and in doing so find peace within themselves." – Johanna (18)

"I hadn't been into politics until the terrorist attacks. This situation forced me to think about our world. Now I feel a little bit insecure and distrust. Human personality is complicated – from one side people are intelligent but from the other they are the most stupid creatures in the world. Generally, I don't believe politicians because they are making too many mistakes to trust and be sure of them.

The future of our world depends on us. People must realise that when they're destroying our world they are destroying themselves. I'm dreaming of a peaceful world because war is a dramatic and painful thing." – Olga (16), Wroclaw, Poland.

"I'm really angry that I might not be able to have kids. I feel as if I've let God down in a way because I don't do anything. I'm scared. I wish there was something I could do." – Beth (15)

"It makes me pissed off with the world and with what's going on. I feel afraid and frustrated. The way things are going we, so many people must have been unconscious. So many people are bloody annoyed but it is our fault and we ought to get off our arses and do something about it." – Daniel (13)

"I feel really angry about the way some people are treating the world and frustrated because there is not a lot I can do to stop it. I am scared about the future and what it will bring for me and my family if greed and pollution and all the other bad things don't stop soon. I feel really mad at a lot of the world leaders and now they are creating a war. What they really don't seem to realise is that if we kill this world there is nowhere else to go. They don't seem to know how to care. I sometimes wonder if they have a heart." – Melea (15)

"Innocent people get killed and then armies go to kill other innocent people. I think it's stupid. War is in general. You don't get much out of having a war. Just dead people." – Kintasha (14)

"It seems that humanity is unable to learn from its mistakes despite the repercussion of the countless wars we've had. I fear that if we don't learn before we go to war again we will never learn. With the advent of nuclear weapons there will be no Earth to fight over anymore. This level of conflict is not synonymous with human nature: rather it is a product of our society. There are a few fundamental aspects of this society that must be changed if we ever hope to achieve World Peace. I don't have a viable model to achieve this, but I believe that for it to happen the quest for economic wealth and the yearning for fulfilment via conquest must be changed from the root of society not just on a personal level." – Thomas (18)

"My greatest fear is that some terrible disaster will happen and change the life of everyone forever. Whether it will be some mad man blowing up the Earth or an ecological catastrophe, it can be anything, but it's something we won't be able to stop or control. It's horrifying. Another thing is, of course, the lack of natural resources. They'll soon be over and it is now when we should be worrying about that and figure out how to live normally without them."
– Agnieszka (16), Wroclaw, Poland.

"I feel incredibly angry that we, the human race, have taken the Earth into our own hands without any consideration for any other life forms or beings. I feel disillusioned because I don't know why we destroy and chop and kill. I feel frustrated that I cannot right all the wrongs and take back all the hurt. I do feel hopeful at the growing awareness on this planet, at all the people who are doing good and protecting our world. I feel a passionate need to do something for the good of all people. I desperately want to help save this world, to spread goodness and happiness and love." – Will (16)

"I feel hope because the people who have discovered love are radiating that energy and will transform all the unhappy people." – Bradley (16)

"If we appear a bit Hesitant to embrace the belief that we can go on behaving in such an irresponsible manner without paying the inevitable price, perhaps it's because we live on a planet on which five to ten species of life are driven to extinction every day, over 30 hectares of trees are cut down every minute, one-third of the land area has become desert and life-threatening droughts and floods are becoming increasingly common year after year. In Antarctic waters, the ozone hole has caused an estimated twenty-five percent reduction in phytoplankton – the basis of all life in the ocean.

Go to the natural world, watch and listen. It tells us that a Great Storm is rising and that before long things will become very interesting, very interesting indeed.

We would like to pass along something that we've learned from the Earth as well as from Taoists, Tibetan Buddhists, Native Americans, the writings of the prophet Isaiah and others. A new way of life is coming – one so unlike today's that it would be difficult, if not impossible, to describe it in today's terms.

Before it begins its approach we'd say to those people who haven't had the inclination or the time to become acquainted with the natural world: Never mind – you'll be getting acquainted with it anyway. Because over the next few years, the natural world will be coming to you (although not necessarily in the way you'd like it to). Perhaps you might benefit by beginning your acquaintance with it now. Just a suggestion."
– TE OF PIGLET, Benjamin Hoff.

Listen to Yourself

Some of you may be confident about life and your place in it. Others may be feeling fearful and helpless. Some of you may prefer not to get involved in world politics. However you can work on a small scale – doing what you can by empowering yourself and connecting to your Essential Nature – the whole World can change.

When revenge and war is spoken about, ask yourself: What are the implications of that in my life and that of others? Men and boys and some women too, are sent to fight in wars that are being waged from greed, ignorance, spite, ego and power-hungry minds where innocent people are killed. Is this a war that is worth fighting or dying for? Think clearly, listen closely and make up your own mind.

Let your HEART guide your thoughts and actions.

The following suggestions support you to stay centred within yourself and remain optimistic:

DO NOT lose hope.

DO NOT allow yourself to die emotionally in order to survive.

DO NOT allow yourself to harden or become bitter and resentful. If feelings of despair, sorrow or anger come up, find someone who you can talk to about how you feel.

DO NOT stay involved in conversations that distress you if they don't offer you a chance to express what you are feeling. Take yourself away from situations that aggravate you.

DO NOT accept a world that is full of injustice and shattered dreams. This is not how it has to be. Hold in your heart the possibility of a different World.

DO NOT deny the tragic events that are happening in the world. When you become aware of such events anywhere, send loving thoughts to those people, situations and places as soon as you can.

DO NOT get caught up in fear, media distortion, revengeful thinking, despair – these emotions feed off each other and take you on a downhill depressive ride.

DO NOT watch television when repetition of horrific events dominate the screen. These images are fed into your subconscious mind and can become addictive as well as emotionally disturbing. Turn the TV off.

DO NOT watch the television at all if you are particularly sensitive.

DO NOT go along with media hype! Listen and look carefully and discover what is true for you. Be your own authority. Decide on what actions to take and do them… in your own life, in your own way.

DO contact your local and national TV channels, magazines and newspapers and let them know that you do not agree with over-dramatised reporting. Let them know they are making people fearful, angry and immobilised.

DO let your elected government representatives know that you do not support them if you sense they are not acting for the good of everyone.

DO allow your feelings of powerlessness, sadness, sorrow, anger and pain to emerge. Give them time and focus. They are a part of you. Find someone to talk to about how you are feeling. Give yourself an opportunity to express what is going on for you. Make a safe space available where you and others are heard. There are suggestions in this book about how to do this.

DO ask for spiritual guidance and help. Pray if this makes you feel better. The good feelings we generate in times of trouble help establish balance more quickly.

DO let the Wise Ones who have walked longer on the Earth carry and transform conflict. They can handle it!

DO offer heart-opening opportunities for yourself and your friends. Find out what is going on for those around you. Find safe places and kind-hearted people to support you.

DO stay connected to your Essential Nature and do what you can, in whatever ways, to make it a better World. Your gifts are essential.

DO keep your dreams and visions alive. Don't let them die. Imagine how you would like the planet to be and your place within it. As a young person your dreams are vital for the World right now. They are what can see us through.

Doing some of these things may help you to deal with the changes that are happening.
You may also gain a tremendous amount of self-respect and can establish a strong sense of who you really are.

Spend time with caring people. By being together we can offer our humanness. We are able to shed our tears and offer ears that hear the soreness in others' hearts. Give comfort, hugs, support, love and smile with each other.
This is a healing balm.

It's a wondrous World and Life is precious.

It is vital that we each generate as much love and peace as we are able.

Planting Peace Seeds

Someone asked the Dalai Lama, "Why didn't you fight back against the Chinese?"

The Dalai Lama looked down, swung his feet just a bit, then looked back up at us and said with a gentle smile, "Well, war is obsolete, you know." Then, after a few moments, his face grave, he said, "Of course the mind can rationalise fighting back... but the heart, the heart would never understand. Then you would be divided in yourself; the heart and the mind and the war would be inside you."

Walking in the bush one day I became aware of all the weeds that are growing that are hard to get rid of. I noticed that my neighbours had planted lots of trees but they were hard to see because of the weeds.

It's like the people who are praying and working for peace. Sometimes they are hard to see, but very soon the seeds they are planting will become great big trees that no one can miss.

"This is no longer a world of you OR me. We must recognise that it is you AND me and that together we can create the world, the life that we have dreamed of forever. A world of peace and goodwill amongst men. A world without hunger. A world without threat of nuclear disaster and the possible extinction of humanity. Peace is a conscious choice."
– Foreword by John Denver in THE MAGIC OF CONFLICT, Thomas Crum.

Ask yourself, "What can I do to make it a better World today?"
You can make a difference!

It starts with me. I am the ONE and so are you!

With millions praying for peace, holding the healing power of love in our hearts and doing what we can to make it a better World, we are bringing in a New Era, a new way of life on Earth!

When all people have peace in their hearts we can live in a peaceful World.

Oneness

Written by Raithe Handiman, author of THE FINAL CHAPTER.

"Our Solar System orbits around Alcione, the central sun of the Pleiades, every 26,000 years or so. Perpendicular to our orbit is a band of Photon Light that takes about 2,000 years to pass through, twice in every circuit around Alcione.

So humanity experiences alternating periods of 2,000 years of Light, then 11,000 years of Darkness. We are, right now, **emerging from a long period of Darkness.**

While in the Darkness we struggled to evolve by choosing right over wrong and love over fear. As we enter the fringe of the next Age of Light, those of us who have sufficiently evolved have the opportunity of **transformation.**

Thanks to the higher vibrations of the Light, we now have the opportunity to live in a state of Oneness. We do that when we stop living for the gratification of our personal wants and needs and begin to serve our Essential Nature.

Oneness is not about being perfect. It is about celebrating our differences and unconditionally loving whatever we have already become, in such a way that it never, ever, needs to change. The Galactic Cycle is currently empowering us to do just that.

In this situation we will be looking to our young for guidance, for they have not been overloaded with decades of belief systems, preferences and judgements. They are still free and know the ways of an open heart – the only thing that ever really mattered.

The New World

What will it take for those who helped create the world mess, to realise that they can't fix a problem with the same thinking that created it in the first place?

What will it take for those who cling to control through fear, to step aside, leaving the indigo and violet children of today to show the way into Oneness?

Perhaps we will witness, in the very near future, the cyclic return of Planet X, the Nibiru of the ancient Sumerian texts and the Wormwood of the Book of Revelation? Some say it is returning soon to cause Earth changes. Perhaps then we could start again with a fresh understanding of the way life can be in Oneness.

These matters are not really our concern. The Galactic cycle has decreed that only those who can live in Oneness may live on Earth in a decade or so. So be it!

All we ever have is the moment – this moment – and we have a choice – always the same choice. Open or closed. Will we serve our Essential Nature and unconditionally love the way we are? Or will we try to control the moment, try to change it into something else that we prefer? Oneness is based on openness.

Our young people are the messengers and founders of the coming Age of Light.

May books, such as GETTING REAL... about growing up! help them to understand how to prepare for this magnificent opportunity."

In this World

Alexie (15)

In this world I see the children, children of the skies.
The help and love and wonder, is bursting from their eyes.
They don't know no killing, they don't know no fate.
They don't know what war is 'cos they don't feel the hate.

In this world there is laughter, although there is pain.
It's all part of life, through the sunshine and the rain.
Life is a miracle, with magic everywhere.
The joy and love and friendship is filling up the air.

One great fear that lurks in all of our minds,
Is the shadowy fear of death, it brings shivers to our spines.
How will it happen? Will it be painful? When will we know?
But don't let it destroy your life or you'll never learn to grow.

Some people have hard times, that we don't really know.
Every day is a struggle, life is like a bitter blow.
They all have their beauty, uniqueness of their own.
If you start by loving, you will find your way home.

In this world there is laughter, although there is pain.
It's all part of life, through the sunshine and the rain.
Life is a miracle, with magic everywhere.
The joy and love and friendship is filling up the air.

Alexie died in a motor bike accident five years later.

THE LAST WORDS

*GETTING REAL... about growing up! is suspended in the
twilight zone – in between the dark and the Light.*

*It is indeed time for us to grow up, to be true and to bring
the manifestation of All Love into existence.*

*Some who read, sit in the dark and are able to see the Light
shining ahead.
Some are standing in an in-between-place.
Perhaps they are more in the Light than the dark.
They can see the dark places they have come from.
Some dance fully in the Light.*

*Twilight, the in-between-breath, awaits the
magnificence of dawn.
The pink, purple and orange hues of a new day.
Full of wonder, awe, adventure, magic and joy.*

*Leaving the old world behind,
As if awakening from a deep sleep,
we brush the dream from our eyes.
There is a choice each one of us can make.
We can embrace the invitation of a sunrise – like no other.*

*In between two worlds – the old and the new,
GETTING REAL... about growing up! beckons
all of us to live the Love and the Light that we are.*

AFTER THE END NOTES

This section has information in it that may be of interest to you. There is information for parents and a note for teachers, youth workers and others interested in understanding and working with young people.

There is an article about 'queer' extended families. This arrived too late to be included in the main body of the text.

Amrita has worked with hundreds, perhaps thousands of young people, she offers understanding, guidance and a deeper look at life in this fast-changing world.

Details about workshops and seminars can be found on the last page.

NOTES TO PARENTS

I have not been a parent. What I offer here is from my experience of listening to young peoples' stories and from talking to parents.

My Mum and Dad not long after they were married

Some of the following has been taken from a number of different resources which are mentioned later.

Things to consider about teenagers:

- They are in a curious, experimental, questioning time of life. They play around with ideas, clothes, friends and possibly smoking, sex, drinking and drugs.
- It can be agonising to watch them make mistakes you can see coming a mile off. If in danger, warn them, otherwise let them go ahead – this is how they learn. They are in the process of becoming an individual – this is a natural process.
- Think about the issues they face, examine your values and communicate your feelings and thoughts with them.
- Anything you do for them that they can do for themselves is robbing them of an opportunity to grow up.
- You may find them at times selfish, narrow minded and then affectionate and a pleasure to have around. This stage of their lives can be difficult, hard to understand, annoying or a delight.

They may feel the same way as you do!

Your children are not your children.
They are the sons and daughters
of Life's longing for itself.
They come through you but not from you,
And though they are with you yet
they belong not to you.
– THE PROPHET, Kahlil Gibran

Preparing Yourself and Your Teen

By giving them a good education about the biological, physical as well as emotional upheaval they may go through during adolescence, you are emotionally and psychologically preparing them for their changes. This gives them a good start. Schools may not do this, unless they are very good ones. Make sure you know they are doing the best possible job otherwise don't rely on them. As they grow and your teenagers ask questions, do your best to give them honest and accurate information. Back this up from your own experiences, especially as they get older. You can use GETTING REAL... about growing up! as a resource to open up awkward conversations by reading it together and talking about the issues that are raised.

Teenagers can be fragile during this stage of their development. Parents too!

Develop a Positive Sense of Self

In workshops I ask young people to tell me things they like about themselves. Some teens can think of nothing.

The implications are that they:

do not value themselves or
do not believe what has been said about them or
have not been given praise.

To change this – when you notice them behaving courageously, kindly, generously or if they are listening well – let them know that you see them doing this. **Examples:** Jenny, I noticed you held Sarah's hand when she got upset. That was a very loving thing to do. Peter, when that elderly lady slipped and you helped her that was very kind of you.

This gives them a language base for identifying themselves and a vocabulary to describe their good qualities. **Praise them often.** This helps them to create a healthy self-image. Adults can assist teenagers to bring their gifts and talents into consciousness.

Growing Up and Sexuality

There is one talk you can have when they are about ten years of age. This is to prepare them for the bodily and emotional changes that will be happening for them very soon.

The other is at about thirteen. Talk about what puberty was like for you with all the details. Tell them some of your funny stories or dramas.

By about fourteen, if not before, it's the sexuality talk that is helpful. The chances are they may not look like they are listening. You may be amazed how interested they are underneath their cool exterior.

I encourage all parents, if you are not already doing so, to open up the sexuality conversation. There is still so much that is not discussed about sexuality. When you notice your teenagers' sexual energy kicking in, make a special effort. I suggest you take them out to dinner. Talk about your own sexual experiences. Let them know how it was for you as a young person and is now.

During an evening talk with fathers, I suggested that they talk to both their sons and daughters about male sexuality. One man already had shared in graphic detail with his daughter how, when he was a teenager, his friends used to talk about and come on to females. He prepared his daughter well for her experiences with boys. Unlike her friend who didn't know about some boys just wanting sex. She thought they were after her because they liked her. She became sexually promiscuous at an early age. When her horrified parents found out, they called her a slut, as did her classmates. She had not been warned and then found herself condemned. Who's responsible for that?

Who is responsible for preparing our children and teens for sexual activity if it is not the adults around them?

Informed young people can take better care of themselves. Their transition from child to sexually educated young adults can be made easier.

About abuse: Listen to children and young people if they tell you they have been abused in any way. Accept what they say and take steps to protect them. Sometimes they lose their voice or an accurate memory about what happened. Stay alert. If their behaviour suddenly changes – they become shut down, anxious, self-harming, obsessive, unhappy or depressed – investigate. Do everything you can to find out what has happened.

If they show signs of fear around an adult or young adult who they have spent time alone with, ask questions. If this person asks to spend time with them, make enquiries from other people before entrusting your child to his or her care.

Sand play and art therapy are great tools for unlocking memories that may go into the subconscious mind if they are too traumatic for them to talk about.

Early intervention can save a lot of distress.

Are They Doing Drugs?

Let them know when they do things that can damage their heart/body/mind/spirit – they can only get away with it for so long.

It has been discovered that the most likely factor for drug abuse during adolescence is the level of self-esteem at ten. Helping children and teenagers feel good about themselves can be an investment for their safety as they grow up.

There are books available for parents about teenage drug use that may help you.

Helpful hints:

- Make rules about drug use while they are young. It is your responsibility to protect them. They can make their own decisions in their late teens.
- If you have been or are a drug user it helps to own up to it. This gives you credibility in their eyes.
- Don't go searching in their room if you suspect they are using drugs.
- Communicate with each other about drugs when you are all relaxed.
- Find out what is happening in the lives of other families, then approach your teenagers indirectly by saying, "I was talking to… and her son is taking drugs. What do you think about that?"
- If you support them in reaching their goals and they know that you are behind them they are less likely to get involved in drugs.

As long as adults have an easy-going attitude about drug use some young people will go on using them. Drug use causes a great deal of damage. It is up to the adults to take a stand on issues that cause harm to the growing adolescent.

Set Limits

Because adolescence is a confusing time, teenagers look for stability and boundaries. They may act in rebellious ways to test you and the boundaries you set. They may not be equipped to deal with too much freedom, so set appropriate limits, then negotiate and be flexible. This way they gain valuable negotiating and communication skills for later life. If you give up control around them, you may not be an effective guide in difficult times. They do not welcome too much freedom in spite of outward appearances.

The idea of road markings is a useful way to think about how rules may help. It is easy to go over the lines, but they make it quite clear when it is dangerous to do that. A rule of not smoking at school does not stop them from smoking, but it lets them know what is acceptable and what isn't. It also lets them know that their actions have consequences or penalties. If they don't have those lines marked out they don't know whether they're on the right track or not.

Authoritarian Doesn't Work

It's useful to find new ways of relating to your teenager – no longer children, they demand something different from you. You can consult with them rather than tell them what to do. If you are being too authoritarian, you may meet with rebellious behaviour. During adolescence you can only earn their respect, you cannot demand it. If they don't respect you already, you may not easily earn it when they reach their teens.

To become a consultant:

- Be prepared to negotiate.
- Listen with an open heart so that they can talk to you.
- Provide some objectivity to their experience.
- Be willing to set clear boundaries and allow flexibility.
- Don't make a big deal out of little events. Use your authority for more serious misdemeanours.
- Aim to create win/win situations in their struggle to grow up. Teach them about becoming responsible for their actions. Negotiate agreements and work out consequences when these are broken. **Be consistent.**
- Discuss with them about: pocket money, curfews, bed times, TV viewing, use of the phone, attendance at parties, homework and anything else.

Helpful Hints:

- Be protective of younger teens. Loosen up as they get older and show they have become more accountable and responsible.
- Don't hide your weaknesses. Be willing to be vulnerable – in that is great strength.
- Reveal to them who you really are, not someone you would like them to believe you are. Who you are speaks louder than any words you speak. Walk your talk.
- Don't ask them to do anything you are unwilling to do yourself.
- Be a role model for taking care of yourself – they learn from you how to take care of themselves.
- Trust the process of their lives. Give them everything to allow them to become responsible for their own lives.
- Give young people the freedom to find out who they are. They often reject parents' values in order to do this. **Don't take this personally.**
- Set fair limits on how they behave and how they treat you. Some are abusive and threaten parents with physical violence. If this is the case why do you allow them to live in your home while treating you like this? It is inappropriate that you are intimidated in any way by your teenagers. Seek professional assistance and find ways to change behaviour that is disrespectful to you. In this way not only are you caring for yourself but also you are a role model for them.
- Talk to them. Ask questions about what they are going through. Even if it appears that they don't like to talk. The chances are they may be grateful when you keep open and lovingly onto them about their lives and yours.
- Always know where they are and make sure that they can get home safely.
- Check that parties have adult supervision.
- If you had a difficult childhood, take steps to heal that now. If things get really tough, find a counsellor.
- Learn new ways to communicate with them if it does not come naturally to you. The numbers of people attending workshops and buying parenting books is increasing. There are numerous seminars, Parent Effectiveness Training programs, workshops and therapies available to expand your communication and parenting skills and also your awareness.
- Do everything you can to stay in a difficult marriage where children are involved. For everyone's sake. Sometimes seeking support from close friends or a Marriage Guidance Counsellor can save a marriage that is on the rocks.

I have worked with hundreds of young people from separated families and witnessed the emotional damage and devastation. I encourage couples to do everything possible to reduce fall-out.

Teenage Problems or Problem Teenagers?

Generally teenagers are not the problem. They are working out how to work with life's problems. When they are behaving unacceptably or being destructive in their environment, be careful not to immediately assume they are the problem. Their actions may be the symptoms of problems within the family or society, rather than the problem itself. They are acting out their discontent. They are often not given the kind of support, direction and guidance they could benefit from.

"Nothing makes up for failure in the family." Sam Keen, a workshop leader and author of many successful books read the message above on a billboard one-day. "After considerable meditation on the matter, I have come to believe that the message on the billboard is both true and prophetic. In watching my children struggle with the hurts and dis-continuities that are the inevitable result of irreconcilable differences between their parents, I have learned what many men learn only after divorce – there is nothing more precious than our children. In the quiet hours of the night when I add up the accomplishments of my life – I know the three that rank above all the others are named Lael, Gifford and Jessamyn. In the degree to which I have loved, nurtured and enjoyed them, I honour myself. In the degree to which I have injured them by being unavailable to them because of my obsessive preoccupations with myself or my profession, I have failed as a father and as a man."
– FIRE IN THE BELLY, Sam Keen

Parenting children in queer extended relationships

My name is Christine Devine. I am writing about my experience as a woman who happens to be attracted to the female gender. My story is one of many women who have chosen to become a mother without a heterosexual marriage. To be a queer mother has been a positive challenge. It has opened up to me a world of love and respect within this society. It has given me choices and direction for my future and my children's future.

I chose to have children by myself. Of course with the help of a gift from two aware men.

I offered them the gift of being involved if they chose to be in an exciting extended family unit and they gave me the gift of life. I am now blessed with two beautiful children – Zac who is 10 years old and Dellilah who is 8 years old.

Both children are well-adjusted and live life with joy and love along with passion. They support each other in their daily lives and love each other immensely. I encourage them to be in their power and to achieve their goals in life.

Zac visits his father and his two brothers every second weekend. This arrangement is very positive. Zac feels love from all who come into his life. He excels in tennis and all his school projects. His father is a positive role model for Zac's development and I encourage this arrangement.

Dellilah's father chooses to be an uncle figure. We have regular picnics at the beach with him and this appears to be satisfactory for her needs at this stage of her life.

Community wise, the children are well known for their intelligence and artistic qualities. They are associated with my friends and family. Also an extended family of artists, spiritualists and teachers – all mentors for their wellbeing and journeys in their lives.

I offer them a great home environment with abundance of encouragement and beautiful love. I give them the space to grow and allow them to express themselves and to live their dreams as they wish.

The life path of eleven years I have chosen has been so rich and fulfilling that I couldn't imagine life without my children. I feel happy about my choices and celebrate motherhood and all its challenges. I support the children equally, I feel so blessed to have a child of each gender. My life has been enhanced and enriched.

The information for parents was found in:

A BOOKLET FOR PARENTS, Talking to Teenagers about Drugs. Author unknown.
PARENTING – THE MOST IMPORTANT JOB IN THE WORLD, The Department of Community Services, NSW.
TEENAGERS AND ALCOHOL, A parent's guide. National Alcohol Campaign, Australian Government.
IT'S TIME TO TALK STRAIGHT, Australian Government.

A Note for People Working with Youth

To Teachers, Youth Workers, Scout and Guide Pack Leaders and anyone who works with or has anything to do with young people.

GETTING REAL... about growing up! is written for young people to read. Many young people will enjoy it and work through the suggestions in it. Many others could be assisted with group and adult support to receive the most benefit from it.

GETTING REAL... about growing up! is a valuable teaching tool and provides processes, suggestions and resource materials. These can be applied to any group situation – with young people and also with adults.

My aim is that this book is shared as widely as possible. However, some schoolteachers have asked that the material be used exclusively by them. It is my wish that this book is not withheld from young people as a resource for only the teacher to use.

I can design a Teacher's Resource Kit offering different material which expands on the current content. I also work with people who are working with teenagers.

May this book be of service to you in your work and to the young people you also serve.

I travel around the world responding to invitations from communities everywhere. If this or the Resource Kit is of interest to you, please make contact.

See page 232 for information about workshops and programs.

Create a Caring World

We, as caring adults, can do great things to improve life for our young people.
We are all responsible! Let's care enough!

In the Family

- Make time for them in your life. Listen to their point of view.
- Welcome their friends into your home and get to know them.
- Provide opportunities to develop trust.
- Keep a sense of humour – this diffuses charged emotional situations. Laugh and have fun together!
- Be willing to risk staying closely connected with them – even when they push you away.
- Create support groups with other parents to help you do your job well.
- Change your emphasis in life if it is materially and money focussed. What are your priorities?
- Take care of the intellectual, psychological, emotional and spiritual life of your self, family and community.

Caring Adults in a Caring Community

- Look out for, protect and support young people. Caring for them even if they are not yours.
- Organise a Community Watch so that abuse of children and teenagers is stopped.
- Give support to families that are struggling and less well off than you.
- Help renew hope. Share your love. Be generous with your spirit.
- Organise social events so that teens can get together – to play games, swim in your pool, just hang out and have fun.
- Invite young people into groups so that they can speak from their hearts, express what's going on for them, shed their tears and share their laughter.

In School

Ask your school council or board if it is willing to:

- Do what it can to change the emphasis in schools from academic achievement, to focus on their relationship skills and psychological, emotional, social and spiritual wellbeing.
- Create a TIME-OUT ROOM of safety and provide staff to support young people who are having difficulties, so that they feel cared for. This could become a place where they can talk from their sore hearts and be relieved of the burdens they sometimes carry.

It's Our Society

Are you ready to create a new paradigm where caring for all people and the Earth takes priority over everything else?

- Focus on the quality of your life rather than the things you have that decorate it.
- Challenge authority when it is not serving humanity and the good of all children. Use your voice to speak out about injustice.
- Approach those who seem troubled or in pain and ask if they would like support. Reach out your hand with an open heart and feel what it is like to do that.
- Be willing to take on responsibility as a custodian of this Earth so that young people know that they are safe.

***TAKE A STAND!
YOU CAN MAKE THIS
A BETTER WORLD.***

AFTER THE END... AFTER THE END...

Recommended Books

TEEN INC – Our voices our visions – Written by Teens. Health Communications Inc., Florida, 2000.
CHICKEN SOUP FOR THE TEENAGE SOUL – J. Canfield, V. Hansen and K. Kirberger. Health Communications Inc., Florida, 1999.
THE 7 HABITS OF HIGHLY EFFECTIVE TEENAGERS – Stephen Covey. A Fireside Book, New York.
THE ALCHEMIST – Paulo Coelho. Harper Collins, New York, 1995.
SEX-WISE – What every young person and parent should know about sex – Janet Hall. Random House, Sydney, 2000.

The New Children

EMISSARY OF LOVE – James Twyman. Hampton Roads, USA, 2002.
CHILDREN OF THE NEW MILLENNIUM – P.M.H. Atwater. Three Rivers Press, New York, 1999.
THE INDIGO CHILDREN – Lee Carroll & Jan Tober. Hay House, USA, 1999. Website: http://www.indigochildren.com

Menstruation

A BLESSING NOT A CURSE – Jane Bennett. Sally Milner Publishing, Australia, 2002.
THE WILD GENIE – Alexandra Pope. Sally Milner Publishing, Australia, 2001.
WALKING WITH THE GENIE – The Modern Woman's Menstrual Health Kit – Alexandra Pope. Sydney, 2002.
THE RED TENT – Anita Diamant. Allen and Unwin, Sydney, 1998.
WOMEN'S TROUBLES – Kaz Cooke. Allen and Unwin, Sydney, 1998.
HEALING WISE – Susan Weed. Ashtree Publishing, Woodstock, 1989.
DAUGHTERS OF COPPERWOMAN – Ann Cameron. Vancouver, 2002.
THE LUNAR CYCLE – Franceska Naish. Nature and Health Books, Australia, 1998.
NATURAL FERTILITY – Franceska Naish. Sally Milner Publishing, Australia.

Sexual Abuse

ANNIE'S LEGACY – Ken McCoy. Piatkus, London, 2001.
OUT IN THE OPEN – A Guide for Young People Who Have Been Abused – Q. Bain and M. Sanders. Virago, 1990.
THE ME NOBODY KNOWS – Barbara Beana and Shari Bennett. Lexington Books, 1993.
THE COURAGE TO HEAL A guide for women survivors of child sexual abuse L. Davis. Harper Perennial, USA, 1994.
(Also THE COURAGE TO HEAL WORKBOOK)

Suicide

VERONIKA DECIDES TO DIE – Paulo Coelho. Harper Collins, Sydney, 1998.
TEEN SUICIDE, TOO YOUNG TO DIE – C.C. Lewis. Enslow Publishers Inc., N.J., 1994.
STRAIGHT TALK ABOUT ... Teenage Suicide – B. Frankel and R. Kranz. Facts on File, New York, 1994.
LifeForce – a Wesley Mission program. Contact web site: www.wesleylifeforce.org

For Adults and Parents

WHY DO THEY DO THAT? Understanding teenagers – Nic Polland. Lion, Oxford, 1998.
EMOTIONALLY HEALTHY TEENAGERS – Jay Kesler. Word Publishers, Nashville, 1998.
EMBRACING PERSEPHONE: how to be the mother you want for the daughter you cherish – Virginia Rutter. Kodanska International, New York, 2000.
SPLIT ENDS: Teenage stepchildren – Ruth Weber. ACER, Melbourne, 1996.
SIBLING SOCIETY – Robert Bly. Vintage, USA, 1997.
RAISING A DAUGHTER – Jeanne and Don Elium. Celestial Arts, California. (Also RAISING A SON)
YOUTH SUICIDE – A comprehensive Manual for Prevention and Intervention – B. Hick. National Education Service, Indiana, 1990.
HOMECOMING – John Bradshaw. Bantam, USA, 1992.
CONVERSATIONS WITH GOD – Neale Donald Walsch. Hodder Headline Group, Sydney, 1996.
MAGICAL CHILD MATURES – Joseph Chilton Pearce. E. P. Dutton, New York, 1985. (Also MAGICAL CHILD)
GETTING THE LOVE YOU WANT – Harville Hendrix. Schwartz & Wilkinson, Melbourne, 1988.
MANHOOD – Steve Biddulph. Finch Publishing, Sydney, Australia, 1994.
IN THE NAME OF THE FAMILY – rethinking family values in the postmodern era – Judith Stacey. Beacon Press, Boston, 1997.

Where They Came From

The quotes, stories and poems included in GETTING REAL... about growing up! came from the following books. The author and publisher thank these authors and publishers for permission to quote from these books. Permission is requested if not already granted.

THE TE OF PIGLET – Benjamin Hoff. Penguin, USA, 1993.
VERONIKA DECIDES TO DIE – Paulo Coelho. Harper Collins Publishers, Sydney, 1998.
FIRE IN THE BELLY – Sam Keen. Bantam Books, New York.
RAISING BOYS – Steve Biddulph. Finch Publishing, Sydney, Australia, 1998.
WOMEN'S BODIES, WOMEN'S WISDOM – Dr Christiane Northrup. Piatkus Publishers, London, 1995.
THE ELEMENT GUIDE – Anorexia and Bulimia – Julia Buckroyd. Brisbane.
THE FIFTH MOUNTAIN – Paulo Coelho. Harper Collins, New York, 1999.
EMBRACED BY THE LIGHT – What happens when you die? – Betty J. Eadie. Bantam Books, USA.
REAL MAGIC – Dr Wayne Dyer. Harper Collins, Sydney, 1992.
THE ANIMAL SCHOOL – Dr G. Reavis. Crystal Springs Books, USA, 1999.
CHICKEN SOUP FOR THE PARENT'S SOUL – J. Canfield, V. Hansen, K. Kirberger, R. Aaron. Health Communications Inc., Florida, 2000.
MAPS TO ECSTASY – Gabrielle Roth. New World Library, California, 1998.
WHY MEN DON'T LISTEN & WOMEN CAN'T READ MAPS – Alan and Barbara Pease. Pease Training International, Sydney, 1998.
MEN ARE FROM MARS, WOMEN ARE FROM VENUS – John Gray. Thorsons, London, 1993.
DEAR LOVER – David Deida. Plexus, USA, 2000.
THE WAY OF THE SUPERIOR MAN – David Deida. Plexus, 1997.
CHALLENGE OF THE HEART – John Wellwood. Random House, USA, 1985.
SIBLING SOCIETY – Robert Bly. William Heinemann, Australia, 1996.
GOD, THE SUBSTANCE OF ALL FORM – Joel Goldsmith. Citadel Press, Canada, 1962.
THE FINAL CHAPTER – Raithe Handiman. The Oracle Press, Australia, 2001.
THE MAGIC OF CONFLICT – Thomas Crum. Simon and Shuster, New York, 1987.
100 WAYS TO ENHANCE SELF–CONCEPT IN THE CLASSROOM – J. Canfield and H. C. Wells. Prentice-Hall Inc., New Jersey, 1976.
ILLUSIONS – Richard Bach. Heinemann, London, 1977.
THE INDIGO CHILDREN – Lee Carroll & Jan Tober. Hay House, USA, 1999.
I SEND A VOICE – Evelyn Eaton. Theosophical Publishing House, Illinois, 1978.
THE LITTLE PRINCE – Antoine d'Saint-Exupery. Piccolo Pan Books, 1945.
THE PROPHET – Kahlil Gibran. William Heinemann, London, 1926.
INITIATION – Elizabeth Haich. Seed Centre, California, 1965.
YOU CAN HEAL YOUR LIFE – Louise Hay. Hay House, Santa Monica, 1984.
THE LOVER WITHIN – Julie Henderson. The Talman Company Inc., New York, 1986.
THE 7 HABITS OF HIGHLY EFFECTIVE PEOPLE – Stephen Covey. A Fireside Book, New York, 1989.
THE TAO OF POOH – Benjamin Hoff. Octopus Publishing Group Library, England.
THE BOOK OF CHANGES AND THE UNCHANGING TRUTH (I CHING) – Taoist Master Ni Hua-Ching. Union of Tao and Man, Los Angeles.
TO LOVE IS TO BE HAPPY WITH – Barry Kaufman. Fawcett Crest Books, 1994.
SEX, IF I DIDN'T LAUGH I'D CRY – Jess Lair. Doubleday, USA, 1979.
THE GREATEST MIRACLE IN THE WORLD – Og Mandino. Bantam Books, New York, 1975.
THE EDUCATION OF THE CHILD – Rudolf Steiner. Nachlassverwaltung, Switzerland.
WOMEN AND RITUALS – Celeste Fremon. Yoga Journal Articles, World Goodwill Commentary, June 1984.
KINSHIP WITH ALL LIFE – J. Allen Boone. Harper and Row, New York, 1954.
THE LOVE CLUB MANUAL. Baraka Educational Foundation, Australia.
LOOKING AT THE BODY – David Suzuki. Wiley, USA, 1991.
MUTANT MESSAGES DOWNUNDER – Marlo Morgan. Harper Collins, New York. 1991.
IRON JOHN – Robert Bly. Vintage Books, USA, 1992.

From booklets and pamphlets:

A BOOKLET FOR PARENTS – Talking to Teenagers about Drugs.
PARENTING – The most important job in the world. The Department of Community Services, NSW, Australia.
TEENAGERS AND ALCOHOL – A parent's guide. National Alcohol Campaign. Australian Government.
IT'S TIME TO TALK STRAIGHT. Australian Government.
A GUIDE TO QUITTING. National Drug and Alcohol Research Centre, University of New South Wales.
LIFE FORCE – Suicide Prevention Programme. An activity of Wesley Mission, Australia.

ABOUT AMRITA'S WORK

TeenSpeak

… is a one-day program for parents and teenagers. It offers a unique experience to build bridges between the generations. It allows open and honest communication and supports young people to find their voices.

Girls Growing Up!

… is a special day of honouring and sharing for mothers and their daughters. It marks the transition from childhood to adolescence. Girls become more confident about themselves and their changing bodies. Growing Up Great! is for teenage girls with their mums.

Reclaiming Puberty Rites for Women

… is a one-day program assisting participants to re-examine their entry into womanhood and to experience their own Puberty Rites. Puberty is a gentle blossoming and an opening of the physical, psychic and spiritual bodies into female hormonal cycles that last a lifetime – it is time to celebrate this.

Reclaiming First Rites

… helps people to reframe past experience and reclaim lost power. It fulfils subconscious yearnings from childhood. First Rites can provide a retrieval at a Soul level of things not given and received as they grew up. It is an Initiation into Womanhood. This program is also available for men.

Wise Woman Healing

… is a one-month residential training program. It challenges Woman to fulfil her potential, take committed action and find form for her love and her dreaming. It is a Rite of Passage and Initiation. It's for women who are ready to make a difference in the World. As we step into the unknown, the Mystery unfolds. Miracles happen!

School Programs

... these include Teenage Relationships and Sexuality, Creating New Gender Ground, Dare to be Different and specially designed programs on request. Amrita is available to work at school or youth camps with groups of teenagers. She also offers in-service training for teachers and youth workers.

The Getting Real Foundation

... is aiming to fund youth projects and activities, to assist young people to realise their dreams and to support disadvantaged youth to reach their potential. After costs, a percentage of the sales of this book will establish The Foundation. It will become the umbrella organisation for Amrita's Vision.

A Youth Centre

... is Amrita's Vision. This is to create a youth centre to make residential facilities available for extended programs and camps. It will provide short and long term residential options for selected young people. Interested investors can make contact or check out the website for information.

Amrita is available to speak to community groups, at Conferences and to facilitate programs in your community, business or schools both in Australia and overseas. She offers private sessions and personalised rituals.

For further information Email: info@amritahobbs.com Website: www.amritahobbs.com

Or write to AMRITA HOBBS, PO Box 76, Mullumbimby, NSW 2482, Australia.